Queen
of the Pulps

*The Reign of Daisy Bacon
and* Love Story Magazine

LAURIE POWERS

D1573389

McFarland & Company, Inc., Publishers
Jefferson, North Carolina

LIBRARY OF CONGRESS CATALOGUING-IN-PUBLICATION DATA

Names: Powers, Laurie, 1957– author.
Title: Queen of the pulps : the reign of Daisy Bacon and Love Story
Magazine / Laurie Powers.
Description: Jefferson, North Carolina : McFarland & Company, Inc.,
Publishers, 2019 | Includes bibliographical references and index.
Identifiers: LCCN 2019032454 | ISBN 9781476673967
(paperback : acid free paper) ∞ | ISBN 9781476636948 (ebook)
Subjects: LCSH: Bacon, Daisy, 1898–1986. | Women editors—
United States—Biography. | Women publishers—United States—Biography. |
Women authors—United States—Biography. | Romance fiction, American—
20th century—History and criticism. | Street & Smith's love story magazine.
Classification: LCC PN4874.B218 P69 2019 | DDC 070.92 [B]—dc23
LC record available at https://lccn.loc.gov/2019032454

BRITISH LIBRARY CATALOGUING DATA ARE AVAILABLE

ISBN (print) 978-1-4766-7396-7
ISBN (ebook) 978-1-4766-3694-8

Front cover: Daisy Bacon, editor of the nation's most popular romance
fiction magazine, in an undated photograph (Daisy Bacon Collection)

Printed in the United States of America

McFarland & Company, Inc., Publishers
Box 611, Jefferson, North Carolina 28640
www.mcfarlandpub.com

To Kimberly Marlowe Hartnett—
mentor, cheerleader,
and friend

Table of Contents

Table of Contents

Acknowledgments

There is simply no way to overstate the following: Without Elaine Knowlden reaching out to me in 2011, and without Bill and Nora Haagenson's willingness to share Daisy's personal papers, this book would never have been possible. Their generosity and their trust in me—a total stranger when we first met in 2011—has always humbled me. Their exemplary patience over this much-delayed project is something for which I will always be eternally grateful.

Kimberly Marlowe Hartnett, to whom I dedicated this book, was my advocate and advisor through the painful process of writing. She encouraged me when I was ready to give up. She didn't think it was a suicidal undertaking for an absolute rookie to write a biography, much less one that encompassed such a huge subject. Her critiques kept me honest but, at the end of every conversation, still excited about writing. That is the definition of an excellent mentor.

Colleagues in the pulp fiction collecting, research, and writing community provided me with multitudes of material, information, knowledge, and encouragement. Ed Hulse gave me my first window into the pulp fiction world, and he patiently answered my questions that led to my learning about Daisy. Will Murray, who is the world-renown expert on the Street & Smith hero Doc Savage, provided me with reams of information on Street & Smith, Doc Savage, The Shadow, and the interactions between author Lester Dent, Walter Gibson, and Daisy. As a reviewer, he gave me much information that I needed to tell a much richer story about Street & Smith and Daisy's last days as an editor there. At the risk of sounding melodramatic (but then this is a history of pulp fiction stories!), Will may write stories about a superhero, but he's a hero himself.

The same can be said about Anthony Tollin, the expert on The Shadow, who generously lent me an original copy of the last issue of *The Shadow*, as well as valuable information on Daisy's last year as the editor of *The Shadow*. And, during the dark days of winter when I felt this project would never end, Tony regaled me with many stories of his beloved dachshunds. It helps to have distractions occasionally.

Many colleagues were generous in their lending of hard-to-find publications and documents essential to knowing Daisy's full story. Nicky Wheeler Nicholson gave me early encouragement and thoughtful ideas on resources. She advised me to contact author John Locke, who provided me, generously and without reservation, dozens of articles with information on Daisy that I needed. Doug Ellis gave me valuable feedback in the review process, and his ideas help me turn the corner of this book. Sheila Ann Vanderbeek, pulp fiction historian and love pulp aficionado, had the rare copies of *Real Love* and *Smart Love Stories* that I needed. Without those issues, this book would not have been the complete and thorough study of Daisy's career and the romance pulp industry.

Walker Martin's knowledge and experience in the pulp fiction world are without peer, bar none, but he was always willing to spend time with me and discuss the progress of the book. As a friend, Walker Martin provided encouragement and enthusiasm. As a reader, he gave me valuable feedback and reinforcement.

Some helped by providing me details and documentation that helped enrich Daisy's story with hard-to find information. Jack Cullers lent me a copy of another pivotal publication in Daisy's history, the 1975 issue of *Round Up* magazine that includes her essay, "The Golden Age of the Iron Maiden." Ann Parker spent an afternoon in the dead of winter at the Brooklyn Museum—when she had much better things to do. Lucie Fielding spent several days at Harvard University's Houghton Library reviewing correspondence between Alice Duer Miller and Alexander Woollcott, pouring over letters full of indecipherable handwriting. William Lampkin hunted down two very compelling photographs that I needed, even though I gave him parameters that seemed impossible to meet. David Saunders provided me with early newspapers that filled some important holes in Daisy's early life. His detective work solved more than one mystery. Lori Biederman generously lent me scarce copies of *Romantic Range*, and she shared with me the story of her grandparents who met through the pen pal column of that magazine. Harry Mulry helped with information on Daisy's years in retirement and her scholarship fund. Dr. Steven Lomazow provided me with an image of the cover of what is considered the rarest of *Love Story Magazine* issues, the very first issue, and Jessica Blackwell, Librarian at the Dana Porter Library at the University of Waterloo, provided me with important correspondence between Daisy and Gerard Chapman. Daryl Danforth provided me with a revealing short story that Daisy wrote in 1932.

Friends helped me in many ways with their extensive knowledge, by their own projects, or just by their interest and friendship. Michelle Nolan's book *Love on the Racks* was instrumental in my initial research, providing much needed statistics on the love pulps. In addition, her ability to tell a compelling story about a little-covered topic was the evidence I needed that, yes, these are stories that deserve to be told. Rich Harvey and Audrey Parente have always supported this project and their reprint of *Love Story Writer* has given the public another chance to read Daisy's long-forgotten book. Barry Traylor, Karen Davis Cunningham, Scott Hartshorn, Lohr McKinstry, Richard Paul Hall, Richard Moore, Sai Shankar, Alexis Francois-Poncet, Frank Schildiner and Mike Chomko all provided information, friendly support, and a listening ear.

Brooks Hefner provided circulation numbers from his and Ed Timke's digital project *Circulating American Magazines,* a new project to collect a century's worth of hard-to-access circulation data to document the histories of major American magazines. The data he gathered while at Syracuse University and his research on Gertrude Schalk have been of tremendous help. In addition, his interest in the project and willingness to share information has buoyed me many a time. Brooks, Jeffrey Shanks, David Earle, Lynn Eaton, and Brian Flota have all provided support and opportunities to speak on Daisy Bacon and *Love Story*, which have opened up opportunities to network with other people with the same interests.

The Galactic Central website is one of the most comprehensive databases in the world that provides information on pulp fiction magazines and their publishing companies, authors, editors, and artists. Those who volunteer their time, especially Phil Stephenson-

Payne, to maintain this website are providing enthusiasts and scholars alike much-needed data. Phil's hard work, combined with everyone's willingness to share information, has turned Galactic Central into an extremely valuable tool for collectors and academics alike.

Several institutions were instrumental in my research. Patterson Library in Westfield, New York, provided early family history and the photographs that are in Daisy's childhood chapter. John Paul Wolfe and Christie Herbst at the McClurg Museum in Westfield spent an entire snowy afternoon with me discussing Westfield and Barcelona history. Syracuse University's wealth of information on Street & Smith quickly provided me with the data I needed on several occasions. Shannon O'Neill at Barnard College generously sent me information on Alice Duer Miller on more than one occasion, even after I had visited the college. The staff at Macculloch Hall in Morristown, New Jersey, opened up their archives and let me look into their historical documents pertaining to Henry Wise Miller's family. The licensing team at Condé Nast helped me navigate the permissions journey and quickly provided me with what I needed to make this book a complete and rich history of one of their legacy publications. The staff at Camera Pro in Charlottesville, Virginia, took extraordinary care of 80-year-old negatives and developed them into some of the striking photographs included in this book, and the staff of the City of Staunton library put up with my long hours at the microfiche machine (the loading of which I could never master).

I owe a tremendous debt of gratitude to historian Roger Huss and Monsignor Carroll of the Our Lady of the Magnificat who were kind enough to meet with me and graciously take me on a tour of the property that was donated to the church by Henry Wise Miller.

And finally, I'd like to thank my dear friends, family, and colleagues—Linda Souza, Becky Miles, Pat Binkley, Jeanie Morgan, Maureen Morgan, Rick Olmstead, Kris Feldman, Sara Feldman, Timna Pilch, Dan Horowitz, Helen Horowitz, Ellie Goldstein, Sabrina Wainio, Jody Grams, Karen Thorsen—who always had a listening ear and who put up with my absence at so many activities in order to get this book done. All I can do is thank you for your support and patience.

Preface

If you are familiar with the pulp fiction magazines from the early 20th century, you probably connect them with hard-boiled detectives, scantily clad women, gunslinging cowboys, and crime-fighting heroes. You might be surprised to learn that the pulp fiction magazine, far from being the dismal and shabby publication bought only by the poor and read by the barely literate, was the nucleus of a blockbuster industry that produced a massive variety of stories, many written by the most famous writers of that age or any other and read by millions of readers of all ages and economic classes. Here's another surprise: The biggest selling, most popular pulp fiction magazine of the period wasn't one that featured superheroes or private-eyes or monsters. The most successful pulp fiction magazine was full of love, tears, romance, and happily-ever-after endings: Street & Smith's *Love Story Magazine*.

Queen of the Pulps: The Reign of Daisy Bacon and Love Story Magazine is the story of Daisy Sarah Bacon, the editor of that magazine from 1928 until 1947. Under her management, *Love Story Magazine* hit a rumored circulation of 600,000 copies a week in the late 1920s and early 1930s, a record never surpassed by any other pulp fiction magazine. Under her guidance, *Love Story* became the go-to magazine for hundreds of thousands of readers every single week for almost twenty years. *Love Story*'s success ushered in a wave of imitators that fueled the red-hot romance magazine industry that began in the 1920s and didn't die away until the 1950s.

Daisy wasn't the editor of just *Love Story Magazine*. She was not a one-magazine wonder. Over her twenty-three career at Street & Smith, she was manager of seven other periodicals, some of which were the most storied icons to emerge from the pulp fiction phenomenon. Some were under her management for their entire runs: *Real Love, Ainslee's Smart Love Stories*, and *Pocket Love*. For others, she replaced their previous editors: *Romantic Range, Detective Story Magazine, The Shadow*, and *Doc Savage* magazines during their last years as pulp fiction magazines.

Daisy was a media darling, appearing in dozens of newspaper articles, social columns, and magazine interviews. She used those opportunities to push her ideas about the "modern girl"—a girl who had options, who could be independent and emboldened—in what was still a man's world. Daisy may have peddled a formulaic, artificial idea of romance to hundreds of thousands of women, but she also championed their right to go to work and even to make more money than their husbands. Thirty years before Helen Gurley Brown told women in *Cosmopolitan* they could have it all, Daisy was vociferously saying the same in newspapers across the country.

At the same time, Daisy was a paradox. She supported a certain image of herself in the newspapers, but privately lived a very different life. She ran a magazine notoriously clean-cut in its image, one that never portrayed heroines as immoral or salacious. Yet, for well over a decade during the heyday of *Love Story Magazine,* Daisy was involved with a married man. She projected an image of an impervious, opinionated, strong and successful woman who ran her office like a well-oiled machine. But privately she suffered and her loyal half-sister, Esther, was the real backbone of the office.

The *Queen of the Pulps* is a biography, a love story, and a history of a particular pulp fiction title that has never been told before. Daisy's story is introduced with the beginning of my search for her life, a search that began with an offhand remark, then was placed on ice, then reignited with a casual email, and then became a full-blown obsession when I was entrusted with her personal papers. The epilogue covers events after Daisy's death, interlaced with one of my research trip, when I took a pilgrimage to the only place that she ever truly felt happy.

It behooves me to explain what this book is not: It is not a history of the pulp fiction magazine in general. There are plenty of well-written and thoroughly researched books written by experts already published on the subject. The industry was so vast and so rich, both in stories it produced and the back story of those that wrote and produced them. For the sake of my sanity, I made a calculated decision early on that this book would only discuss the magazines that Daisy managed in her employment at Street & Smith, and only during the time period in which she was involved with them. I hope that I have given the reader enough information into the whys and hows of the industry in general and it will whet her appetite to read more on the subject. If so, many of my favorite histories on the subject are listed in the bibliography of this book.

It is also not a study or survey of the romance genre or the structure of the romance story. I only wished to address a gap that has long been needed to be filled: The history of the romance pulp fiction magazine, a commodity that filled a need after the Victorian romance story paper declined and before the romance paperback novel came into being. The door is open for someone else to dive deeper into this exciting period of American cultural history.

Daisy Bacon was a woman before her time who didn't think twice about taking over the helm of a national magazine before she was thirty years old and who wouldn't shrink away from speaking her mind in front of a newspaper reporter. Yet she was also a woman of paradoxes, who was warm and welcoming to some who knew her, but guarded and impervious to others. She projected an image of the career woman who had it all together, but her private life was full of secrets. She championed her writers, helping them hone their work and eventually get published, but she struggled to find her own writing voice. But Daisy was consistent in one aspect: she believed that the modern woman in America could have it all: in business, in social life, and in love.

Author's note: Many periodical titles include the word "magazine." For the record, each magazine is given its full name in the first mention in this book. Afterward, for ease of reading, the word "magazine" is then dropped from the periodical title except for an occasional reference.

Introduction

Why read a book about a woman who died over thirty years ago and who was forgotten long before that? A woman whose only major accomplishment was being the editor of a pulp fiction magazine, a magazine that printed highly formulaic and forgettable stories? A magazine that, as far as most people are concerned, belongs in the dustbin of history?

Because the woman in question, Daisy Sarah Bacon, was an editor whose magazine, *Love Story Magazine*, probably touched more women during her twenty-year career than any other woman of her generation. Her influence was felt far and wide by a group of readers who suffered silently through the Great Depression, who had very little leisure time on their hands, and whose only source of entertainment was the family radio, an occasional movie, and reading pulp fiction magazines that sold for a dime or fifteen cents.

Daisy was the defender of the "modern girl." She told them it was okay to work and be married. She presented the possibility that they could even make more money than their husband.

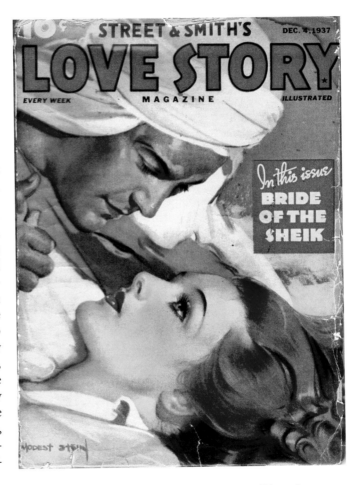

The cover for the December 4, 1937, issue of *Love Story Magazine.* Almost all stories in *Love Story* were based around the everyday "modern girl," with trials and tribulations to which most readers could relate, but set in exciting locations. The heroine of this cover story discovers that the man of her dreams is disguised as a sheik (*Love Story Magazine* © Condé Nast).

3

She told them that they could have it all but, in no uncertain words, they needed to buck up and not wait for a man to hand it to them. She was what one journalist called a "violent, vociferous feminist," decades before the term "feminist" even became part of the common lexicon.

In a nutshell, the heroines that appeared in *Love Story Magazine* were relatable to the women who read their stories. Heroines are secretaries, store clerks, seamstresses. They can also be in occupations that 1930s readers could strive for: Movie stars, lawyers, pilots, artists, business owners. They struggle with money, difficult bosses, recalcitrant boyfriends, and roommates who don't have their best interests in mind. But the reader could always count on the heroine and the hero ending each story with a kiss and the promise of love that would last forever. But before that can happen, the heroine always comes to a reckoning of some kind—a personal moment of growth if you will—that affects her actions in the end. The heroine always comes out the winner, and she always figures it out on her own.

That's why I think the stories were so popular, and why I think Daisy Bacon deserves more recognition than she has ever received.

Named for the cheap paper it was printed on, the pulp fiction magazine was undoubtedly the wildest, strangest, and most thrilling reading material sold to the public during the first half of the 20th century. Each and every week, these gateways to the world were sold to millions of readers, crowding newsstands with stunning and sometimes shocking art and titles in as many settings and genres as could be imagined. Inside the covers were roughly 128 pages chock full of adventure, detective, western, science fiction, weird, and fantastical stories. Iconic figures like Tarzan, Zorro, Conan the Barbarian, The Shadow, The Avenger, Hopalong Cassidy, The Continental Op, and Doc Savage were all born in pulp fiction magazines. At least one in twenty Americans bought a pulp fiction magazine at the price of a dime, during a time when a dime really meant something. During the Depression, when money was scarce and thriftiness was everything, these magazines of frail, rough paper were passed around between friends and family until they literally began to fall apart.

Known first as "pulpwood" or "fiction magazines," the format was born in the late nineteenth century, and the first magazines to gain prominence were full of mainly high adventure stories that encompassed a wide variety of genres and audience appeal. With the Roaring Twenties, the magazines became leaner, and many magazines focused on one specific genre, like the detective story or the western story. The term "pulp fiction" didn't gain traction until the mid–1930s, just about the same time that an avalanche of low-quality magazines—focused more on violence and shock rather than quality— engulfed newsstands. The stigma behind "pulp fiction" was solidified during those grim days.

Love Story Magazine started the phenomenon known as the romance pulp fiction magazine, or otherwise known as the "romance pulp" or the "love pulp." Launched in 1921, *Love Story* was an immediate success, moving from a monthly to a bi-monthly schedule almost immediately to meet demand. Sales continued to increase, and after two years it became a weekly magazine. It was a solid seller its first six years, but after Daisy Bacon took over as editor in 1928, the circulation soared to a rumored 600,000 copies per week, a number that would never be met by any other pulp fiction magazine—before or after, regardless of genre.

Love Story was so successful that a stream of copy cats followed. At the height of their popularity in the 1940s, there were an average of twenty different magazines, featuring nothing but love stories, appearing on newsstands across America. Over three million readers bought a romance magazine every single month. When you consider that six million Americans were reading pulp fiction magazines every month, that means that roughly half of those were buying a romance pulp. So many bought them that the romance, along with the western, became the two most popular genres of pulp fiction sold during the Depression and World War II.

These romance fiction magazines employed dozens, if not hundreds, of people and kept freelance writers, illustrators, and poets fed and clothed when America was grappling with a unemployment figure that would reach twenty-five percent. In an era when many pulp fiction magazines barely profited $500 an issue, a publisher could be confident that a romance magazine would help keep the company afloat. The love pulp may have been the quiet embarrassment of the pulp fiction publisher and contained stories that men wouldn't be caught dead reading, but they paid the bills.

And yet, in the seventy years since their demise, almost nothing has been written about them.

I entered the field of pulp fiction history reluctantly. My grandfather had been a pulp fiction writer for almost twenty years, writing over 400 stories for the western pulps in the heyday of the pulp fiction phenomenon. But after the pulp magazines disappeared from newsstands in the early 1950s, he never discussed the pulps nor his career writing for them. Divorce, family estrangement, and eventually his death in 1971 resulted in my knowing almost nothing about my grandfather until the late 1990s. When I first learned of his secret career, it seemed like a horrible irony: I was finally learning about my grandfather, but what I was learning was, to me, somewhat embarrassing. A pulp fiction writer? Why couldn't he have been a writer of more thoughtful and aesthetic fare?

As I researched my grandfather's life and read up on pulp fiction, I discovered how wrong I was about the stories. Pulp fiction magazines were made with low-grade pulp paper, but the stories were highly entertaining, even addicting at times. They had also been the breeding ground for many a writer who would go on to literary immortality and, contrary to their shoddy reputation, many of the stories were skillfully and expertly crafted—so much so that some are considered the best examples of their genres.

I also learned that the publishing company that bought most of my grandfather's stories, Street & Smith, was the company that produced by far the most pulp magazines in history. Street & Smith had been around since before the Civil War, when they had prospered publishing dime novels. Over the first fifty years of the twentieth century, they published so much material that if there was any company that met the description of "fiction factory," it was Street & Smith. Indeed, the book they published to celebrate their 100-year anniversary is called "The Fiction Factory." I bought a copy of the book online, only to find out that this was a writer-for-hire book, full of accolades of the company's successes and also riddled with errors. Still, it is one of the few books devoted to the company's history, albeit a flawed one.

My grandfather was primarily a writer for Street & Smith's *Wild West Weekly* magazine, so in preparation of publishing his memoir, *Pulp Writer: Twenty Years in the American Grub Street,* I had focused on reading westerns. After *Pulp Writer* was published, I attended PulpFest, the annual national conference for pulp fiction collectors. Here was a world-wide community made up of namely historians, collectors, and writers. Most of them had, for decades, collected, studied, and written about pulp fiction magazines, the stories printed in them, and the writers who wrote them. I was lucky enough to be taken under the wing of pulp historian and writer Ed Hulse, who patiently answered the questions that I threw at him.

The dealer room, where the buying and selling of the old magazines took place, was full of tables covered with copies of *The Spider, Adventure, Western Story, Dime Detective, Argosy, Dime Mystery, Western Story, Amazing Stories, Battle Stories, Operator #5, G-Men, Gangster Stories*. Pulp fiction magazines appeared to be a male-focused industry and were now collected, appreciated, and researched mainly by men.

So when I asked Ed for the name of the biggest selling magazine—the big honcho, the big Kahuna, the powerhouse of the industry—I expected the answer to be a magazine with "Detective," "Thrilling," or "Adventures" in the title, or a magazine like *The Shadow* or *Weird Tales* that had traveled through history as the icons of the pulp fiction phenomenon. But his answer shocked me.

"*Love Story Magazine*," he answered.

Love Story Magazine. The answer was so unexpected that I would have been less surprised if a woman in a bridal gown had marched into the dealer's room at that moment.

It was a Street & Smith magazine, he said. And its editor, Ed added, was a woman named Daisy Bacon.

Well, with a name like that, I just had to do more investigating.

I learned from someone else that Daisy had never married herself, which, to me, was another fascinating nugget of information. Here was a woman who was immersed in the romance story—a story that almost always ended with the promise of a ring—on a daily basis, but never walked down the aisle herself. Had she been hurt at some point? Was she just convinced that she couldn't have both a career and a relationship? (I would very quickly learn how wrong I was in that last assumption.) Or was she leading a private life with someone?

I had found my new adventure.

After the conference, dozens of newspaper articles in which Daisy was interviewed gave me some of basic information about the woman herself. I learned that Daisy had written a book in 1954, *Love Story Writer*, a few years after most pulp fiction magazines had disappeared from newsstands in the wake of comic books, television, and paper rationing during World War II. But after I bought a copy and began to read it, I realized that the book is more of an instruction on how to write love stories and is not a memoir or autobiography. She does pepper the chapters with some personal stories here and there, but not enough to reveal her true nature. Convinced that I would find nothing else about this woman who seemed to be destined to be an asterisk in the annals of publishing history, I wrote a few pieces about Daisy on my blog and then shelved the project.

Until one day in 2011, when a woman named Elaine Knowlden sent me an email.

> I just found your blog posts on Daisy Bacon. I was Daisy's and Esther's caretaker during the last few years of their life.

A few months later, Elaine and I stood in the basement of a house on Long Island. Daisy had moved to the quiet enclave of Port Washington from Manhattan after she left Street & Smith in 1949. Elaine had arrived to take care of Daisy and her half-sister Esther early in 1986. Bill and Nora Haagenson, who lived next door, looked in on them as they advanced in age. Before Daisy died in 1986, she entrusted them with her personal papers and, like the good people they are, kept them in their basement for the next 25 years.

With the home in which Daisy lived the last 35 years of her life perched like a sentry next door, we descended to the basement of the Haagenson home, where two dusty boxes greeted us at the bottom of the stairs.

These were what remained of Daisy's life: Discolored and stained manila folders, 25-year-old tax returns, fistfuls of utility bills, check stubs, receipts. Photographs of every size and type. Faded Polaroid snapshots, duplicate head shots by the dozen, small portraits encased in cheap gold frames and hazy glass, and countless negatives of photographs stuffed into envelopes. Scrapbooks, fragile photo albums. A pencil stub with teeth marks. Journals, manuscripts, notepads, browned newspaper clippings, a few magazines, memo pads, envelopes, hundreds of slips of paper, and old address books. Typed essays. A few short stories. One of the most unusual finds was a set of three heavy long-playing phonograph records, a recording of one of Daisy's radio interviews from 1941.

But the most valuable find were almost twenty diaries. Some were written by Daisy, some by her half-sister Esther, and some by their mother, Jessie. Each one was stuffed to the point of exploding, full of brown and crumbling newspaper clippings and scraps of paper.

I noticed a small black metal box with gold trim on the bottom of one box. I pulled it out and opened it. A burgundy American passport was tucked into the middle of a bundle of tightly folded deeds, letters, and small memo paper. I opened the passport. It was Daisy's, and it was dated August 29, 1929.

The photo inside was of a woman in her late twenties or early thirties. Her clothing looked smart and tailored: A cream silk shirt, pearls, and a floppy hat in the style of the day. Her mouth was set in a half-smile as if she was trying to hide a pleasant secret. Her large, luminous eyes projected confidence, but with a hint of melancholy. This was Daisy Bacon, the darling of the New York publishing world during the 1930s, who edited the biggest selling romance magazine during the Great Depression, who had earned the title "The Queen of the Pulps."

I began to thumb through the passport, interested in the places to which Daisy traveled. There were only a few stamps in the visa section—Cherbourg, Calais, Southampton—and they were all from 1929. As I reached the back cover of the passport, I found three small photographs. They were all of the same man.

One photograph is a professional shot, the man posing in a military uniform from World War I. He has wavy brown hair, close set eyes, a strong nose and chin and a healthy mustache. He could have been in his forties at the time the photo was taken. With his arms folded and looking solemnly off into the distance, he has a look of distinction, of a gentry class lost to the nineteenth century. The print had been carefully and almost perfectly trimmed with scissors into an oval shape. In the next photo, he stands in profile on the shoreline of a mountain lake. In the third, he is standing on a ship deck, arms folded, shuffleboard court in front of him. His eyes are cast downward, but there's a hint of a smile as if he is harboring a secret.

Daisy had locked these away in a metal box and separated from the rest of her photographs, most of which were carelessly scattered amongst her other papers. Who was this person whose memory she had kept separate from all others?

"That must be Henry," Elaine commented as she looked at the photos. "Henry Miller, her lover. She was involved with him for a long time, I think. He was married to a famous writer, Alice Duer Miller." After a minute, she added, "And from what I remember, Henry had built Daisy a house, a 'love nest' somewhere out in the country."

If this was true, the dichotomy was painfully obvious. Daisy, whose magazine featured only chaste and highly conventional stories that frowned on extra-marital sex, was herself involved with a married man. Daisy, who had proclaimed that the "modern girl" of the 1930s could call the shots when it came to relationships and her own destiny, had chosen to stay in a relationship that had the poorest odds of giving her any kind of long-term happiness.

I felt overwhelmed. There was much more information than I had ever expected. Daisy was proving to be a much more complex and challenging subject than I had anticipated. Nevertheless, I took a deep breath, packed up the materials and entrusted them to the local UPS store, and then headed back to California.

1

Holding Court

It didn't matter what part of the country you lived in. If you lived in the United States between 1930 and 1955 and you read a newspaper, the chances are that you came across an article about Daisy Bacon.

Some of these newspapers were based out of small towns, like the *Hammond Times* in Hammond, Indiana, and the *Florence Morning News* in Florence, South Carolina. Others had significant readership, like the *New York Evening Post* and the *New Orleans Times-Picayune*. *The Boston Globe* and the *New York Times* both carried pieces about her. Followers of Walter Winchell's national gossip column—from Logansport, Indiana, to Madison, Wisconsin, to Port Arthur, Texas, to Humboldt, California—could catch stories of Daisy thumbing her nose at the competition and raising eyebrows with her opinions. Readers in San Bernardino and Spokane were treated to feature interviews about how she dressed, what kind of man she dated, and what the "modern girl" wanted in her love life. Readers from Binghamton, New York, to Lowell, Massachusetts, to Portsmouth, Ohio, learned that the "Love Expert Has No Love Herself." Readers of *Parade Weekly* nationwide saw photos of her with her feet up on her desk, surveying her kingdom.

Most articles were accompanied by a photograph. She had translucent skin and softly curling brown hair in the style of the day. Her large, luminous eyes always seemed to be looking down her slightly prominent nose at you, challenging you to even dare to make fun of her, her magazine, or its readers. She had the air of an aloof and no-nonsense woman, and she almost never smiled.

The general backstory ran like this. Daisy Bacon was the long-time editor of Street & Smith's *Love Story Magazine* that had sold heart-throb love, marriage, and happily-ever-after stories to millions of readers since 1921. Stories in the magazine were centered around romance, yes, but they were also packed full of adventure, mystery, and misunderstandings, devious friends and relatives, lost fortunes, and poverty-stricken parents who depended on their daughter's resourcefulness to survive. Sales were respectable when it first appeared on the newsstands. After Daisy took over as editor in 1928, circulation exploded. It was, by all accounts, the model that all other romance magazines attempted to copy, usually unsuccessfully, and was the magazine that more readers bought than any other romance fiction magazine.

This could be attributed, the articles claimed, because Daisy had an uncanny instinct for knowing what her readers would want in their stories: what kind of heroine they liked, what kind of story lines they wanted to read, even what words the hero would use to proclaim his undying love at the end of the story. She had, as one reporter would write,

Daisy in her office at Street & Smith in 1942, sitting behind her famous roll top desk with an equally famous collection of ceramic cats. The portrait on the wall of a woman wearing a straw bonnet, by cover artist Modest Stein, was the cover art for the January 15, 1938, issue of *Love Story* (photograph: W. Eugene Smith, reprinted with permission from Black Star).

"an unfaltering finger on the feminine pulse." She could help those broken down by the Depression or the war forget "physical weariness or an aching heart."

The formula worked. In 1941, thirteen years after Daisy had taken the helm, a journalist claimed that *Love Story* was said to be "larger than *Harper's Magazine, The American Mercury,* and *The Atlantic Monthly* rolled together, and as a business investment, rivaled the biggest industries in the nation."[1] *Love Story* was, by many accounts, the biggest selling pulp fiction magazine of all time. Bigger than *The Shadow,* than *Black Mask,* than *Doc Savage, Western Story, Weird Tales, Argosy, Dime Detective, All-Story, Adventure,* and any of the other roughly 900 pulp fiction titles that appeared between 1896 and 1950.

She was the wonder of the magazine world, who managed to turn out a quality product every single week for twenty years. Year after year, publishers released imitation magazines, only to slink back to their offices once they realized that their efforts didn't make a dent in *Love Story*'s circulation. Other magazines showed some longevity, but they never had the name recognition that *Love Story* did.

Daisy seemed to do it all on her own, or at least it seemed like it. Her closest assistant was her half-sister Esther, who seemed content to stay in the background, handling all of the logistics of managing the magazine while Daisy concentrated on piling through sacks of manuscripts, reading a reported million words a week, picking out the stories that had the right magic for her readers. She alone decided what stories would appear.

Newspaper accounts always included a stock set of interesting tidbits about Daisy. She was an unlikely candidate to oversee a magazine that most would consider sensational. She came from an impressive family heritage: On her mother's side, she was a descendant of leaders of the Puritan settlements, including Captain John Holbrook of Weymouth and William Bradford, five-time governor of Plymouth County. Her father was a descendant of a cousin of Sir Francis Bacon on her fathers' side. A distant relative founded Bacone College in Oklahoma. She lived in an upscale Fifth Avenue apartment, was known for her exquisite taste in clothes, and was rumored to be considered one of the best dressed women in the country. She loved cats, the country, and was a champion for the working girl.

The accuracy of other items seemed to vary with the reports and some were downright fables. Some wrote that she was already successfully making a living as a writer before she came to work at Street & Smith. (She had two articles published in the *Saturday Evening Post* two years before, hardly enough to live on.) They described her as a "tall, pretty blonde." (She wasn't tall, and she wasn't blonde.) She hadn't gone to public school and had been home-schooled. (Only partly true. Her grandmother taught her to read when she was a child, but she ended up the valedictorian of her high school.) She had been at Street & Smith for only a few months before taking over as editor. (It was two years before she was promoted.)

And she was single, either because she was too busy to have a love life or hadn't found the right man. (She was single, but the reasons why were a bit more complicated and rather scandalous.)

She never asked for corrections or retractions. It was as if she enjoyed the mystique of no one really knowing the true Daisy. But the journalist was expected to get a few things correctly or face her wrath afterwards. She hated the term "pulp fiction" because she believed it had been coined by a group of snobbish writers who looked down on the stories that appeared in these magazines—stories that entertained millions of readers every week and ran circles around their literary journals in sales. She preferred the terms "pulp paper" or "pulpwood magazines," terms that accurately reflected that yes, these magazines were made from pulp paper, but that didn't have anything to do with the quality of the words inside.

She didn't believe in denigrating her readers, and they were never looked down upon in any of her interviews. Thousands of letters from readers arrived every month, and from those she knew that her readers weren't from any specific class of people, and the journalist better not pigeon-hole them either.

For the many journalists who visited the *Love Story Magazine* office to meet the legendary Daisy Bacon in person, coming face to face with the actual woman was a shock. They may have been expecting a tough dame or a seasoned smart-talking city reporter-type who could hold her own with the boys, holding a cigarette between ink-stained fingers and with a bottle of whiskey stashed in the top drawer of her desk—someone you would expect to be in charge of a pulp fiction magazine.

Instead, here was a woman who could pass as a socialite or a young matron of the country club set. She dressed impeccably, in suits and dresses more fitting for afternoon soirees. She was soft-spoken and spoke with the air of one who had studied at a storied university. There were no wisecracks about slamming together pulp-paper magazines full of stories snickered at by the social set. She greeted them in her pleasant, clipped voice, maybe even smiling at their little jokes. She had manners and was brought up to always act like a lady.

She certainly didn't look like she fit in her surroundings. The office always looked like it had been fighting a battle with piles of paper since the dawn of time and it was losing the war. Her desk was situated so the back of it faced the middle of the room; most likely to hide the explosion of papers that continually covered it. The condition of her desk looked like it would have belonged to a "crossroads justice of the peace,"[2] as she colorfully admitted. A long mahogany table held stacks of manuscripts, waiting for her judgment on whether they would be printed in *Love Story* or be whisked back to their owners via the U.S. Mail.

The office was almost always freezing. Rumor had it that she kept it that cold on purpose, to keep unwanted visitors from staying too long. Having been raised on the shores of Lake Erie, Daisy didn't seem to even notice that her guests, huddled in their coats, were shivering. She would graciously offer them a chair next to her roll top desk, the top of which was covered with several dozen ceramic cats. But, she wasn't afraid to be forward, even rude with visitors. She had a habit of covering her nose with a handkerchief when male visitors arrived.

Reporters came armed with plenty of questions, first about her magazine and its readers. What did she think about the state of love in America? What did the "modern girl" want in her love life? Why did she stick to the soft and sentimental in her stories, when so many movies, and books were becoming more and more sensational and revealing in their descriptions of love? What kind of man was the American girl wanting? And could a "modern girl" *really* keep working after getting married?

The braver ones asked about her own love life. Did she really do much of her daily work from her own bed? Was it true that she believed in astrology and the supernatural? What kind of man did she find attractive? Why hadn't she ever gotten married herself?

Once the questions started, the pleasantries would have stopped and Daisy Bacon would have gotten down to the business of the interview. And she had plenty to say.

French Novels

According to legend, even Daisy's birth was romantic.

Her parents had planned to name her Sarah after her maternal grandmother. But, according to a newspaper story printed forty-four years later, the attending physician did not feel that "Sarah Bacon" was glamorous enough. He had just finished reading a romantic English novel centered around a woman named Lady Daisy Bacon. He became a little misty-eyed, thinking of the book that had transported him to a place full of castles, heroes rescuing damsels in distress, and kisses under the moonlight.

The name Sarah wasn't fitting, the physician argued, for an infant that was beautiful and "destined to flower into gorgeous womanhood."

"Name her Daisy," he entreated.[1]

Whether it's myth or fact, it's quite the fitting beginning for the woman who would eventually become queen of the pulp romance story.

In reality, Daisy's early life was anything but a fairy tale. It didn't begin in an English castle, nor in a New York penthouse, nor a southern plantation. It began in a nondescript town with a less than memorable name, Union City, that was perched on the far western border of Pennsylvania where her father, Elmer Ellsworth Bacon, ran a general store.

Elmer was a humble man, a merchant of goods who may not have been overly wealthy, but still took great pride in the role he played in his community. He was well liked. He was a hard worker. He traveled far and wide to see relatives and friends, even though he wasn't healthy much of the time.

In the only surviving photograph of him, he wears a wool coat, a natty diamond-pattern scarf, and a waistcoat pin. His strawberry-blonde handlebar mustache is so large that it dominates his face with its curled ends extending far out into space. His slight

Daisy's father, Elmer E. Bacon. Born in 1864, he was 34 when Daisy was born (Daisy Bacon collection).

build, prominent cheekbones, slightly asymmetrical jaw, large ears, and small chin give him a friendly, almost comical demeanor. While Elmer doesn't smile in the photograph, there is no hiding his clear, penetrating eyes that shine mischievously, as if he's about to tell the photographer a great joke he heard at his store that day.

Elmer was born in 1864 in Spafford, New York, to David and Ruth Bacon. David was reportedly a descendant of a cousin of Sir Francis Bacon, the scientist, author, philosopher, and Attorney General and Lord Chancellor of England in the seventeenth century. Eventually Elmer's parents settled in Westfield, New York, a few miles inland of Lake Erie, where David ran a profitable farm. When the 1880 census was taken, Elmer was the fourth of five children in the household.

Westfield was a thriving town with businesses that included general stores, taverns, paper mills, tanneries, breweries, and banks. Churches with imposing steeples in brick and wood frames were abundant. Grape growing and farming were the area's main industries, and furniture making was a thriving industry in the nearby Jamestown area.[2]

Westfield had already earned fame for being the town where an eleven-year-old Grace Bedell had gained notoriety in 1860 for writing a letter to presidential candidate Abraham Lincoln. In the letter, she advised him to grow a beard, assuring him that more women would urge their husbands to vote for him if he did. "All the ladies like whiskers,"

Downtown Westfield, New York, during "Old Home Week," ca. 1909 (from the Patterson Library archive collection).

she confided in the letter. One month after receiving the letter, Lincoln was growing a beard. Later, a dentist-turned-farmer named Thomas B. Welch, a steward in the Methodist Church, would move his burgeoning grape-drink industry to Westfield, and the town would become the centerpiece for the Welch Grape Juice Company.[3]

Daisy wrote later that her father was self-conscious of his hair coloring and dyed his mustache a dark brown to hide his Danish lineage, although if there was Danish ancestors, they were several generations removed. Regardless, he needn't have worried about how he was viewed by others; he was regarded in town with respect and was noted by the local newspaper to be a young man "of honor and integrity."[4] In 1888, Elmer married Carrie Thompson, a "very estimable young lady" who had migrated to Westfield from Ohio about two and a half years before. The couple stayed in Westfield until 1894, at which time he moved to Waterford, Pennsylvania, about 38 miles from Westfield, where he opened a grocery store. The route between Waterford and Westfield became a familiar one for Elmer who continued to maintain his strong emotional and familial ties that he had formed in there.

But, in 1895, Elmer Ellsworth Bacon showed the guts and boldness that his daughter would duly inherit. He stood up to his family and announced the unthinkable, that he and Carrie were getting a divorce. Elmer had fallen in love with another woman, Jessie Holbrook.

Even though Elmer had his own impressive lineage, he took on an equally if not more distinguished family line when he became involved with Jessie. Jessie's father, Simon Bolivar Holbrook, was a descendant of Thomas Holbrook, who arrived in Massachusetts in 1634 from Weymouth, England. Several generations later, another ancestor married a

Daisy's mother, Jessie Holbrook. Born in 1870, she had five older brothers and a twin sister, Maude, who died in infancy (Daisy Bacon collection).

descendant of William Bradford, who had arrived on the Mayflower and had been governor of Plymouth Colony five different times. Another ancestor was reportedly John Holbrook of Vermont, a publisher in colonial times.[5]

Simon and his wife, Sarah Ann, were farmers in Barcelona, a small fishing village adjacent to Westfield and on the shore of Lake Erie. Once a sea captain, Simon then turned to dealing in cattle and selling horses. He and Sarah eventually took over the running of her father's farm in nearby Barcelona.

Jessie was a sprite of a young woman with large, heavy-lidded eyes and brown hair that curled tightly around the base of her neck. Despite her petite stature, she was a tough little nut, unafraid of standing in the way of danger to protect or help a suffering animal. Later in life, even when she was suffering from debilitating health issues, Jessie would still make the effort to join with fierce New York animal activists, including Mrs. George Bethune Adams, who eventually founded and managed a hospital for animals. In boiling New York summers, they would stand on Third Avenue in New York City with pails of water for the delivery horses. Jessie thought nothing of bounding into the traffic and grabbing a horse's bridle and launching a tirade at the driver of a coal wagon over the mishandling of his team. "My good man, listen to what I am saying about those reins," she commanded. "I've forgotten more about horses than you will ever know."[6]

Jessie's bravery no doubt was ingrained in her by being the youngest of six children and, after her twin sister died in infancy, the only girl. If anything, having five older brothers taught her to be tough and to fight.

And fight the family did. They were a formidable, quirky, passionate family, especially when it came to animal welfare. Daisy would write later that the Holbrook family "was notorious for getting into hot water about animals and a street fight was such a common occurrence among them that it was never given a passing thought."[7] The family's passion towards helping animals that were abused, neglected, or abandoned ran strong. It was a philosophy that would resonate deeply with Daisy for her entire life.

After they married, Elmer built up a lucrative grocery trade in Waterford while Jessie set up housekeeping. In 1896, Elmer and Jessie moved to Union City in Erie County, Pennsylvania, again not far from the Westfield area, and set up another mercantile there where he and a partner sold everything from flour and sugar to nuts and bolts and supplies to the Union City Chair Company.

It was there, on May 23, 1898, that Daisy Sarah Bacon was born.

In Daisy's earliest surviving photograph, she is roughly six months old, wearing a crisp white frock and sitting on a fur blanket in a photography studio. A small black dog sits next to her, marking the beginning of a life-long bond with canine and feline companions. As in most later photographs, she doesn't smile. Instead, she quizzes the photographer with direct, inquisitive eyes as if to ask, "tell me, what is the point of all this?"

Life was idyllic during the summer and fall of Daisy's first eighteen months. Every day Jessie painstakingly wrote on small lined memo paper of Daisy's activities: Playing on the front porch, riding a toy horse, observing baby chicks with wonder, and greeting visitors who arrived almost daily. When "Papa" came home from the store, they took the horse and buggy out and went for a drive so Daisy could soak in the wonders of the countryside.

Daisy and the first of many four-legged companions in her life, ca. 1899 (Daisy Bacon collection).

But, in October 1899, Jessie noted in her journal that a doctor had paid a visit, but she left out any other details. In the next few days, the doctor returned and "stayed a long time." It was the last entry in Jessie's diary of Daisy's babyhood. Elmer was sick, and apparently had been sick for some time.

On November 6, 1899, Elmer checked into the Invalid's Hotel and Surgical Institute in Buffalo, a supposedly "state-of-the-art facility" that advertised itself as being equipped with all of the latest medical machines and patient therapies to help those with chronic diseases. The hotel was owned by Doctor Ray Vaughn Pierce, one of the richest men in Buffalo, who had become very wealthy selling questionable medicine by mail-order and through the sale of his book *The People's Common Sense Medical Advisor*.[8]

Elmer seemed to be truly frightened when he wrote his wife after his arrival.

My Darling Wife:

I arrived here all right at noon today. I am somewhat tired but stood the journey pretty well. My case is so much worse than they thought at first I have got to stay for some time. I don't know what to do but I might better stay and try and get some help if I don't I may not live a year. I have had a thorough examination. They are very careful and didn't hurt me much. There isn't any stone in the bladder. The inflammation is contracting my bladder and in a little while it won't hold any water at all.

… I am worried most to death about you. I only hope your mother is there. If she isn't have her come at once. You can come and stay with me a few days later on I must mail this card I think you will get it in the morning…. Write soon. Keep up good courage.

May God bless you and Daisy.

Elmer[9]

Even with its modern technology, the Invalid's Hotel could not help Elmer, and after six weeks they sent him home. There, on January 1, 1900, the very first day of the new century, Elmer passed away. He was just shy of his 35th birthday. The account in the local newspaper, the *Westfield Republican*, reported that he died of Bright's Disease.

"Mr. Bacon was a man of good habits, enterprising and progressive in business affairs, and was respected by all who were honored with his acquaintance," the *Westfield Republican* printed on the 10th of January.[10] His fellow grocer's merchants association acknowledged Elmer in a separate tribute in the newspaper and declared that they would shut their businesses for his funeral.

Jessie and Daisy, who was just about to turn two, eventually moved back to the family farm in Barcelona, a small village on the perimeter of Westfield. Positioned right on the shores of Lake Erie, residents of Barcelona always had to brace for winters, when bone chilling winds swept snow into drifts against houses that banked the Portage Trail. But the lake was also a source of income for the thriving village. Hotels and stores that sold goods, hardware, food, and fishing supplies flourished. Passenger boats brought people across the lake to work, visit, or to play. Fishing was such that young men were regularly excused from school to work on the boats. Barcelona was, by one local historian's account, "a glorious, noisy, bustling village of activity."[11]

Indeed, fishing and transporting passengers had become such a large industry that Barcelona had become an established port of entry by the U.S. Government, with a lighthouse that was the first in the world to be lit by natural gas. But after railroad transportation became more readily available, the industry of ferrying passengers dried up, and the lighthouse was deactivated in 1842. Still, the lighthouse continued to be a centerpiece of the town and would even be included in one of Daisy's early pieces that appeared in *Love Story*.

Barcelona Lighthouse, ca. 1900. The exact location of the Holbrook farm was close to the light-house, although the farm's exact location isn't clear in the historical record (courtesy Patterson Library, Westfield, NY).

The Holbrook farm was the centerpiece of Jessie's family. To Daisy, "the farm" was always present in her memories of childhood. By the time Jessie and Daisy moved in, Simon's passion for the welfare of animals had resulted in the property becoming something of a menagerie. Daisy's earliest memories were of raccoons taking up residency, along with a various assortment of abandoned animals including cats, a three-legged dog that ran away from a circus, and friendly crows that took refuge there.

As Daisy grew up on the Holbrook farm in Barcelona, another important part of her childhood began. Her grandmother, Sarah, who had a weakness for reading French novels, took it upon herself to teach Daisy to read and write when she was three years old. She began to instill in Daisy a strong appreciation for literature as provided for in romantic and risqué French romance stories.

Daisy's memories also reveal that, from an early age, she considered herself to be something of an editor prodigy. In later interviews she recalled that, at the age of five, she altered the Lord's Prayer in the family Bible—an heirloom that her mother had cherished for years—from "Our Father which art," to Our Father, who art." She also rewrote the ending to *Little Women*. Angry at the original ending, she had Jo marry Laurie.[12]

As for Jessie, she managed to move forward despite her grief. The date of Elmer's death would be a dark anniversary that Jessie would commemorate in her diary thirty years later. In her quiet moments she wrote poetry, and in the months after Elmer's death, she wrote a poem that she would eventually turn into a song. She paid to have sheet music published, with Daisy's photograph embossed on the cover page of the song.

The Child's Lament

A little child from her sleep one night
    Awoke in sad alarm—
"Mama, I'm afraid and dreaming,
    Please take me in your arms.
I thought I heard papa coming,
    He sure must be near;
I guess he would think me a big girl now,
    It's so long since he was here."[13]

Jessie either continued with Elmer's grocery or set up her own in Westfield. She kept the same ledger that Elmer had used for his grocery business and continued with entries from her own business.

It's questionable if Jessie was ever accepted into the Bacon family. She may have been considered a "homewrecker" due to Elmer's divorce from Carrie. This rift didn't seem to improve even after Elmer's death. Sometime during the next year, a dispute began between her and Elmer's father David. The back page of the ledger shows the following entry:

David Bacon accused me of stealing April 3, 1901.

On May 2, 1901, a notice of judgment, entitled David Bacon vs. Jessie Bacon, appeared at regular intervals in the *Westfield Republican*, declaring that property owned by her late husband was now in foreclosure. On July 3, 1901, David bought that property, by referee, for $2,725.

Small towns being what they are, it must have been extremely difficult for Jessie to not cross paths with her father-in-law or his family. But it appears that the break between Jessie and David Bacon was a permanent one. Daisy never mentions her father's side of the family in any of her papers, other than to mention the lineage from Sir Francis Bacon.

In the early summer of 1904, David Bacon was surprised by his family and several dozen other guests with a birthday party. The paper listed every relative and friend who had traveled far and wide to surprise the patriarch. But there is no mention of Jessie or her family attending the party.

There was, however, another notable guest: A certain George E. Ford, minister and widower, who had the honor of presenting the birthday present on behalf of the entire group, a "beautiful Morris chair," to Bacon. Ford gave a few "fitting remarks" to the crowd. A minor note, but Ford would later have a monumental impact on Daisy's life, as he would eventually become her stepfather.

By the time George Ford had arrived in Westfield to celebrate David Bacon's birthday, he had already made a name for himself in the previous towns in which he lived, and not always in a positive light. Born in England around 1858, Ford immigrated to the United States and, by 1900, was living in Bridgeton, New Jersey.

George had changed jobs at least four times since arriving in America: First as a Baptist minister, then a leader of American volunteers, then as a member of a "faith curist" religious cult, and then a second Methodist minister in Paterson, New Jersey.[14]

He had also survived a serious accusation of improprieties with a young woman in this last church, causing him to flee town. Pastor Ford made the front page of the *Philadelphia Inquirer*, but apparently the church dropped their accusations and Ford returned to the church.[15]

By early 1903, Ford had moved his wife Gertrude and family again to West Portland, New York, and Ford spent time in nearby Westfield, attending services there and baptizing churchgoers. Now 42, he was responsible for either six or seven children in his household, although it wasn't clear whether the children were his or his wife's from a previous marriage. Now, Gertrude was pregnant again.

But on March 31, 1904, Gertrude died after giving birth. Three months later, George attended David Bacon's birthday party. After that, nothing is reported on his whereabouts until November, at which time the newspaper reported that a financial donation was being taken up for George Ford. None of his children from his marriage

George Ford, Jessie's second husband. George seems to have been a wanderer, in and out of towns and careers (Daisy Bacon collection).

with Gertrude were mentioned as being part of his household.

George Ford may have had a colorful and somewhat scandalous past. But Jessie Holbrook Bacon saw something in him, because sometime between 1906 and 1908, George and Jessie began a relationship. In early 1906, they were married. On October 1, 1906, Jessie gave birth to Daisy's half-sister, Esther Joa Ford, who would become Daisy's lifetime friend, supporter, work colleague, and confidant.

If there was any marital or family happiness in the Ford household, it wouldn't last. George died shortly after Esther was born, on January 24, 1907. Esther stated later that her father died from tuberculosis. The *Jamestown Evening Journal* was short and to the point when reporting his death, and the children from his previous marriage were not mentioned. Esther would mention in diaries decades later of a "Sis" that was not Daisy, and it is possible that this person was one of her half-siblings. But, for the most part, any children born to Ford before he met Daisy's mother disappeared from her history.

By the summer of 1908, both of Jessie's parents were also dead. Daisy, now ten years old, undoubtedly was affected by the grief and discord surrounding her. She had already been subjected to the death of her father, disputes between her mother and grandfather, her mother's financial difficulties, upheaval with her mother's remarriage, the death of her beloved grandmother and tutor in 1906, the death of her stepfather, and then, in 1908, the death of her grandfather, Simon Holbrook. Then, in October 1908, Daisy's other grandfather, David Bacon, was killed at the age of 80 when he walked in front of a train.[16] So many tragedies experienced by such a young person in such a short period of time undoubtedly had a profound effect on her psyche.

After the death of Simon Holbrook, Jessie's older brother Henry took over the farm, and it wasn't long before Jessie felt the need to move. In 1909, Jessie moved into a multi-family unit on Jefferson Street. By 1915, the family had moved again, and then again that year moved again to an apartment on Washington Street. But for the most part, the family of three appeared to have enjoyed some semblance of stability after 1910. They were only mentioned in the town newspaper when Jessie's poems were printed, when Daisy lost a fountain pen and placed a notice in the classifieds, and when Daisy and Esther made the high school's honor roll—a regular occurrence.

Many articles about Daisy claimed that Daisy had been home-schooled, and one even claimed she had "never seen a classroom" and had been privately tutored in some subjects. But elementary school became compulsory in New York State after 1867, so more than likely Daisy attended the Barcelona School for the elementary grades. In both 1909 and 1913, the *Westfield Republican* acknowledged her as a student with perfect attendance. In 1913, the paper showed Daisy as a member of the public-school rolls who passed the entrance examinations to be accepted into high school, earning scores in the 90s for reading, English, and writing. In 1917, Daisy won a Daughters of the American Revolution contest with her essay "The Louisiana Purchase, Its Extent and Influence," that was published in the *Westfield Republican*. And the school district's commencement pamphlet issued in

Daisy (left) and her half-sister, Esther Joa Ford, who was her best friend, confidante, and supporter for most of her life (Daisy Bacon collection).

1917–1918 show that not only did Daisy graduate from the high school in Westfield (then known as the Westfield Academy and Union Free High School) in 1917, she was also the valedictorian.

In the spring of 1917, the United States had entered the war in Europe. During the subsequent months, a feverish pitch of patriotism spread across the country, and Westfield was not immune to the fervor. As part of her responsibilities at commencement, Daisy was requested to deliver a special speech at graduation. Philander Priestly Claxton, United States commissioner of education, had issued a request to all high schools that their commencement programs should include "an important place be given to the expression of patriotic sentiments." His directive, accompanied by a "gift" of a watercolor of the Washington Monument, stressed that "...It is highly important that at this time that every American should be fired with patriotism." Daisy dutifully gave her address, in which she proclaimed, "This is the most critical time in our history, probably in the history of the world." Daisy unveiled the gift and when she delivered the speech, "The climax of patriotic fervor was reached, for she transmitted the spirit of the majestic shaft upon which the eyes of the audience rested to her hearers and echoed its message in simple but effective language."[17]

Daisy herself became caught up in the patriotic fever. She created a scrapbook filled with war sentimentality, pasting poems that touched subjects like the loss of love, secret love, Fate, sorrow, and of the loss of war; editorial illustrations; and newspaper and magazine clippings.

At the end of her schooling in Westfield, Daisy had been awarded a small scholarship to attend Barnard College, a women's college affiliated with Columbia University. But the scholarship was for only $100, a paltry sum even in 1917. Daisy never made it to Barnard College, and there are no indications in her papers that she went to any other college either.

By this time, Jessie needed to find a job that would meet the needs of her and her daughters. Daisy had dreams of becoming a writer and, like many others, felt that living in a city would provide her with more opportunities. Jessie and her two daughters—Daisy fresh out of high school and Esther barely ten years old—packed up and moved to New York City.

Daisy in what is most likely a commencement dress. Newspaper accounts later claimed she was schooled at home and never attended public school. Records show she attended the high school in Westfield and was valedictorian (Daisy Bacon collection).

3

City of Promise

Even though the women probably had already visited New York City on more than one occasion prior to moving there, it still must have been a shock to the system to be planted into the sounds, smells, and sights of the city permanently. The farms and vineyards of Westfield must have seemed worlds away as they took in the whistles of policemen directing traffic, the honking of horns, and the clanging of trolley cars that competed with the noise of commerce everywhere. The sight of skyscrapers—ten, twenty, even thirty stories high—filled the horizon.

New York City, ca. 1920. Daisy, Esther, and Jessie arrived here about the time that this photograph was taken. The city was already experiencing a population boom that began before the turn of the century, and over the next ten years an explosion in building, especially skyscrapers, would change the city landscape (courtesy Library of Congress).

Encroachments on old New York were occurring everywhere. The Trinity Church, a Gothic church built in 1846 in lower Manhattan and one of the highest points on the New York skyline for several decades, was already dwarfed by life insurance buildings, such as American Surety and Bankers Trust, on either side, some of which were at least twice its height.

The city was choking with new arrivals from other parts of the country, a wave that had began roughly ten years prior. In Times Square, crowds of hurried businessmen moved on to their next destination. Farther south, automobiles careened around the intersection of Fifth Avenue, Broadway, and East 22nd Street, oblivious to the magnificent centerpiece of the Flatiron Building that overlooked the constant flow of people and the incessant noise of automobiles and trucks.

Along with the throngs of Americans who were moving to the city, businesses were migrating as well, including publishing houses that began to centralize in New York from other cities such as Boston and Philadelphia. Most of the famous publishing houses we know today either moved to or came into existence in New York in the 1920s.

Newspapers in 1919 were full of headlines of the looming Paris Peace Conference and the treaty of Versailles and how it was going to strangle the German people. Yet newsboys, already savvy to what sold papers, knew people wanted to read more sensational news: the bombing of eight cities, the disappearance of aviators who attempted long-distance air flights. And, every day, the looming nationwide prohibition of alcohol was in the news. By October 1919, the Volstead Act was in effect and everyone was preparing for the final act to go into effect the next year.

Jessie, always the horse lover, spent time on the streets of New York campaigning for the rights of animals (Daisy Bacon collection).

Even with the excitement of living in Manhattan, the sobering reality of economic need pressed on Jessie. She needed to find a job. But even with the vast changes occurring in the city and the granting of women's right to vote quickly approaching, women's opportunities in the working world were slow to change. For Jessie, a fifty-year-old woman with no skills, job opportunities were limited. She may have had a historic family background, but pedigree was of little use when it came to job skills.

A few years later, Daisy ghost-wrote an article, "On the Fourteenth Floor," a first-person account of a woman—a mother of two daughters—who has run out of money and moves to New York City in search of a job. Retail work is available, but she wisely decides that she would not be a good candidate to be a saleswoman. One day, she lunches with a friend at a large hotel in the city and notices that the hotel is bursting with business. Foot traffic in the lobby is thick and without letup. The woman realizes that this is a thriving operation and most likely has job positions available. On a whim, the woman applies for a job, not really knowing what position they would place her in. The manager says she can begin the next day as a chambermaid for thirty-six dollars a month, along with room and board.

"On the Fourteenth Floor," rich in detail as to the woman's responsibilities and day-to-day activities, is sprinkled with descriptions of her interactions with the clientele. The author also writes of a friendly co-worker named Zayda with whom she becomes close friends. Daisy would give homage to Zayda later in her early career at Street & Smith.

Forty years later, Esther would tell stories of the time when the three women lived at a hotel in Manhattan. They lived at the Hotel Astor, Esther said, and socialized with Arturo Toscanini's wife Carla. Esther remembered Mrs. Toscanini cooking traditional Italian dinners for her and her sister in her suite, much to the consternation of the hotel management. Although there is no documentation proving this, and neither Jessie nor Daisy mention living at the Astor in their journals, Esther's reminisces about socializing with the wife of the legendary conductor line up chronologically with the time that she lived at the hotel.

Working as a chambermaid and living at the Hotel Astor and rubbing elbows with celebrities don't really add up. But anything is possible, and it could have been that Jessie was working at the Astor and given room and board.

Daisy was moving through a couple of jobs of her own, none of which she cared to remember when she jotted down her early years in her journals decades later. "Tried a lot of things and didn't care much for it," was her recollection ten years later.[1] She then dabbled at being a model, and even sat for a photographer for an instructional article. Surviving photographs show her even posing partially nude in one photo, tastefully standing with long swaths of chiffon draped over her sloping shoulders and falling to the ground. She stands on her tiptoes, holding a small sphere in her hands,

Daisy, ca. 1923. One of her earliest jobs was as a model (Daisy Bacon collection).

her hair pinned up. But she was too short to make a go of modeling, she would say later.

The late 1910s were a transient time for the three women. Eventually the women had enough financial security that they could move to an apartment. By 1920 they had moved to 605 Lexington Avenue, in an area just north of what used to be called Turtle Bay, and rented an apartment above stores that lined the street. Just a few blocks to the east was a neighborhood with one of the most harrowing histories in New York City. Just a generation earlier, the area had been packed with slaughterhouses, cattle pens, coal yards, and breweries. But the neighborhood was already going through transition, and by the time they had moved there the slaughterhouses had disappeared. Daisy, Esther, and Jessie rented an apartment above stores consisting of jewelry shops, the occasional antique shop, and a drug store. An immense building resembling a Russian orthodox church towered over the corner, and a YMCA occupied a large portion of another block south of the apartment.[2]

Eventually Daisy landed a job at the Harry Livingston Auction Company, which specialized in auctioning off luggage abandoned by patrons at some of the city's bigger hotels. On auction days, Daisy's job was to tally and collect the money from buyers. Her job may have been a dead end, but she stayed there for at least a few years. The terminal boredom of keeping books gave her time to exercise her imagination and write various short stories and articles, and experience on this job would eventually give her material to write another article that would be her biggest break up to then.

Summers in New York City were close to unbearable for many. The humidity, compounded with the heat from cement and the choking pollution from automobiles made it hard to breathe. In the early 1920s, it appears that Jessie was working at resorts outside of the city, possibly even going back to the Chautauqua Lake area where tourism was booming in the summer months. She took Esther with her, while Daisy stayed in the city to work. It was during one of these long hot seasons that Daisy entered a romantic relationship that would be the most influential and longest-lasting she would have. On July 10, 1922 or 1923, she met Henry Wise Miller.

Henry was twenty-two years older than her, a dapper, well-bred, and Harvard-educated man of high society and expensive tastes. He was of slight build, a little under 5 feet 10 inches tall, and so thin that in photos his suits and overcoats are well tailored but appear to be too big on him. He looks like a ten-year-old boy dressed up in his father's overcoat and bowler hat. His close-set eyes, high set forehead, and prominent mustache gave him a sensual look. He had the appearance of someone who looked down on the middle and working classes.

Henry was born in 1875 into a well-established New Jersey family. His father, Jack, was a Naval Lieutenant commander. Henry's mother, Katharine Wise, was a granddaughter of Edward Everett, a legendary orator who also served as president of Harvard University from 1846 to 1849. Everett also has a place in history as being the first speaker at a ceremony held to honor those that had fallen at the Battle of Gettysburg. Everett's speech, which was 13,000 words and ran for two hours, was followed by the 272-word speech given by President Abraham Lincoln.[3]

Eventually the Miller family settled in the home of Jack's family, Macculloch Hall in Morristown, New Jersey. Named after the family of his paternal grandmother, Mary Louisa Macculloch, the house is a large colonial mansion situated on expansive acreage, and in the 19th century was a center for Whig politics and later the Republican party before the Civil War. Eventually it became a historical home and museum. Mary ruled over Macculloch Hall as grand matriarch. Her large and domineering personality was the first strong female role model for Henry.

Henry's family was wealthy but, more importantly, they were also old money, and Henry never forgot it. It was an insular, select society in which money was not enough to admit. Breeding was more important, and yet, even that was not enough. You had to be accepted by the "inner circle," a group of people with money, society, and name. Henry looked at it as a golden era. "They were not intellectuals, they were the reverse of strenuous, but say what you please about them, no one ever had a better time."[4]

Henry was married to Alice Duer Miller, a writer who became quite successful in the early 1910s with her column in the *New York Herald Tribune*, "Are Women People," which championed the suffrage movement through humorous and satirical essays. The column would put the public on notice that this was a woman with a biting sense of humor who did not give an inch even to the highest of public servants. Writing novels and poetry as early as the 1890s when she was studying mathematics at Barnard, Alice then found success with her novel *Come Out of the Kitchen* in 1916, a romantic comedy which eventually became a play and movie. She began to sell stories to *The Saturday Evening Post*, firing off short stories just as frequently as those of a pulp fiction writer.

Henry Wise Miller. Henry attempted several jobs before going off to Paris in World War I as a Red Cross Officer. He managed a factory that manufactured artificial limbs for the French military (Daisy Bacon collection).

Henry, on the other hand, struggled to gain a foothold in a career. He returned from the Great War facing the fact that he didn't have a lot of experience in keeping a stable job. "The first ten years after I left college I had and lost I don't know how many jobs. At a class dinner I made second place for numbers of failures so far. It became second nature to me to look at any employment as temporary only. I got expert in jumping before the ship sank, in quitting before the business collapsed or before I was fired."[5] Eventually, Henry became a stockbroker and, in 1918, bought a seat on the New York Stock Exchange with money lent to him by his wife.

By the time that Daisy met Henry, he and Alice had settled into a life of comfort and tony social circles. Both Alice and Henry were regulars at the Algonquin Round Table, which was at its height of fame. Some were surprised by the radical turn of Alice's interests, from being a staunch and fierce suffragette to a member of a group that prided itself on its lack of work ethic, biting joke sessions, and non-stop party atmosphere. While Alice had progressed into middle age and was considered the matriarch of the Round Table, she could hold her own with the sharp-tongued group and became close friends with Alexander Woollcott, George Kaufman, and Harpo Marx. Her relationship with Woollcott was almost as close as her marriage with Henry. Alice was much loved by many: She was a successful and hard-working writer, but with a witty sense of humor. She traveled in the highest circles and was connected with the upper echelon of authors, playwrights, critics, and publishers. She was instrumental in getting her niece Ellin's family's approval so Ellin could marry Irving Berlin, because Ellin's parents didn't approve of her marrying a Jew. Alice lent money to Harold Ross so he could get his brainchild magazine, *The New Yorker*, off the ground. She later ushered in a few relatives to work on the magazine.

Henry was a frequenter to the Round Table, too, and played poker upstairs with the famous Thanatopsis Poker and Inside Straight Club. But he was seen less frequently at the Round Table gatherings. Henry gave off the impression of being rather snooty, giving off an aura of one who doesn't mingle well with others, much less those of a different economic class.

Henry and Alice had developed a habit of living separately. It seemed that almost as soon as Hollywood began to emerge as the world's centerpiece for

Alice Duer Miller: Author, poet, suffragette, screenwriter, member of the cynical and free-wheeling Algonquin Round Table (photograph: Alice Duer Miller Papers, Binder 20, Collection BC-17-Photographs, Barnard Archives and Special Collections, Barnard Library, Barnard College).

moving-making, Alice spent several months a year there writing screenplays for Cecil B. DeMille. She also began taking long trips to Europe. Many times, as soon as she returned to New York, Henry would leave for his own trip. He admitted later that their living apart wasn't necessarily just because of career choices.

> Throughout our married life we were separated for considerable lengths of time…. We found by experience that such partings were salutary. We came to believe that marriage did not preclude a certain amount of freedom, or better still a holiday. Yes, I mean a holiday from each other.[6]

He alluded to their conscious decisions to live separately and perhaps in an open-marriage arrangement saying, "Our married life was successful, but whether because we broke all the rules, or in spite of that, I do not know."[7]

Still, their lifestyle wasn't without controversy or objection. Henry noted several years later that his in-laws didn't particularly care for their choices.

Many people—and that included members of our own family—thought we were crazy. My mother-in-law told me a few days before we were married that it was still not too late, if I wanted to change my mind. And thirty years later, my mother remarked at a large family luncheon: "Alice, I don't see why you haven't divorced Harry years ago." This at my own dinner table.[8]

By the time Daisy met Henry, he must have appeared to have emerged from a time capsule: He was very much an example of the genteel, wealthy life of the 1890s. This was a man who had grown up with chauffeurs, butlers, and valets, and he had very prescribed and exact notions on how they should behave. "A servant, opening the front door, should let go the handle, not clutch it as if poised for flight," he would note later. Taxi drivers should mind their manners. "I don't like a chauffeur or taxi driver to ask me: "Where to?" Let him start the car as soon as I am in and keep on driving until I tell him what to do." He chafed at those who didn't consider his needs above their own. "Servants are naturally guided by their sense of what is orderly rather than our own comfort. My effort has been to reduce the working of that sense to a minimum."[9]

Above all, he was a lover of fine material possessions, such as antique furniture, silver, jade, and porcelain. Still, he wasn't above scouring wrecking yards and, perhaps, auctions of abandoned luggage to look for treasures. Knowing this, it's very possible that Henry may have met Daisy while attending a Harry Livingston auction.

Daisy must have been dazzled by the older man. Being well-heeled and entrenched in high society, he could steer her into circles that she would never have been able to encroach before. In Daisy, Henry saw another brilliant woman who instinctively knew how to travel in well-heeled circles, but much younger and more malleable. He himself was awed by brilliant women. Henry might have been a snob, but he was a strong supporter of suffrage and the advancement of women in society.

And despite his stuffy demeanor, he loved a practical joke, and he shared Daisy's love of animals. He also fancied himself a writer at times, and had co-written at least one play with his sister-in-law, Caroline Duer, that appeared in *Ainslee's* magazine in 1903. He also had a few humor pieces published in *People's Magazine* in 1908. Both of these magazines were published by the company that would soon be Daisy's employer, Street & Smith.

Only a few photographs remain of Daisy and Henry together; those that did survive are blurry or of poor quality. But, early on in their relationship, the two began a tradition of posing for "paired" pictures: Each one would sit in the same exact spot, or a spot neatly opposite the other's, with almost identical poses and sometimes holding the same objects. The first pair shows a twenty-ish Daisy sitting on a bench outside a house and holding a kitten. Henry poses in the other photo, sitting on a bench next to what is very likely to be the same house and holding the same kitten.

By the mid–1920s, Jessie was showing evidence of suffering from a melancholia that would arrive and debilitate her for days. She mourned in her journals, marking anniversaries of losses. "I am all alone tonight & no one to care. When I think of all those that have loved me, but they are gone away now but I think of them."[10] At the same time, some of her notes from that time period hint that Daisy may have begun to suffer from the same malady. "Labor Day. Dais called me & said she was near crazy" she wrote at the beginning of September of 1923.[11] Many years later, Daisy indicated in journal entries that she was beginning to suffer from depression during this time as well.

In 1924, Daisy's luck in writing began to change. The article "On the Fourteenth Floor" was sold to the *Saturday Evening Post*, as well an article of her observations of

Daisy and Henry began a tradition of taking matching photographs of each other, placing both of them at the same time and place. There is no exact date document when the two met, but there are some hints that it could have been as early as 1923, and Daisy's youthful appearance in this photograph indicate that this pair was taken around that period (both photographs Daisy Bacon collection).

working at the auction company, "With Contents Unknown." In the latter she shows an early flair for the dramatic: "If only these bags and trunks could speak, they would tell us exciting adventures of being abandoned in strange hotels, of being fought over and then passing into other hands."

It must have given Daisy some satisfaction to know that her pieces would appear in the same publication as the one that published much of her lover's wife's work. But she didn't have the pleasure of seeing her name in print, because both pieces were printed without bylines. Getting published in the nation's most popular magazine was a heady accomplishment. Her two *Post* articles were mentioned frequently in future interviews after she became editor of *Love Story*, as if to validate her literary chops: She had, for a moment, been part of higher literary circles. These articles would supply her with plenty of mileage in that respect.

By 1925, the family was living at 735 Lexington Avenue in an apartment above a pet store. During this time Daisy's only appearance in print was when the store below caught fire, forcing Daisy to evacuate the apartment along with the family's pet monkey. Her adventure eventually became front page news for her hometown newspaper, the *Westfield Republican*. But she could not get published again. "Worked like slaves to get into *Liberty* and never made it," she recalled later.[12]

Jessie's physical ailments would eventually force her to quit working and stay at home. Esther had graduated from school, but had no work experience yet to speak of. Daisy found herself, at twenty-eight, the bread-winner of the family and, once again, looking for work.

On February 22, 1926, she opened up the Help Wanted section of the classified advertisements in the *Sunday New York Times*. In the "Young Lady" section, buried amongst jobs for typists, telephone operators, and "young girls," was a snippet of an ad.

YOUNG LADY, well educated, in publisher's office; desirable environment and personnel; state age, experience, if any, and salary desired.

The Greatest Publishing House in the World

In March of 1926, no less than forty-five different pulp fiction magazines crammed every square inch of newsstands across the country. Titles covered the alphabet, from *Action Stories* to *Western Story*, with wildly dramatic covers painted with vivid reds, yellows, and greens, promising stories of escape and adventure of every kind and located

Pulp fiction magazines dominated the reading market for almost fifty years, as can be seen in this newsstand in 1938, with pulp fiction magazines filling up every inch of space (courtesy Library of Congress).

in every corner of the world. The number of different magazines could fluctuate at any given time, with new titles showing up and disappearing just as quickly. Profit margins were razor-thin, but the market was wide open and the public's appetite for thunderous stories was insatiable.

If a person had enough gumption, they could start a magazine with as little as a couple of thousand dollars, provided they could survive the first white-knuckle months of uncertainty. Pulp fiction magazines may have been known for lowbrow culture, but they were also a rousing example of the American dream at its very best.

Known in the 1920s as "pulp paper magazines," "pulpwoods," or simply "fiction magazines," some titles like *Blue Book, Flynn's, Railroad Stories*, and *The Popular Magazine* had been around since shortly after the first pulp magazine, *The Argosy*, appeared in the late 1890s. Others were barely a few months old, and some would disappear within a few months more without fanfare, axed by their publishers who moved on to the next best thing.

But the pulp fiction magazine that centered around the romance genre, the "romance pulp" or the "love pulp," was a late comer to the circus. Even though women were a large proportion of readers of the romance fiction of the nineteenth century, pulp publishers were slow to find a title that would click with the public, which was ironic, considering that the biggest publisher of the group, Street & Smith, made its early fortune on romantic stories printed in early newspapers and libraries.

Street & Smith was forged in 1855 when two young men, Francis S. Street and Francis S. Smith, met and became close friends while both were employed by the *New York Weekly Dispatch*. When their employer, Amos Williamson, offered to sell the *Dispatch* to his two employees with a payment plan to cover the $50,000 sales price, the two men saw their chance, despite the risks of taking on a business that had a very small market share. As part of their agreement with Williamson, Street and Smith were allowed to take home only a $20 weekly salary until the loan was paid off. But what the two lacked in cash flow they made up in ambition.[1]

By this time, women had already become a very powerful consumer group. Before the Civil War began, there were over one hundred magazines for women, and publishers early on began to include romantic fiction in many of them. Cultural historian Russell Nye named four types of fiction that were dominant during the late 18th and 19th centuries: Sentimental, satiric, gothic, and historical romance. Historical romance usually featured a young heroine and a plot in which she had to find a way to her true love.[2]

Many of these periodicals were created by female writers and editors, but magazine owners were usually men. These publications struggled at first, but after 1830, they were established as standard reading of educated women who could afford to buy periodicals. Some of the more famous periodicals of today—namely *Ladies Home Journal, Good Housekeeping*, and *McCall's*—are descendants of these early journals.[3]

As romantic stories proliferated in these publications, social and religious leaders heavily criticized the content. They argued that those who bought these periodicals could be easily swayed towards immoral thoughts and behaviors. To appease these leaders, publishers took pains to ensure that the romantic stories were heavily painted with morals that followed the social norms of the day. This practice would have a far-reaching effect long after these magazines were gone.

Most of the earlier stories could be categorized as what is called the "domestic" novel, in which the theme and plot are centered around the home and family. But in the

1860s, a national uproar over the working conditions of the sewing factories and the women that worked in them resulted in a new heroine that could be exploited by publishers like Street & Smith: the working girl.

Francis Smith, who himself was a supporter of a local working women's union, took the opportunity and wrote *Bertha, the Sewing Machine Girl: or Death at the Wheel*, a story so popular that it was adapted to a stage play. These working girl stories, which would eventually dominate the fiction peddled in story papers, dime novels, and libraries, had less Christian undertones. The romantic story was not a love that sprang out of godliness, but rather from the hands of Fate. In these stories, as Michael Denning wrote, "One is more likely to find tags from Shakespeare than from the Bible."[4]

As Street & Smith gained a foothold in the New York market, they churned out sentimental romantic serials every week about poor waifs against the world, written by writers such as Mary J. Holmes and May Agnes Fleming. One of the most prolific writers was Charlotte M. Brame, who had been a well-known author in the *New York Ledger* and in British story papers. Street & Smith recruited Brame to write for them, but the company was cautious of running against any exclusive agreements Brame may have had with British publishers. They solved the problem by using a pseudonym for her work for the *Weekly*. They flipped her initials from CMB to BMC and came up with the name Bertha M. Clay.[5]

After Brame died in 1884, Street & Smith took the position that the Bertha M. Clay name was a "house name," a term used for a name that they had created and owned for stories printed in its publications. Later, in the pulps, house names would be used liberally when one author was responsible for more than one story in an issue; the house name would be used for the excess stories to make it appear that a wide variety of authors contributed to the issue.

The pseudonym Bertha M. Clay was used by dozens of writers, many of which were men, for hundreds of stories, well into the twentieth century and would have a dominant role in the first issue of *Love Story*.[6]

Francis Street died in 1883, after which Francis Smith's son Ormond bought out Street's interest. Francis Smith died only four years later, leaving the four Smith children with a company that had grown into a powerful force in the popular fiction field. Ormond then placed his brother, George Campbell, as vice-president of the company. Two years after that, the brothers decided to diversify and enter the dime novel market, competing against Beadle & Adams, the originators of the format. As dime novel companies began to fall away as the market changed and fluctuated, Street & Smith was there to pick up the pieces.

Street & Smith then took these popular heroes and reprinted them extensively over the next several decades. For example, the character Frank Merriwell originally appeared in *Tip Top Weekly*, then the *New Tip-Top Weekly*, the *Tip Top Quarterly*, the *Medal Library*, the *New Medal Library*, the *Tip Top Semi-Monthly*, the *Wide Awake Magazine*, the *Sport Story Magazine*, the *Fame and Fortune Magazine*, the *Fortune Story Magazine*, and finally the *Top Notch Magazine*. The Merriwell name was then used for reprints in the *Merriwell Baseball Stories*, the *Merriwell Football Stories*, in a complete edition between 1921 and 1930 as the *Merriwell Series*, and then another reprint for the *Burt L. Standish Library* and the *Merriwell Library*. He then finished his career with a comic book appearance, a Big Little Book, radio programs, a movie, and a novel in 1941.[7]

A common misconception is that pulp fiction magazines were a direct descendant from just one source of reading material, the dime novel. Dime novels were 5 × 8½ inch pamphlets that became a sensation almost as soon as they were created by the Beadle & Adams publishing company in 1860. In reality, the true ancestors of the pulp fiction magazine weren't one format, but at least three: story papers, which were eight-page weekly newspapers full of serials and a hodgepodge of articles; the dime novel; and the "libraries," which were collections based around a theme or author. Libraries, which were 8 × 11, and consisted of 16 or 32 pages, more closely resembled the format that the pulp magazine would follow.[8] The libraries, along with the dime novel, would be the foundation on which Street & Smith would amass their fortune.

In 1896, a small fiction magazine with a plain yellow cover appeared on newsstands. Frank Munsey was the owner of an ordinary magazine, targeted at young working-class readers, called *Golden Argosy.* He knew that his readers liked fiction stories but shied away from the price of slick magazines. He used uncoated paper for the first issue, and then lowered the grade once again to woodpulp grade paper for the next, then changed the name to simply *The Argosy* and put a price of ten cents on the cover. The pulp fiction magazine was born.

Roughly around the same time, other changes were in play that would drastically affect the production of periodicals in the United States. Technological advances, such as rotary printing presses, sped up the production process. The advancement of the railroad and later the automobile provided new and easier distribution avenues. And new postal requirements granted periodicals a special second-class postage rate provided they followed certain parameters: They had to be released with stated intervals, a date of issue, numbered consecutively, and be formed of printed sheets without substantial binding. All of these advances gave publishers more than enough incentive to crank out as many periodicals as they could with as little money as possible.

The decision that Munsey made to use pulpwood paper would distinctly differentiate these fiction magazines from the more mainstream and expensive magazines that catered to a wide swath of the paying public. Magazines such as the *Saturday Evening Post* and *Good Housekeeping* used paper with a slick coating that advertisers loved. Just like pulp magazines would be given the nickname "pulps" for the type of paper they used, these more expensive magazines would be given the nickname "slicks" for their coated paper.

Pulpwood paper carried both advantages and disadvantages. Because it wasn't coated, it was cheaper to produce and purchase and, because it was lighter than slick paper, it was cheaper to ship and mail. But advertisers shied away from the dull appearance of the paper and would only display their wares on the back and inside covers of the pulpwood magazines, which were the only elements of the magazines that used coated paper. And the uncoated paper was never meant to stand the test of time, and the paper crumbled into flakes after just a few years. As a result, pulp fiction magazines were thrown away rather than kept.

This last characteristic was not so much a concern to the publisher or the reader of the early 20th century, because the whole idea behind these magazines was to read what was considered "disposable fiction." But the fragile nature of magazines has been the nemesis of collectors and historians ever since, because a large number of issues, especially those of short-run magazines, have been extremely hard to find. As for the reading quality being worthless, well, anyone that has studied these magazines for any length of time knows that some of the fiction these magazines carried was anything but disposable.

With a low price and a hefty number of fiction stories to make it appealing to those who liked the idea of getting value for their money, *The Argosy* doubled its circulation to eighty thousand within two months. Over the next four years, Munsey absorbed two more of his magazines into the fiction magazine, eliminating some of its own in-house competition. After that, circulation soared until it would hit half a million in 1905.[9] With *The Argosy* gaining momentum, Munsey was on his way to becoming a multi-millionaire. Eventually he would build a publishing empire that would make him one of the richest men in America.

Street & Smith eventually followed Munsey's new direction in format. But with a well-stocked library of weekly serials, dime novels, and paperbound books, including the Diamond Dick, Buffalo Bill, Nick Carter and other dime novel heroes that had made wild profits for the Smith brothers, they were slow to adapt everything to the format that would be the standard for the pulp fiction magazine. In

The new Street & Smith building, ca. 1906, located at 79 Seventh Avenue. Designed by Henry Kilburn, the company boasted that the building was "the most complete plant of its kind in the world" (courtesy Special Collections Research Center, Syracuse University Libraries).

the meantime, they bought the rights to stories that had originally appeared in Beadle & Adams dime novels, the George Munro and Norman L. Munro libraries, and, later, Frank Tousey's old holdings. They bought *Ainslee's* magazine, a magazine that would print many substantial writers over the years. But their first pulp-format magazine wasn't created until they launched *The Popular Magazine* in 1903, which was converted to an all-fiction pulp magazine after four issues.

In 1905, the company built new headquarters at 79 Seventh Avenue, on the corner of Seventh Avenue and 15th Street on the southern end of the Chelsea District in Manhattan. It seemed fitting that the company would be located between Greenwich Village, an area rich in history of the written word and famous for its artistic residents, and the gritty realism of the working-class neighborhoods of Chelsea, where the docks, on the edge of Eleventh Avenue, were the biggest employer of the region.

Chelsea was a neighborhood in transition. Ornate Victorian streetlamps dotted every corner. The smells from the National Biscuit Company drifted through the

The printing department, ca. 1906. Street & Smith was one of the few publishers that produced their magazines almost completely in-house, and they prided themselves on their state-of-the-art printing machines (courtesy Special Collections Research Center, Syracuse University Libraries).

neighborhoods. But it wasn't long before R.H. Macy had opened a store on 14th Street. More stores followed suit, such as Siegel-Cooper's store at 6th and 18th that became a landmark store with its fountain that became a central meeting place for ladies to meet for a shopping day. The famed Chelsea Hotel, one block over and six blocks up, had already gained a reputation as a haven for writers, artists, and musicians.[10]

But the area was still a mix of wealthy and poor residents.[11] Storefronts in the neighborhood consisted of nondescript and bargain clothing stores: ("Furs! ½ price! Coats! ½ price!"); a shoe outlet, a coat shop, men's clothes, a barber. Just one block south, the Rhinelander apartments, an enormous complex of imposing and dark walkups that catered to German immigrants, was beginning to decay. But from every viewpoint, skyscrapers could be seen on the horizon, promising higher and taller buildings that would eventually encroach on the neighborhood.

The Smiths, proud of their new building and their fiftieth anniversary, published a celebratory pamphlet entitled "The Greatest Publishing House in the World."

> The new Street & Smith building, the most complete plant of its kind in the world, is solid and substantial and typical of the firm itself. In outward appearance it is simple in architectural treatment, yet showing how cleverly plain bricks can be put together to form an imposing structure.[12]

The book department, ca. 1906. The amount of paper probably increased dramatically over the next twenty years due to the Smith brothers' reluctance to throw anything away (courtesy Special Collections Research Center, Syracuse University Libraries).

Over the next fifteen years, Street & Smith printed and reprinted hundreds of romantic stories in the format of dime novels and libraries. They produced at least twelve series after the turn of the century that focused on romance stories, or their contents included romance stories. Many of them were reprints from the original *New York Weekly*. Out of the 41 publications that Street & Smith launched after 1900, a third were romances. The remaining 29 contained adventure, suspense, detective, western, frontier, sports, and juvenile stories with a young man carrying a rags-to-riches theme, such as the Horatio Alger and Frank Merriwell stories. But converting the romance story to a standard or pulp magazine format that would be an unqualified success continued to elude the company. Two magazines created in the early part of the century, *Smith's Magazine* and *Women's Stories*, were targeted to women and were favorites of the Smiths, but they failed to grab the public's attention.

Years of publishing experience had resulted in the company adopting practices that remained part of the bedrock of the company's reputation as a fiction factory. For better or for worse, Street & Smith had certain company-wide rules when it came to submissions. One was their efficiency and promptness in paying authors. They paid an author upon acceptance of a story, as opposed to other magazines that had the aggravating habit of paying an author only once the story was published. The Smith brothers also made it known that they were willing to shop manuscripts between their magazines, so if a story didn't work for one it might work for another.

By this time, a young executive had begun to make more of the creative decisions involving the pulp fiction magazines. Henry William Ralston, or Bill as he was called, had joined the company during a college summer break of 1898. When autumn and the new school year arrived, Ralston decided to stay on. A handsome man with pronounced cheekbones that gave him a cherubic appearance, Ralston was the quintessential people person who could talk to new employees as well as the old-timers. By the early 1910s, he was taking on more responsibilities, including the creation of new publications. As the years continued, many of his decisions would be ground-breaking and change the face of popular fiction.

When dime novels began to lose popularity in the early 1910s, Ralston transferred the struggling *Nick Carter Stories* dime novel into a standard pulp size—7 inches by 10 inches—and changed the title to *Detective Story Magazine*. The new pulp was the first of the fiction magazines to specialize in the detective story, and it became so successful that other publishers soon followed suit. Over the next forty years, over 250 detective-story-specific magazines would appear on newsstands at one point or another. Then, in 1919, Ralston performed the same act with the Buffalo Bill dime novel series, changing its title to *Western Story Magazine*. *Western Story* would eventually become the biggest selling western fiction periodical of its time, and home of some of the genre's most famous writers such as Frederick Faust, writing as Max Brand, and Ernest Haycox.

By the end of the decade, the company had founded two very popular magazines in an attempt to retain their male readers. The formula of offering magazines that were genre-specific and in the pulp format was definitely working. But their female-focused magazines still lagged behind.

5

"They Are Our Shakespeares"

The legend of the creation of *Love Story Magazine* is much like many of the stories that appeared in the magazine. It's a dramatic tale of the dreams of a company owner in which ambitions that are fulfilled through inspiration and perspiration and all ends well. But, when exposed to daylight, there are some holes that make the story a little suspect.

The established story is that during the 1910s Ormond Smith was obsessed with owning a successful woman's magazine, one that would recapture the female audience that "wasn't particularly interested in higher culture or in reading the slicker magazines of the day." He wanted to corral the readers that had so loved the *New York Weekly* romances; readers with what *The Fiction Factory* calls the "mass-circulation mind."[1]

It's true that the Smiths mulled over creating a new publication for women for several years, as can be seen by their previous launches of *Women's Stories* and *Smith's*. According to *The Fiction Factory*, sometime in 1920, Ralston assigned Amita Fairgrieve, an associate editor of the company's *People's Favorite Magazine*—a young woman with "charm and editorial acumen"—with creating a new woman's magazine. In this version, Fairgrieve holed herself up in an office, armed with nothing but a collection of the company's old dime novels. After six months, *voila*. Fairgrieve emerged from her cave with the concept for *Love Story Magazine,* and the rest is history.[2]

But at closer look, I found other factors at play.

For one thing, in 1919, *True Story*, the first confession magazine, hit the newsstands. Created by Bernarr Macfadden as an afterthought to his flagship publication, *Physical Culture*, the magazine would usher in the confession magazine craze that would peak in the 1950s and 1960s.

True Story owes its existence to Macfadden's older magazine, *Physical Culture*. Macfadden had noticed that many *Physical Culture* readers were writing in to the magazine, describing their experiences in a range of love, romance, and marriage subjects. Macfadden, acting on a hunch, launched *True Story*. Stories were written in the first-person, penned by staff in the beginning, and accompanied by photographic illustrations. Macfadden used gimmicks such as submitting the magazine to "men in the street" for reading. The magazine was also supposedly scrutinized by a board of clergyman who reviewed the "moral fitness" of the stories. As John Bakeless would dryly note in his book *Magazine Making*, "Judging by the results, the clergy have broader minds—in several senses of the word—than one would ordinarily expect."[3]

The magazine was an immediate sensation. Within a few years, *True Story* had a circulation of over a million readers a month. It wasn't long before other publishers scrambled to produce copy-cats.[4]

The Smiths and Ralston undoubtedly knew about Macfadden's product that was conquering newsstands across the country. *True Story* was creating a sea change in the market, one in which magazines leaned towards sensationalism rather than sentimentalism. If Ormond wanted a successful woman's magazine, *True Story* may have made him sit up and realize that the world was moving on, with or without his dream being fulfilled.

As for Amita Fairgrieve, she had graduated from Smith College eight years before, where she had been an honor student and a member of the literary society and the mathematics club. After graduating in 1912, she co-wrote a play with Helena F. Miller, "Purple and Fine Linen: A Prize Play in Three Acts," and in 1913, the play was published by the Samuel French Company. By 1920 she was working on Street & Smith's *People's Favorite Magazine*, which she described in the *Smith Alumnae Quarterly* as "the greatest undiscovered periodical in America."[5] But she had little if no experience in running a magazine, much less launching a new one.

It wasn't unheard of for the company to put a rookie in the role of editor of a magazine, as would be seen by Daisy's example later in the decade. But to give the responsibility of coming up with a new concept for a national magazine, one that would require substantial sums of money to launch and distribute, to an associate editor and one who had not published any romance-themed stories of her own, sounds unlikely.

Bill Ralston was the idea man, and by the time he plucked Amita to oversee the new project, he probably already had done the math: a magazine that would be similar to the smash hits *Detective Story* and *Western Story* but geared for women. And as far as the company was concerned, women wanted romance. It was well documented by the dozens of romantic stories they published in the nineteenth century, sold by the hundreds of thousands.

A genre-specific magazine for women. Full of stories of romance.

The old story is that it took Amita six months to come up with the idea for the magazine. I believe that it was probably Bill Ralston that came up with the idea, and it probably took him six minutes to come up with the idea of *Love Story Magazine*—right after *True Story* hit the newsstands. Amita might have been holed up in an office, but it was probably as a manager-in-training, assigned to get up to speed with the kind of stories that the Smiths wanted in their new magazine.

The day that the first issue of *Love Story* appeared is in question, too. The issue is dated May 1921, but there are different accounts as to when the issue was released. In the Smith College alumnae newsletter of November 1921, Amita commented that the first issue appeared on July 25.[6] To make the historical account even foggier, in an anniversary issue of *Love Story* twenty-one years later, the "Love Story Notes" column declares that the first issue appeared on the newsstands on April 20, 1921.[7]

Regardless of its release date, Amita was fairly bursting with excitement when she updated her classmates in the Smith alumnae announcements:

> I don't know what Miss Jordan would say if she knew the new job I've tackled. I'm editing *Love Story Magazine*—the new Street and Smith publication—the first issue appeared July 25. (Perhaps this notice ought to go among the births!) I shall be glad to have any modern Mary J. Holmeses or Bertha M. Clays communicate with me either by letter or interview. They are our Shakespeares. I'm having a wonderful time, am very enthusiastic about the work, and only hope I'll be able to swing it.[8]

The first cover, showing a rosy-cheeked brunette blissfully picking out a long-stemmed rose from a flower box, proclaimed that the magazine was "FIT FOR ANY

HOME." Contents include Part One of a serial, "Love Triumphant," by Ralph Kaye Ashley, three short stories, three poems, various "News & Notes" fillers, and one column, "Heart Talks with the Troubled," by a Mary Mead. The price: 15 cents, a price that would be fixed for the next sixteen years.

The feature story is a classic Street & Smith concoction: a story printed using a byline of none other than the house name Bertha M. Clay. "A Final Temptation" had originally been printed in a British magazine, the *Family Herald Supplement,* in 1883 under Charlotte Brame's real name.[9]

As such, the first feature story in *Love Story Magazine* is the perfect example of what Street & Smith produced in the grand tradition of their early years: It is a reprint, it originally appeared in another company's publication, it was written by an author who had been dead for 37 years, and the byline was a pseudonym used by an untold number of other writers.

Love Story also carried what would become some of the hallmarks of the pulp fiction magazine: those famous

First issue of *Love Story Magazine* dated May 1921. The cover artist is unknown, but it could be Modest Stein, who began painting covers for the magazine soon after this and normally signed his work. This cover is indicative of what Street & Smith was trying to accomplish with the magazine: clean, wholesome entertainment that was "fit for any home" (courtesy Dr. Stephen Lomazov/Great American Magazine Collection).

(some might call them infamous) advertisements to cure piles, relieve hernias, lure men for traveling sales jobs, increase male vitality, and the like. These ads were obviously tailored for a more male audience and seem misplaced in a magazine targeted to women. The reason behind this is simple: Those companies that advertised in pulp fiction magazines bought their space in bulk. The ads that are so out of place at the back of *Love Story* are identical to those that appeared across other, more male-oriented titles like *Detective Story, Western Story, Sea Stories, The Popular Magazine,* and almost every other pulp fiction magazine on the newsstand.

The second issue of *Love Story* wasn't out until mid-summer, with the date of August 1921 stamped on the cover. The editorial column in the second issue made a point of expressing what the editor, or her managers, thought was the vision of perfect love:

> And so we have taken love for the theme of all our stories—the love of the One Man for the One Woman, the kind of love that ends in happiness and the warm human joys of home. To be happy you must learn the difference between True Love and False, between the baser feelings which end in suffering, and the right and noble ones which bring real joy. Our ideal is to publish fiction which portrays the True Love in this magazine.[10]

Directly below this editorial column was an announcement that due to overwhelming reception, *Love Story* would immediately become a semi-monthly. *The Fiction Factory*, which is full of glowing and sometimes unverified declarations about the company, states that the original circulation was approximately 100,000 copies.[11] That may sound impressive, but the author failed to mention that this number was within the standard circulation run for a first issue of a pulp fiction magazine. We can only assume that the magazine had very few returns.

Company management ran with it. The third issue was dated August 10. After that, the dust settled, and it remained a semi-monthly, faithfully appearing with the cover dates of the 10th and the 25th for the next year. In September 1922, the publishers again responded to demand and changed *Love Story* to a weekly, which it would remain for the next twenty-one years.

In an attempt to grab some of the *True Story* audience, the August 25, 1921, issue includes photographs to illustrate stories rather than the standard line-cut drawings, and the cover advertises "Illustrations by direct photos from Living Models." Then the cover of the sixth issue is a colorized photograph of a couple, a medium that Street & Smith had used frequently before, especially in magazines like *The Popular Magazine*. The photograph of a couple interlocked, as if contemplating a serious situation, appeared as if it was pulled right out of a silent film.

But *Love Story* was as staid as *True Story* was daring. This Street & Smith product was in the tradition

Volume 1, #6 issue. A colorized photograph was used for this cover, more than likely a black and white photograph that was then hand-painted. This method, which was used rarely on *Love Story* issues, was probably employed to compete with *True Story's* photographed covers and illustrations (courtesy Brooks Hefner).

of the old, grand *New York Weekly*: a magazine full of nothing but dramatic but respectable romance stories featuring orphaned women who needed to be rescued.

The early issues have various columns which appear for short periods, such as "How To Be Beautiful," but also columns that would last for almost the entire lifetime of the magazine, such as the advice column "The Friend in Need." Within a few years, "The Friend in Need" would profoundly affect Daisy's life.

Early on, *Love Story* staff received letters from readers giving them feedback on the contents. Like many fiction magazines, editors relied heavily on these letters to guide them as to what to include, what to leave out, and what to adjust in the storylines. One letter featured in just the fourth issue questioned the policy that all stories in the magazine end happily with the heroine and hero finding true love. The decision was quickly and staunchly defended:

> Notwithstanding all this, notwithstanding that writers should hold a mirror up to nature, humanity shrinks from an unhappy ending will not read stories which close in misery, and insists on at least a prophetic ray of light falling athwart the gloom…. If we believed there are no happy endings at all in life—which we don't—we would still believe in them unshakably for stories, particularly LOVE STORIES![12]

And perhaps because of confusion in the market over the difference between *True Story* and *Love Story*, a full-page ad was inserted in an early issue that clarifies exactly what kind of content was carried in *Love Story*.

> *Love Story* is *not* just another of those sex-problem magazines, which have done incalculable harm.
> *Love Story* is clean at heart, and its stories are written around the love of the one man for the one woman.
> Civilization has been built upon this sort of love—all the great accomplishments of mankind have been inspired by good women who were greatly beloved.
> *Love Story Magazine* will take a place in your life that no other magazine can occupy, because *Love Story* has an irresistibly human appeal.[13]

Amita Fairgrieve left Street & Smith in 1923 to become editor of *Cupid's Diary,* a new competitor published by Dell Publishing. She was replaced in the *Love Story* offices by Ruth Agnes Abeling. Abeling had newspaper editorial experience in Indiana working as a society reporter and had written several short how-to articles and some serial and short fiction for Midwestern newspapers and, at one point, was named managing editor of the *Terre Haute Post*. That job didn't seem to last very long. Before she could make a dent in the editorial page, Abeling, noted as "sweet and bright little woman," was assigned to be the Newspaper Enterprise Association women feature's editor. From 1921 through 1922, her work appeared in newspapers in Missouri, Indiana, and Pittsburgh.

The record isn't clear on why or when Abeling relocated to New York City to become the editor of *Love Story*. But it's easy to assume that the job of managing a nationwide woman's magazine, albeit a pulpwood magazine, was far more exciting than her previous job, one in which the highlight assignment was reporting on a Harrington, Illinois, woman who had been fasting for twenty-two days in an effort to religiously convert her husband.[14]

Once Abeling got to Street & Smith, she planted herself in the office and made very few changes to the magazine over the next five years. The status quo seemed to be working. Why change it?

By the time Daisy arrived, the cover art on *Love Story* issues featured women in beautiful 1920s fashions, but the stories inside were still mired in the 1890s. By most accounts, the magazine was selling well, but its good circulation numbers could be attributed to its breathtakingly simple name, its publisher's power in the industry, and its ability to bridge the gap between the female reader and the pulp fiction magazine. It also enjoyed very little competition. Out of the roughly 45 pulp magazines issued in 1926, only six were devoted to the romance story. Out of those six, three were issued monthly, two issued every other week, and only one—*Love Story*—was issued weekly.

This cover from a 1922 issue, painted by Modest Stein, is a typical example of a common theme for early *Love Story* covers: A woman cringes or "shrinks back" in horror or fear from what she views as a threat. This theme would be used frequently through the 1920s and into the early 1930s (author collection).

6

First Days

Secure behind an iron fence, the Street & Smith building dominated the corner of Seventh Avenue and 15th Street. Four large marble columns, two on each side, overpowered the small steps to the double doors beyond. The exterior, seven stories of deep red brick, was described later by *Doc Savage* author Lester Dent as being the color of congealed blood.

On March 13, 1926, Daisy arrived at the building for her first day at work, wearing a seal skin coat for the occasion. She was there for her first day on her new job as the reader for the *Love Story Magazine* advice column, "The Friend in Need." Daisy's salary was $35 a week.[1]

Stepping inside the front doors, official visitors made their way to the waiting area, a room designed to impress with portraits of the company founders hanging from paneled walls, thick Oriental rugs, richly upholstered benches, and tables adorned with a sampling of the company's magazines. But Daisy, like many employees, entered the building through a less impressive, more utilitarian entrance with the required time clock installed close by. After punching in, employees headed straight for the elevator, a steel trellis cage with the nickname of The Iron Maiden. Operated by a gentleman affectionately known as Louis the Fourteenth, The Iron Maiden rattled up and down the seven floors of the building continually throughout the workday, a relic from a slower, more peaceful age. Daisy was bound for the sixth floor. With her slim stature, sculpted cheekbones and glossy curly brown hair, she must have made quite an impression on those that encountered her that morning.

The sixth floor had no resemblance to the quiet and orderly scene of the waiting room. Paper—stacks of manuscripts, sacks of mail, books, magazines, letters, files—were piled high in hallways and shoved into every crack and corner. Amidst the din of clattering typewriters and ringing phones, workers hurried by wear-

Daisy in a 1923 portrait. Photograph by John Weiss (Daisy Bacon collection).

ing green shades and carrying armfuls of papers. In the deep center of the building, hallways took unexpected turns and small stairways led to other hallways that led to other stairways that led to annexes. Rolls of paper, as tall as a man's torso and almost as wide as his outstretched arms, were stacked in the middle of rooms like monuments, reminding editors and artists that they needed to be filled with stories and art—sooner rather than later.

Several months later, Daisy wrote a twenty-six page essay that describes her first job at the magazine.

> You ought to see my mail. You would think that I was a movie actress or philanthropist, a millionaire or at least a murderer. Every morning the mail trucks back right up my door and throw quantities of letters off. Most of them are addressed in long hand and they are postmarked from every state in the Union; all the large cities and every hick town west of the water tower.[2]

"The Friend in Need" was a popular advice column in *Love Story*; so popular, in fact, that it frequently hogged several pages of each issue. No less than ten questions were answered each week, sometimes up to twenty were addressed. The letter written by the person seeking advice could stretch from one to several pages, as if writer needed to reveal every detail, every incident, that led to the situation at hand. Questions were answered in length by the "author" of the column, who used the fictitious name Laura Alston Brown.

Daisy's essay, "Dear Mrs. Browne," is not dated, but more than likely it was written in her first two years at the company, when reading for the column was her only responsibility and she still had the time to write a twenty-six page essay. She might have intended to sell the essay to the *Saturday Evening Post*. In order to protect her employer's privacy and to keep her from getting fired, she changed the name of the column to "When You Need a Friend," the writer of the column to "Louise Winston Browne" and the name of the magazine to "Love Affairs Magazine." But there is no record that she sent it off anywhere, a decision that in hindsight was a good one. The Smith brothers wouldn't have taken kindly to a newcomer writing about company doings, even if they weren't scandalous or revealing company secrets.

Daisy's lack of experience and maturity certainly didn't stop her from taking on the awesome responsibility of advising people on making major decisions that could affect them for years to come. In fact, according to her, she felt she was better qualified to answer the letters than a woman over thirty, because she could "better understand the hopes and despairs that feminine hearts feel with that age staring them in the face."[3]

The office received about seventy-five letters a day, except during the winter, "when our rural readers—and they made up a good half of our circulation—couldn't get out in the flivver, it sometimes went up to 150." About ten percent of writers were men. She received letters with questions ranging from what kind of shoes should someone buy to whether or not to tell a lover about your past, to what to do with a husband who drinks and becomes violent. Many wrote in confessing serious indiscretions. Some wrote in asking for a matrimonial list, including a few coins to help pay for it. "I have always found it amusing to think that the women expect to pay more for a mate than the men. The women usually send a dollar but the men rarely send more than a quarter."[4]

Abeling told Daisy that the most important rule, which could never be broken, was that she should never suggest divorce as a solution. The second rule was that, if all else failed and Daisy couldn't come up with a viable answer for the problem, Daisy was to

The Friend In Need

Department

Conducted By

Laura Alston Brown

HAS a husband the right to demand that his wife give up all her own friends and cleave only to his? Has he the right to ask her to make herself over in the pattern which is admired in his circle?

In every successful marriage there must be a certain measure of adaptation, of course. To a certain extent, individuality must be smothered in the interest of a pleasant, comfortable home.

There is a limit, though, beyond which lies danger. The first law of nature is: "To thine own self be true." When the bride—or the groom—in the first sweet flush of warm, unselfish love, goes too far and makes concessions which are too irksome to be kept up in everyday life, the consequences are often tragic.

This matter of friends is dynamite for many a luckless pair. Each of the sweethearts is jealous of those lucky persons who knew the other in those scarcely conceivable days before they met; persons who share memories from which the grudging spouse is forever excluded.

And when, as in A Blue Flapper Wife's case, the friends, too, are jealous, when the two sets can't mingle any better than fire and water, then the trouble starts in earnest.

DEAR MRS. BROWN: Just about a year ago, I married a man whom I love dearly. But there is a growing barrier between us. This is how it started: He didn't like my friends, and asked me not to see any more of them. I resented this, especially since I had two girl friends who were as close to me as sisters. But, being in love, I did as he wanted, after a little persuasion, and started going with a few of his friends.

They didn't like me. I wasn't their type. Nor did I like them. But Bud, my hubby, didn't notice anything wrong, and I didn't say anything.

One of his friends I liked, though, and liked very well. She spilled the beans. After we had begun to be chummy, she told me that the rest of the set didn't want Bud to marry me in the first place; they thought I was loud and unworthy of Bud in every respect.

I, a flapper, marrying a homebody like Bud! Oh, it was simply too impossible to them!

At first I only laughed and kidded her about being a busybody in other people's affairs. I told her I didn't know they tried to get Bud not to marry me, but I did know they didn't like me and wouldn't even give me a chance to make good.

Her name was Pauline, and she was a daughter of Bud's best friend. She was wonderful to me, but she finally had to go to school, and I didn't see much of her after that.

Whenever Bud takes me to their home and the rest of his set happen to be there, while the men go out for a cigarette the women tell me over and over how lucky I am to marry a man like Bud. They seem to enjoy making me feel uncomfortable. They seem like a bunch of old cats trying to get their claws sunk into my flesh so they can tear it away and fight over it.

I can't complain to Bud, for he'll think I am trying to knock his friends just because I can't be like them. Oh, it's unbearable! Sometimes I think I'll run away from everything. But if I do, they will all say: "I knew she would. She's just that type."

Daisy's first assignment at the magazine was working on "The Friend in Need" column, an important column of the magazine. It ran for an average of 12 pages per issue and covered a wide range topics and printed letters from both sexes in a wide range of ages. It was Daisy's training ground on which she learned about her magazine's readers (*Love Story Magazine* © Condé Nast).

tell the readers that the answer to their question could be found in stories that would be in an upcoming issue of the magazine. Daisy thought differently.

> The editor and I belonged to different schools of lovelorn letter writers, I could see that, right from the start…. She said they would buy the magazine to get the stories. Perhaps so, but I had an idea, and still have, that most people who wrote and asked a question were more likely to buy the magazine if they received an answer to that question.[5]

She also added that it was doubtful that there would be any follow-up, because the person's letter was soon lost amidst the avalanche of correspondence that arrived daily.

As Daisy worked on the column, she was quickly forming opinions of how she would answer situations differently than those directed by her editor. Before she took over, answers were written in an old-fashioned, Victorian tone, sweetened up with motherly "my dear's," that invoked a kindly grandmother figure. Daisy's style was much blunter. "I tried to answer every question to the best of my ability and if it wasn't always the best solution, at least I never resorted to the purring, milk and water note."[6]

Showing not a little bit of hypocrisy in her essay, Daisy writes dismissively about women who wrote of being in love with married men. "Their letters are all alike," she sniffs. "You don't mean to tell me, Marge, that you are going to fall for that misunderstood line?" she cites as her answer to one such letter. "When a man pulls that, one of these two conditions exists: Either his wife understands him only too well and no longer cares what he does or else a very real affection exists between him and his wife and he is only seeing how much you will believe. Take my tip, he'll never leave his wife for you."[7]

Daisy writes in the essay of spending the first six months at the magazine working on nothing but "The Friend in Need" and lying awake at night, worrying about how to answer particularly pressing questions posed to the column. But Street & Smith book-keeping records show that Daisy might not have been telling the complete story. A Mrs. Alice Tabor was paid $25 per week to work on the "The Friend in Need" column during Daisy's first years. It's not clear as to whether Mrs. Tabor was paid to support Daisy, read the letters, or answer them, but what is clear is that not once in the "Dear Mrs. Browne" essay does Daisy mention another person helping her with the column.

Regardless of how much or how little help she received on the column, one thing is certain: reading these letters day in and day out gave Daisy a priceless education in the magazine's audience. Their letters, covering subjects ranging from what they expected in a relationship in a love story, to what they wanted in a spouse, to how to deal with troublesome family members, became the foundation of Daisy's uncanny ability to know what her readers wanted to read in a romance.

If Daisy was anything, she was ambitious. Even at her previous job—the dead-end bookkeeping job at Harry Livingston Auction Company—she would visit other auctions to observe them and "see if I could learn anything that would be of use to me in my work."[8] Now she wanted to learn about the publishing world, and she took any opportunity she had to learn about the building in which she worked and the products the company produced.[9]

While the Street & Smith building may have been touted as the "strongest printing building in the world" after it was built, by 1926 it was a firetrap. No one was allowed to smoke inside, forcing employees to huddle around small exterior spaces that connected the buildings to sneak a cigarette. Braver souls flouted the rules and smoked inside, keeping a vigilant eye out for a Fire Marshall.[10]

Much of this could be attributed to the packrat tendencies of the two brothers, who had hung on to remainders and monuments of their publishing dynasty for decades. All told, it totaled thousands of pounds of paper stored for up to fifty years. Unsold copies of the *Buffalo Bill, Deadwood Dick, Jesse James, Rough Riders,* and *Nick Carter* dime novels, along with the remainders of twenty-nine other weeklies that had been launched since 1855, were stored on the ground floor, turning it into a shrine honoring the company's leadership as the popular fiction dream machine of America. The books and magazines weren't alone: their original printing plates—23,000 boxes, weighing over a million and a half pounds—collected dust, awaiting the call to be used again.[11] Chances were that, in the twenty years since then, not much had been discarded and more than likely the number had increased.

The ground floor was also where the paper rolls, proud symbols of the volume of production, were rolled off flatbed trucks and then stored until they were sent off to the printing department. Stacked two high, they filled one room in the building, with overflow rolls stacked in the editorial and artist spaces. In 1906, the company had boasted that it enough paper to stretch from New York to Cleveland.[12] Chances are its output of paper would have increased over the next twenty years.

The Smith brothers, despite being in the fiction-creation business for the previous fifty years, still identified the company as a printing company rather than a publishing enterprise. As most pulp publishers contracted their printing processes out to printers, Street & Smith was only one of two pulp publishers who operated their own printing process in-house. Armed with experienced and seasoned operators, many of whom were career and union employees, Street & Smith's magazines were known for their quality in composition and make-up.

Adding to the mountains of paper stored on the ground floor were roughly 900,000 manuscripts that were received and distributed by the mail room in any given year. After manuscripts were received, they would disappear within the building, off to the editorial offices on the fifth and sixth floors.

From the moment that all stories were accepted and the copy editing finished, the process of producing the actual magazine began: a process comprised of dogged human endurance and hulking machines that, as primitive as it seems now today, were marvels of invention in the 1920s.

After each magazine was copy-edited, the contents of the magazine were laid out into a mock layout by the composing department. When a magazine was ready to go into the actual physical production phase, it was sent to the typesetting, or linotype, department. Here, all of the stories, poems, and columns were completely re-typed, word by word, line by line, in a manual process that can only be described as hair-raising.

When the linotype was invented in 1885, it revolutionized the technology of printing newspapers and periodicals. Prior to its invention, the only manner of setting up writing copy for printing was to hand-set the copy using individual letters placed by hand. The linotype mechanized the process, by taking advantage of the typewriter keyboard and the technology behind using and reusing molten metal.

From floor to top, the linotype stood almost seven feet tall and, at first glance, resembled a mash-up of a typewriter, bagpipes, and a witch's cauldron. When the operator (more than likely a man), sat at the machine, he faced a keyboard. Above the keyboard stretched a large curtain canvas that, although similar to a movie projection screen, probably never provided any kind of entertainment. Behind the canvas was a large storage

The linotype department, where noise and heat were the order of the day (courtesy Special Collections Research Center, Syracuse University Libraries).

area, a "magazine" if you will, that stored letters of the alphabet, molded in brass, each one called a "matrix." When the operator pressed a letter key, a brass mold of that letter dropped from the magazine into a holding tray, a process that was continued into a complete line of type (hence "linotype") was in the tray. When a line was complete, the operator would check to see if any extra space was needed. When a space was needed, a spaceband in the shape of a toothpick was inserted in order to "justify" the line. Once the line was completed and justified, the line was delivered mechanically to a casting mechanism, at which time hot metal, comprised of lead, tin, and antimony, was sprayed into the mold and solidified instantly. This new line of hard metal, now called a "slug," would be used for the actual printing of the process.[13]

Obviously, even though the linotype was a gigantic step forward in the history of the printed page, it brought its own set of issues and hazards to the printing factory. If the line was not completely justified even after spacebands were added, the machine would usually sound an alarm and stop operations. But if that safety mechanism failed, there was the risk of 500-degree molten metal spewing through any cracks in the line.[14] A famous "Hell Bucket" was always nearby to be used in such cases. That is, if the bucket itself didn't melt.

Between the typing of the keyboard, the clanking of the matrices, the heating and spraying of metal, and the ringing of bells, it was a loud, hot, uncomfortable environment. Many companies made a point of hiring operators that were either hard of hearing or even deaf to eliminate the nuisance of operators bothered by the noise of the machines. If they weren't hard of hearing, more than likely many were by the time they retired.

Once the slugs for an entire page were completed, they were locked into a frame or galley. These were then used for the printing process. Thirty huge rotary presses churned out the interior pages, and smaller flat presses used for covers and advertising, pounded the building non-stop. The hallways and cubicles reeked of ink.

The ground floor was the final destination for magazines. Stacks of *Love Story, The Popular Magazine, Detective Story, Western Story, Top-Notch, Sea Stories, Ainslee's, Complete Stories,* and others were wrapped in brown paper, secured with twine, and then piled in four-feet-high stacks. Men loaded the bales onto waiting trucks that carted them off to truck distribution centers and railroad shipping points. From there, the magazines traveled to the approximately 50,000 to 55,000 retail outlets across the country. This figure would grow by over fifty percent after 1930, when grocery stores and drug stores slowly began to carry magazines as well.[15]

At this point, it was time for the pulp magazine cover to work its magic. Because pulp publishers relied on the newsstands for most of their sales, it was vital that the cover for a magazine be as attractive and appealing as possible in order to convince a buyer to part with her money. In 1926, a buyer had almost unlimited choices of reading material in which to escape: breathtaking pastoral scenes of men on horseback, schooners docked in front of a stunning sunsets; men confronting all manners of threats from the jungles of Africa, private eyes pulling guns on the mean streets of New York and, yes, young ladies falling into the arms of the man they were destined to love.

Think of Me as Zayda

Knowing Daisy's ambitious personality, odds are that she picked up an issue of *Love Story* prior to her first day at work to familiarize herself with its contents. The March 13, 1926, issue, dated the same day as her first day on the job, is a typical *Love Story* issue of the period. *Love Story*, like many pulp fiction magazines, carried serials as part of its standard contents. Most serials were from four to six installments, and the magazine usually staggered two different serials in each issue. The March 13 issue carried part four of "Honor," by Mary Spain Vigus, and the final installment of six-part "Quicksand." The author of the latter is Victor Thorne, a pseudonym of Frederick J. Jackson, a prolific author who wrote hundreds of stories for various magazines during the 1910s and 1920s under his real name.

Six short stories, some branded as novelettes, were included in this issue. All of them featured heroines stationed in one of two ends of the economic spectrum: very wealthy, or below the poverty line. "The Harbor of Love" features a wealthy young lady, Helen Stevens, who is fully entrenched in the upper classes at her boarding school and only cares for her status until her father is thrown in jail, accused of murder. Helen leaves school and goes back to the city to support her father. During this turmoil, Helen meets a young man who is not of the upper class but is an up and coming assistant district attorney. Ed has a level head on his shoulders and only wants to help Helen. He comes to her apartment later under the ruse of returning a wrap. Having him there is a relief for Helen, as she hasn't any other relatives or friends to help her. He offers to take her to dinner. He is a buddy, not a romantic interest, at this point.

After Ed leaves, Helen thinks of how she would never have appreciated his companionship before. "Oh Daddy!" she whispered, getting to her knees beside her empty father's chair, "to think this had to happen to you before I'd realized what's worthwhile in life!"

Helen, however, must vindicate her father before she can move on to true love. When she visits her father, he tells her that he was framed by a man named Stanton, who may have killed the victim in a jealous rage over a woman named Rita. Thus begins an elaborate game of detection in which Helen infiltrates a nightclub disguised as a "Spaniard," in order to seduce Stanton and get his confession.

At the close of the story, Ed Stoner rushes to be by Helen's side at the apartment.

> She could not speak. The overwhelming emotion of the moment locked the words in her throat. But as his arms closed about her, it was as if a tired little ship had made harbor at last—the harbor of love.
> Their eyes met and smiled into each others,' with a knowing assurance that two souls had met for eternity.

"The Harbor of Love," was written by Mary Frances Doner, whose earlier stories appeared in *Cupid's Diary* a few years before. By 1926 she was writing regularly for that magazine as well as *Love Story* and would eventually write over 250 stories for the romance pulp fiction market. But Doner's focus would eventually be on writing stories centered around her birthplace of Port Huron, Michigan, and she would write over twenty-eight books beginning in the 1930s.[1]

In the other five short stories of the March 13 issue, the heroines live in almost Dickensian conditions and struggle to move up in the world. Almost to the letter, every story ends with the heroines inexplicably forgiving the hero for transgressions without question or doubt. They are, in fact, saintly in their quickness and complete absolution, because they believe their duty and honor is to be in the home.

In "Luck's Darling," Wanda Leigh is a poor young woman who was raised by her father after her mother died in childbirth. Her father, who used to be a famous tenor, raises Wanda to be an opera singer. When Wanda sings in a cabaret one night, a man named Cyril Shane, a promoter, introduces himself. Over the next several months he trains Wanda to be a star and at the same time, the two fall in love. But after a while, Cyril begins to drift away and ignores Wanda. Even when Wanda's father dies and she goes to Cyril, begging for a shoulder to cry on, he turns her away. As Wanda walks away from Cyril's apartment that night, she tells herself that she hates him.

In the very next scene, the story has moved forward five years and Wanda is now an international opera singer. Now with the name of Margot Delaine, she debuts at her American appearance. After the performance, Cyril shows up and, not recognizing her as Wanda, requests that Margot go out with him. She does, but after Cyril falls for her, she rebuffs him, using the same language he used with her five years earlier. Cyril leaves, broken-hearted and still clueless as to who Margot really is. Ten weeks later, Margot receives a telegram that Cyril is seriously injured from an auto accident. Margot goes to him and when she learns he needs a blood transfusion, steps up. "My blood is perfectly pure," she said softly, "use it to the last drop, but save him."

When he wakes up, he now realizes that Margot is Wanda. He asks for her forgiveness. She says she will never leave him. Not only that, Margot gives up her career. "Fame, fortune, adulation of the world," she repeated softly, "I have tasted them all. I have them all. They are only ashes in one's mouth." She goes on to say that despite her fame and fortune, "the poorest woman in the humblest cottage with her man at her side and her babe in her arms was ten thousand times richer than I." The story ends with her in the arms of Cyril.

"Luck's Darling" was penned by Mrs. Harry Pugh Smith, the name used frequently by Anita Blackmon, or also known by her married name Anita Blackmon Smith. Married to Harry Pugh Smith in 1920, she rotated between writing mystery stories for magazines such as *Mystery Magazine* and *Detective Tales*, and romance magazines such as *Love Story*. Like Doner, Smith would eventually move on to writing novels in the 1930s.[2]

Poems were a staple in *Love Story*; each issue had at least four to six. Most were standard—almost boilerplate—three stanzas, but others would fill entire pages. Some poets, such as Vera Hobart, Franklin Pierce Carrigan, and Bert Cooksley appeared for years. Most were the standard "roses are red" fare, such as "A Bit of June," by Willard King Bradley that begins:

The snow is high, in city streets;
  The frost is on the window pane;
And, like lost souls, the north winds shriek!
  But I've got a bit of June, for Jane.

It was obvious that the content in *Love Story* needed serious help. Daisy would look back on these first years later and what she thought. "The heroines were usually paid companions, governesses, or employed in some such genteel occupation and were always so sweet that it made you want to choke them! The rich girls in the story were allowed to be perfectly poisonous, but the working girl never!"[3] But, with Ruth Abeling at the helm, not much would change for the time being. Daisy had to be content with working the job to which she was assigned.

If she wanted to learn more from other employees, she needed to be discreet. The Street & Smith working environment and culture wasn't known for comradery. Editorial assistants didn't socialize much either. According to Richard Wormser, who began as a writer of *Nick Carter* novels and later would be assigned to *The Shadow Magazine*, any assistant who was caught talking to anyone in another department would be fired. Management felt that assistants, who lived on very low salaries, might be tempted to "do a little horse-trading" of stories with assistants on other magazines.[4]

She also probably had limited interactions with the heirs of the original Street & Smith founders, at least in the beginning. Ormond, tall, barrel-chested accentuated by double breasted suits, and cold, penetrating eyes, always looked unapproachable. Employees were too afraid to approach them; there's no guarantee that they would be acknowledged if they did.

By this time the two Smiths were advancing in years, but they still came to the office every day. They arrived in the late morning, with their personal chef at their side, taking notes as to what to serve them for lunch in the private club built into the annex. Later, Wormser reported seeing one of the elderly Smith brothers being assisted by a nephew to the limousine every day. The nephew would shove one side of his uncle's body so the left leg would move forward, then shove the other side so the right leg would move forward.[5]

Austere rules were in place. Time clocks were punched and everyone worked nine to five, and allowed only one minute before and after. Dress code was strictly enforced: Women were required to wear modest-length skirts and subdued colors, and men always wore ties and didn't dare roll up their sleeves. When Ormond came across a man who dared to not wear a coat or tie, Ormond wanted to "get rid of him," until a middle-manager interfered on the worker's behalf.[6]

And while the Smiths were not known to fraternize with subordinates, they were also known for their benevolent policy towards their employees. Workers were treated like family and were taken care of as they retired or became ill. It wasn't unusual for some employees to have been with the company for thirty, forty, or even fifty years.

After she had been working for the company for a few months, Daisy began to write short stories for *Love Story*. This was not unusual for many pulp editors and their assistants. Many, in fact, wrote for their magazine and sometimes other in-house publications on and off for their entire tenure. For Daisy, it was a good way to learn first-hand the requirements needed for a story to appear in *Love Story*. Two months after Daisy was hired, she had already finished her first short story for the magazine, "The Remembered Fragrance," which appeared in the September 11, 1926, issue. It is a simple

The book department in an informal photograph, date unknown. Slightly messier than the staged photographs taken for the company's pamphlet in 1906 (courtesy Special Collections Research Center, Syracuse University Libraries).

story of approximately 5,450 words with the sensibility of a Victorian romance, but it's here we see the resurrection of a name that was of great importance to Daisy's mother.

　　The story is told from the point of view of the hero, Clive Voorhees. He is a criminal attorney who has an innocent hobby of being able to name any fragrance that he smells in his daily travels. As the story opens, Clive has stopped to look at a store-front window when he is struck by the smell of a fragrance that he has never smelled before. He discreetly follows the young woman wearing it, who is dressed in a "severely plain blue frock," for several blocks until she confronts him and threatens to call police. But then she feels faint. Clive, suspecting that she is poverty-stricken, offers to take her to tea. She is a mysterious woman, and when she leaves him and he asks her for her name, turns to him and tells him, "Think of me as Zayda."

　　Daisy's next story, "At the Sign of the Five Jewels," appeared in the January 15, 1927, issue. She pulled in her home town of Westfield in detail, down to the Barcelona lighthouse. The story begins with Bob, an artist living in New York, who is unhappy in the city working in an office. He decides to leave the city for a while to paint. He has $10,000, which he inherited from his uncle who had been an artist. At the Grand Central station, he throws some change on the counter and tells the ticketholder to sell him a ticket that will take him as far away as possible. The ticket agent gives him a ticket to Westfield, New York.

After a long train ride, Bob sees a small town that was "the heart of the grape belt." After a few days he moves to a small harbor town called Barcelona and there he is given the name and address of a boarding house. The boardinghouse is ran by five sisters who also run a beauty parlor and sell a hair tonic invented by their grandmother. Bob is attracted to the youngest, named Laura Lee, who is very shy and says very little to him. He spends most of his time with Catherine, who reveals herself to be something of an opportunist.

This is where the story takes on a distinctive fairy tale tone and sentiment. When Bob and Catherine go for a picnic with the other sisters, Bob hears someone crying softly.

> With the moonlight streaming in upon her, Catherine sat with her beautiful head bowed upon her arms. The lights in her hair seemed almost bright enough to burst into flames.
> In her pale green dress she looked almost ethereal, part of the romantic night, and Bob rushed to her and dropped on his knees beside her.

"Catherine, my dear," said he, "why are you crying? Tell me!"

> "Oh," she sobbed, "I'm crying because I am not clever like my sisters. I'm no good at hairdressing, and when we go to Buffalo I don't know what work I'll do and the girls don't love me, either." She ended in a choking sob.

Bob, feeling sorry for the woman he thinks he loves, proposes to her and suggests that the five women come back with him to New York City and open a salon there.

> "Good! We'll use great-grandmother Jewel's hair tonic recipe!" Said Catherine, clapping her hands together. "And I can take care of the appointments and do the cashiering." To herself, she added, "and I'll really be in charge."

After the four women and Bob move to New York, they open a successful salon and all four women begin to experience their different stories of success. Catherine spends a lot of time with Bob's father and eventually they run off together, a rather surprising and unorthodox ending for a conservative magazine. Don't worry about Bob, though: When he gets a telegram stating that Catherine has eloped with his father, he runs off to propose to Laura Lee.

Daisy went on to write five more stories for *Love Story*. "A Queen for a Day," appeared in the February 5, 1927, issue; "The Girl Who Dared," in the February 26, 1927, issue; "In a Chinese Garden," in the May 7, 1927 issue; "Her Big Boy" in the January 14, 1928, issue; and "Salt Water Kisses," in the January 28, 1928, issue. She also wrote at

Daisy in one of her more relaxed poses before she had the pressures of managing a magazine on her shoulders (Daisy Bacon collection).

least two non-fiction pieces for the magazine: "Know Your Type," and "Don't Wear a Mask."[7]

All these stories were published under Daisy's own name instead of pseudonyms. Many authors of stories that appeared in pulp fiction magazines used pseudonyms for various reasons, such as because they did not want the stigma of being contributors to what was known as "low-brow" reading. For these instances, authors usually used pen names that they personally had conjured up for use across all their publications.

In other cases, publishers had their own pseudonyms that they used at will, such as the house names that Street & Smith had in place for years that were doled out as needed, most commonly when an editor wanted to print more than one story written by an author in one issue. In other cases, a certain author's name began to be an attraction to some buyers, whether the name was real or not. "Vivian Grey" was probably the most commonly used house name for *Love Story*, used by authors including Harry Walter Anderson, Ruth D'Agostino, and Marion Dare, and appeared on the cover periodically for over fifteen years.

Stories by male authors appeared in *Love Story*, but their percentage of the total was much less. Many wrote under their real names, such as Thomas Edgelow, who wrote roughly 100 stories for romance and the "snappy" pulps, and David William Moore.

Occasionally an author would have three different stories in one issue, one credited to their real name, one to their own personal pseudonyms, and one to a house name. But many writers, like Daisy, chose to have their stories appear in *Love Story* using their own names as the author.

When it came to the rate that Daisy received for her stories—one cent per word—she had no reason for complaint. Most beginning authors were getting a penny a word, others less than a penny. The pay rate to authors for *Love Story* submissions was all over the map, and having a literary agent didn't necessarily guarantee a higher rate. A study of the manuscript tracers—the bookkeeping cards that documented the author, title of story, word count of the story and the amount paid to the author—show few patterns in pay rates. Anita Blackmon, who wrote under the name Mrs. Harry Pugh Smith, was getting three cents a word. Other published authors, like Ethel Donoher and Marion Dare, were paid two cents a word. But authors who had almost zero experience writing for *Love Story* were getting the same rate. Other writers, who wrote just as prolifically and were just as seasoned, were getting less than one cent a word.[8]

There's no record of what Ruth Abeling thought of her ambitious assistant, but Bill Ralston was paying attention. In Daisy, Ralston saw a young woman who was a quick study and self-confident. Daisy's and Ralston's working relationship would last for the next twenty years and he would later be dubbed as the man whose job was to "keep Daisy in line."[9] In later years, he was one of the few people who could talk Daisy out of jumping off a ledge.

After being editor for six years, Ruth Abeling was fired. In March 1928, just shy of her 30th birthday and two years after starting at Street & Smith, Daisy was presented to the world as the editor of what was quickly becoming Street & Smith's most profitable product, *Love Story Magazine*.[10]

8

Modern Girl

While others might have been exultant or at least enthusiastic over being put in charge of a magazine with a circulation of a half-million readers every week, Daisy approached her new position in a matter of fact manner and as if it was destiny. Years later, she would downplay the promotion publicly by saying that "the publishers decided to make a change. I was doing the markup and part of the reading anyway, and the publishers just let me go on with the rest."[1] She may have outwardly pooh-poohed the accolades being thrown her way, but inwardly she knew she was the only one that could do the job. She admitted as such when a few years later she would write of her first days at Street & Smith in a compilation of notes about her career.

> ... it was with fear ... that she entered the big brick building at Seventh Ave and 15th.... She knew that, given time enough, she could soon get the hang of things and have the magazine going the way she knew a magazine should run.

But she crossed out the entire passage and replaced it with a declaration that was more fitting of her public image. Daisy would never admit to being anything other than confident.

> But she was just as sure of herself then as she is today.[2]

Daisy took her place behind an enormous roll top desk with a history of its own. Some

Daisy Bacon, editor of the nation's most popular romance fiction magazine, in an undated photograph (Daisy Bacon collection).

records say it was originally used by Francis S. Smith in his early days of writing stories for the *New York Weekly,* others claim that at one time its occupant was Theodore Dreiser when he was editor of *Smith's.* Daisy placed her growing collection of ceramic cats on the top of the desk. She had her desk moved so the back faced the middle of the room. By doing so, she could keep an eye on what was going on in the rest of the office while hidden partly from view, a fitting analogy for a woman who preferred to keep slightly apart from society.

She then got to work and began to make personnel changes. Alice Tabor, who had a hand in helping Daisy during her formative years writing the "The Friend in Need" column, abruptly dropped from sight. Daisy then made a decision that would probably be the smartest one of her entire career: She hired her half-sister Esther to be her associate editor.

Esther, about the time that she was hired by Daisy to be her associate editor. From then on, they would use only their surnames when referring to each other, using "Bacon" and "Ford" both in the office and at home (Daisy Bacon collection).

The two made an odd couple. Esther, short, dark and diminutive, had an outgoing, chatty demeanor that proved irresistible to men. She was already attracting several suitors, many of whom would drop by the apartment frequently to take her out. Photos show her vamping next to a car, her foot on the running board, a pixie haircut and a cigarette finishing the look. Daisy, reserved and serious, wouldn't be caught dead smiling for a photograph, much less playing and acting up in front of the camera.

Esther was just twenty when she started at Street & Smith. Extremely organized, her duties in the office eventually expanded to the point that she touched almost every aspect of producing the magazine, including editing the manuscripts for continuity, making up the pages, proofreading, and ordering and purchasing art.

As early as August of 1928, Esther was following in her sister's footsteps and writing for the magazine. In the November 17 issue, one of her poems, "Wonderment," was printed under the name "Joa Ford," and in the January 26, 1929, issue, a short story, "Hidden Love," was printed under the byline "Joa Humphrey," but Esther was given credit in the company's author records. The pseudonym Joa Humphrey could have been a house name that Daisy and Esther created, as it pops up in issues for poems and stories that were not credited to either Daisy and Esther, and would show up in other places, as we shall see.

All in all, it appears that Esther wrote fourteen poems, stories, and articles for the magazine over the years, along with any columns that regularly appeared in the magazine.[3]

Esther later flirted with non-fiction articles and at least one short story. In a column in the December 29 issue, "Love Talks with Folks Who Know," Esther takes on the topic of women who abandon their own personalities and appearances to attract a man. She uses the example of flappers, who seemed to be the scapegoat of every type of societal blame during that period.

> If they would only take a hand mirror, study themselves carefully, and finally determine their type and use their make-up accordingly there would be springing up hundreds of new flowers that formerly were that dreaded thing called "a wall flower."

The prose is clunky to be sure, and Daisy should have at least smoothed out some of the more egregious errors, but writing the article could have been a testing ground to see if Esther would be suitable for taking over "The Friend in Need." Indeed, Esther's enthusiasm for dispensing advice to young women does shine through the awkward phrasing.

> So, girls, if you think that the boy friend is beginning to lose interest, and you are sure that he is the "only one," take inventory and put some new stock into circulation.

Almost from the minute that that Esther came on board, she and Daisy called each other by their surnames. By following this tradition, Daisy and Esther wanted it clear that they, too, were professionals and would not be considered differently than any other colleagues in the building. From then on, for the rest of their lives, even after Esther married and took on her husband's name, they called each other "Bacon" and "Ford," both inside and outside the office, even in their journals.

The women had other assistants and readers helping them with the production of the magazine and, in many cases, the pulp fiction offices hired readers to go through the masses of stories first. They threw to the side those stories that were beyond hope and those that were literally unreadable, and then pass on to the head editor those that stood a chance. Even after thinning out the piles, Daisy was reading over a million words a week.

While there are no surviving notes or documentation on how Daisy organized or ran her office, it's safe to assume that the editorial process was much like an assembly line. While Daisy was six weeks ahead in reading stories, Esther was working on the issue due out in five weeks, other staff working on the final touches of issue due out in four weeks. The printing, bundling, packaging, storing, loading, and distribution by trucks to train stations of 500,000 copies of a magazine every single week was carefully planned out and schedules closely watched. If the magazine wasn't ready to go by the four weeks before its due date, serious problems could arise.

Daisy's attitude towards her staff was one that could be described as, like many of her relationships with women, cordial yet at arm's length. An article the next year said she ran her office "like a slave driver." But Daisy claimed a few years later that, at the very least, she tried to treat her staff fairly.

Another thing that a woman has to contend with the attitude of the women who work for her. A woman will not put herself out for another woman as she will for a man. The fact that a man treats his secretary more or less like an upper servant seems to make no difference. I have never sent my secretary out to buy socks and ties for a man's Christmas present nor have I ever asked any of my assistants to run around to the cleaners with my clothes. I do not smoke but if I did, I should oil my own cigarette lighter—or whatever has to be done to it. Furthermore, when I want to discharge the people who work for me, I do it face to face.[4]

One of the first lessons editors learned at Street & Smith was that their jobs were no more important than any others in the building. The company was producing fourteen titles, some of them on a weekly basis, and over the course of one year could churn out three hundred and fifty issues comprised of over two thousand short stories, novelettes, and serials.[5] There was nothing romantic or idealistic in what they produced. It was product, pure and simple, as unglamorous as producing canned tomatoes. With that, editors were just one stop in the assembly line. Because Street & Smith considered itself a printing company, as far as the company was concerned, "the only commodity cheaper than paper was editorial talent."[6]

This attitude was displayed in one of Daisy's early encounters with the manager of the composing room, where the process in which the actual layout of the issue's contents was physically laid out in a mock-up. Daisy readily admitted that when she was promoted to editor, she knew "practically nothing" about it.[7] When she approached the head of the composing department, she quickly discovered how her inexperience was viewed.

The composing room, where Daisy received a dressing-down from the silver-haired boss who tested all of the editors with gruff questions and strong language. He probably wasn't used to women editors, either (courtesy Special Collections Research Center, Syracuse University Libraries).

He was a handsome white-haired old gentleman who had been a copy boy for Charles Dana of the old *Sun* and he had two tests for new editors. First he would swear a blue streak—trotting out an assortment of plain and fancy cuss words—and then launch into a tirade about what a nerve you had to fancy yourself an editor. If you did not get offended at the swearing or cry at being told how little you knew, he settled down to helping you and entertained you with stories of what a bad editor Theodore Dreiser had been.[8]

Daisy also learned that not everyone was enamored with her refined dress and her way of speaking. She tended to speak like a professor and with her nasal, soft spoken voice, some staff quickly judged her as someone who thought herself as superior. She eventually learned that to get things done, it didn't hurt to throw a few expletives around. "Well-bred tones did not spell authority to them and after I learned to talk to them in language which I had heard my grandfather's stable boys use, everything was fine. Now they consult me about things which don't belong in my province at all."[9]

It was quickly becoming clear to her that a woman in management needed to adjust to different situations. "In order to accomplish things, she must talk like a lady to some men and be at home in a longshoreman's province with others."[10] She had to learn how to play the game to get her way.

Bill Ralston continued to oversee Daisy's work. Even with his growing responsibilities, including managing the company's imprint Chelsea House and working with American News Company, Ralston was the decision-maker for the company for the next twenty years. As for the owners of the company, Daisy wrote later that Ormond and George Campbell Smith were hands-off owners, and she was grateful for that. "I have them to thank for putting the tools of the trade before me but not dictating how I should use them."[11]

Editors also needed to work closely with the artists who painted the cover art and the interior illustrations for their magazines. When it came to cover art, *Love Story* had relied on almost exclusively one artist since its conception, Modest Stein. Stein's romantic soft brush had become as much a part of the magazine's brand as its name and masthead. But his personal history was anything but sentimental. He had emerged from a dangerous past that could have easily ended up with his life being much different.

Stein, whose birth name was Modska Aronstam, grew up in Kovno, Russia. As a young man, he displayed a talent for art and worked towards becoming a full-time artist. His father, however, disapproved of his passion. Modska, chafing under his father's demands, dropped out of school and emigrated from Russia to America in 1888.

Upon arriving in New York, Modska immediately began to socialize with his cousin, Alexander "Sasha" Berkman, and Sasha's lover, Emma Goldman, both of whom were already activists in what would eventually become the era's most powerful anarchist movement. Emma was struck by Modska's "wavy brown hair, fair complexion, neat mustache, and eyes that held a dreamy expression," and the two began to call him by his nickname, "Fedya." Even though she was still seeing Sasha, Emma began to have sexual relations with Modska. For a while, the three roomed together.

Modska became known as the strong man in their anarchist circles, credited later with beating up at least one informer. But things became even more violent when Sasha became infuriated over the strike-breaking tactics of Carnegie Steel's Chairman of the Board Henry Clay Frick. He devised a plan to assassinate Frick and pulled in Modska to help. The plan called for Sasha to go to Frick's office in Pittsburgh and shoot him. If he was unsuccessful, Modska would follow the next day and blow up Frick's house with dynamite.

On July 23, 1892, Sasha was able to infiltrate Frick's offices and injure the magnate, but Frick and another man were able to tackle and subdue Berkman and quickly had him arrested. Modska dutifully arrived in Pittsburgh two days later to finish the job, unaware that prior to his arrival, police had found out about his part of the plan. In the days before telephones, and before news was splashed immediately across television, newspapers were the lifeline for transmitting news to the public. News that there was a follow-up to Sasha's attempt had already hit the papers by the time Modska stepped off the train in the city. Even though his name had been garbled in the rush to get the news out, the message was clear in the following headline: The police were looking for him.

WAS NOT ALONE. BERKMANN HAD ACCOMPLICES IN HIS MISSION OF MURDER. IS AARON STAMM HERE?

Modska panicked. He ran to a nearby outhouse, shoved the dynamite inside, and then fled the city. "Years later," his grandson recalled, "he told me that if I should ever visit Pittsburgh, I should watch out where I took a shit, because somewhere there was twenty pounds of dynamite under a toilet."

Modska hid out in Detroit for several months before returning to New York. By the time he returned, the search for him seemed to have cooled. He laid low, turned back to focusing on art, and changed his name to Modest Stein. But he apparently never strayed too far from his original circles. Once he began to make a regular paycheck, he helped both Emma and Sasha financially and did so on a regular basis for the rest of their lives. It's not known if either the Smiths or Daisy Bacon knew of Stein's past life or the fact that he had continued to support Emma and Sasha.[12]

By the time Daisy arrived at Street & Smith, Stein was almost sixty and his wavy brown hair now white, but his dreamy eyes remained unchanged. Along with painting almost every single *Love Story* cover, he was accumulating a significant portfolio that included cover art for *Argosy, The Cavalier, Complete Stories, The Popular Magazine, People's Favorite Magazine, Picture Play, Clues, Western Story Magazine,* and *Far West Illustrated.* Stein had become one of the most prolific and in-demand pulp artists in the industry.

Much would be made later of Daisy's ability to work with new writers and steer them towards the proper writing technique needed for writing the formula romance story. But in the beginning, she also had several seasoned writers that she could rely on to give her solid pieces, such as Leta Zoe Adams, Ruby Ayres, Violet Gordon, and Katherine Greer. Some of them, like Maysie Grieg and Ruth D'Agostino, became close friends with Daisy. Having them as sounding boards and using their stories as training ground no doubt helped the young, earnest editor in her first few years. Daisy also kept in touch with Ruth Abeling, going to dinner with her and having her over to the apartment for lunch, until at least 1932. No doubt her old boss provided her with some advice from time to time.[13]

Daisy developed a philosophy of what she thought the successful love story should be, a creed that she would follow for the next twenty years: The story must carry itself as if the romance element was not included. At the same time, a story in which romantic elements were thrown in like frosting on a cake would not be considered either. "A romantic situation and a glamorous setting, some scenes connected loosely by sentimental dialogue and constant mention of love-making do not constitute a love story; yet this is belief held by most writers who start out to write love stories…."[14] Daisy was continually irritated by the young woman who worked in the mail room whose job was to glance at stories upon arrival and send them to the magazine she deemed appropriate. Apparently, every time she came across a story with the word "love" in it, she threw it on the cart destined for the *Love Story* office.

Another aspect was how much—or how little—authors incorporated Daisy's philosophy that the heroine and the hero controlled their own destiny. She began to reject manuscripts in which it appeared that characters were carried along as if they were puppets. "At the beginning of the nineteen-thirties, most of the love stories still contained elements which were a carryover from the Rhoda Broughton and Ouida school.... The authors wrote of love as a controlling force in our destiny. They wrote not of girls and men but of heroes and heroines personified and of Fate."[15]

The *Love Story* heroine needed to be modernized. Women needed to be shown working, not just as seamstresses in sweat shops or servants in remote mansions, but also in the business, entertainment, legal, and services fields. She relayed the message to writers, to agents, and to anyone who would listen that the heroine should be occupied in a job that a reader could relate to, such as a secretary, a beautician, or a clerk. But she could also be in careers that the reader dreamed of obtaining one day, such as a pilot, or a self-employed businesswoman. Glamour was not completely ruled out: readers loved reading stories centered around singers, chorus girls struggling to get a break, models who dreamed of being able to support their own artistic endeavors.

All heroines, however, should be looking for a change. Crossroads were required. They should be restless, unhappy, be at risk of losing their livelihood, or be hiding a secret. Being satisfied in their station in life was always compromised in some way. And they didn't necessarily need to be likable, at least in the beginning of a story.

Gradually, stories in the magazine began to reflect a more modern, emancipated woman: one who is united with the love of her life at the conclusion, but not until she finds fulfillment of her own dream job, or realizes an important life-lesson, or makes a decision that reflects maturity and could even benefit the common good. The falling in love and the declaration of love at the end of the story is, of course, imperative to the conclusion, but it is in no way the only bullseye that is hit.

Daisy was careful not to bring her readers too many changes at one time. "Some of the magazines realized it sooner than the others and some saw it but hesitated to make the change. In *Love Story*, we started a little earlier than most of the magazines; we made the changes gradually so that the readers did not get stories for which they were not prepared and hardly realized that changes were taking place until they were actually in effect."[16]

But some established elements were in for the long haul. Supporting a sick father, being orphaned, having a rich relative appear out of nowhere, or being in servitude to a rich and spoiled relative would continue to be prevalent in the magazine for many years. Going to masquerade parties, cruises, going undercover to solve a mystery, or accompanying a handsome stranger on a trip disguised as his wife or fiancé were all settings and situation that had lasting power and would remain staples for the magazine's duration.

And the issue of money—obtaining it, the lack of it, the imbalance of who had how much of it, or whether the hero and heroine could live without it—was always prevalent. In "The Love Trap," by Anita Smith in the December 7, 1929, issue, Lydia is a manicurist who, after being raised in "sheer heartbreaking poverty," is determined to marry only a wealthy man. She receives a letter from her grandfather, who wants her to come and visit him, but with no explanation why.

Lydia takes the train and is met by a chauffeur at the depot. Lydia notices he is handsome, and they look at each other in the "wind-shield mirror," but they both look away. She goes to the library to meet her grandfather. He is cool and gruff, but Lydia matches him in her comebacks. "Why do you suppose I sent for you?" She shrugged her shoulders, "To give me something, I hope. I hate being poor."

The next day her grandfather gives her a check for a thousand dollars and tells her to go buy some clothes. Lydia is giddy as she gets into the limo, and the chauffeur, who introduces himself as Riley, tells her that a thousand dollars is his "shining mark." He gives her some of his history: he wants to be a doctor. A man he greatly admired when he was young was a doctor, and Riley is determined to be a doctor himself and is trying to save a thousand dollars for his education.

When Lydia returns to the limo, wearing a "new gray coat with orchid hat and scarf," Riley compliments her, but then says nothing else. "Evidently he felt that the aristocratic young lady in the tonneau was not the simple, approachable girl to whom he had blurted out his hopes." Lydia is rather relieved, however. "After all, he was only a chauffeur."

Even with distractions like her grandfather's attempt to marry her off to a wealthy but simpering young neighbor, Arthur, and buying her a sports car, Lydia begins to realize she is drawn to the chauffeur and begins to be conflicted about her new life at her grandfather's. When Riley is assigned to be her driving instructor. Lydia looks forward to her hour a day with Riley, but one day during their lesson, Riley tells her that he is leaving because he is entering medical school. Heartsick, Lydia goes back to the house, and when Arthur proposes marriage, Lydia says yes because it will "please her grandfather," but also because of Riley's apparent disinterest in her.

After tea that day, Riley picks her up. Lydia asks him what he thinks of her getting married. Why shouldn't she be happy? she asks. "No reason at all if money's everything you want," he answered. When she says what else is there, Riley replies "love, and happiness, and health." Lydia scoffs at him, "And I don't believe in love! It—all that sort of thing is tommyrot!"

At dinner that night, a gala affair, Lydia comes to the realization of what is important in life.

> It was with actual dread that she contemplated the evening before her…. What an empty existence it was!

A tear splashed down her cheek.

When she meets up with Riley that night, he confesses his love for her.

> And suddenly she was in his arms, as she had so often dreamed, held close to his pounding heart. He kissed her, and a radiant new world seemed to open before Lydia's wide, happy eyes.

Riley then reminds her that her grandfather will disinherit her if she marries him. Riley offers to give up medical school to support Lydia.

> She shook her head. "But of course you're going to school! Do you think I'd let you give that up for me? Never! But we'll be married just the same. You forget, Riley, that I can work. I—I'll get a job and—and I'll keep it until you're a full-fledged doctor!"

Lydia and Riley's embrace is typical for a *Love Story* piece. The heroine is not carried away by the physical exhilaration and chemistry she feels while kissing the hero; rather, the kiss is the seal of the end of a search, a sign from the heavens that this is a love that would last through the ages and the final answer to all questions in life. The physical aspect of the embrace is never as important as the emotional, almost metaphysical revelation that this was true love. This was a credo that would be the *Love Story* signature even as the years progressed—less sex, more emotion—and would be part of its public persona. Any person picking up a *Love Story Magazine* was guaranteed safe and wholesome fare.

It would also be colorless. Like in almost all mainstream pulp fiction stories, people of color in *Love Story* were either not included or were included as stereotypical characters. Heroines are white, young and, while not always blond, with fair and unthreatening physical characteristics. Occasionally a heroine had olive skin and perhaps may have been a second or first generation American, but they were the minority. Heroes were white, tall, youngish (although many times were of the older, father-figure type), with mesmerizing eyes and square jaws. However, unlike the heroine, they could have darker hair and eyes, to go along with the "swarthy" type so popular in the era of Rudolph Valentino.

The magazine's circulation numbers at the time of Daisy's promotion were sturdy; some historical accounts state that sales were in the 400,000 range by this time, which can be partially credited to the fact that *Love Story* still had very little competition. *Sweetheart Stories* and *Cupid's Diary* were still the two main rival magazines. *Marriage Stories* promised stories of connubial bliss or non-bliss as the case may be. And, of course, there was always *True Story* for those who want to go over to the dark side and read confessionals. But other publishers were slowly joining the "love pulp" foray. In fact, another large publisher, Fawcett Publications, had just launched a brand-new magazine, *Love Affairs*, in February. This unchartered territory for publishers would drastically change within the next year, however.

By this time Daisy, Esther, and Jessie had moved yet again, to 129 E. 23rd Street, a few blocks from the Flatiron Building and much farther south than their previous residence. They may have moved farther south to be closer to the Street & Smith building. Jessie continued to dabble in poetry, and at least one of her poems, "A Picture," appeared in the June 23, 1928, issue of *Love Story*.

Daisy was busy with the magazine, but it didn't keep her from socializing. Occasionally the lines between professional relationships and romantic ones seemed to blur. One acquaintance who wished to see his fiction in print was Elmer Davis, a Rhodes Scholar recipient who began his career as an associate editor of *Adventure*, probably under its famed editor Arthur S. Hoffman. Davis then wrote *The History of the New York Times, 1851–1921.* He was a freelance writer at the time he wrote Daisy in September of 1928.

> Daisy Bacon, woman whose memory I shall ever cherish as my companion in one of the greatest experiences of my life, I wish to God I had a serial, unsold but still salable.[17]

Davis would eventually become the head of the Office of War Information during World War II and would gain a reputation as one of the most respected broadcasters to come out of the Edward R. Murrow period of journalism.

Whether or not Daisy had a romantic relationship with Davis is not known. It certainly appears that way from Davis's mash letter. But one thing is crystal clear: Henry Miller was never far from her affections.

9

The Golden Age

About the same time that Daisy was settling into her new position, Henry was putting the finishing touches on a house he built in western New Jersey near the township of Boonton. He had bought 80 acres there, land consisting mainly of thick and remote woods, in 1925. Officially the unincorporated area was known as Kinnelon, but for Henry, Alice, Daisy, and any family and friends, his property would be known as "Botts." For Daisy, it was Botts, not the skyscrapers of Manhattan, where she really belonged, and she would frequently refer to it in her later journals.

> Beautiful day of kind HW & I so often worked out at Botts
>
> dream: find myself outside of Botts house.

About a twenty-minute drive north of Henry's home town of Morristown, Kinnelon was a heavily wooded area in which a person can barely see the sky for the number of maples, birch and oak trees. The area was flush with lakes and ponds where great blue herons, ducks, screaming blue jays and woodpeckers are plentiful with wild turkeys trotting through the base of forest. The air hummed all day with the sound of crickets, a sound that became deafening once the sun went down.

Kinnelon first appeared as a development during the early 1700s when iron forges and furnaces were established in the area. By the time Henry bought his eighty acres there, the area had turned into more of a haven for the wealthy, initiated by a cigarette manufacturer, Francis Kinney, who bought 5000 acres in 1883 and began the Smoke Rise development. By 1922, Kinnelon had bustling businesses catering to weekenders, including two general stores, ice cream stands, and farmers that sold produce, pressed cider, and firewood.

But overall it was still wilderness where seclusion from neighbors and prying eyes could be obtained. There was train service into the city from Boonton, but the drive to Kinnelon from New York City was a good two hours, with a few scattered restaurants and stops along the way.

Henry may have picked this land because of its remote location, but also because of its link to his childhood. A youthful Henry, his siblings, and a passel of cousins may have trekked and camped on this land and talked about their ambitions, sports, and girls while lying and staring at the stars at night.

Henry built his home in the middle of a clearing at the bottom of a gentle slope. This was a man who was exacting, stubborn, and uncompromising in his quest for quality, and he wanted this house to reflect his passion for perfect workmanship.

> Working over old pieces, washing, waxing, and polishing mahogany and pine, you slowly learn to understand the design, the workmanship, and—most important—what dealers call the quality in

furniture, the fineness of the surface through the choice of woods, the seasoning and use of the grain…. You learn the difference in old silver due to different alloys and centuries of care in varying climates; the perfection of glaze in porcelain, the adaptation of design to utility in particular. It is no easy matter to make a thing of beauty out of a tablespoon.[1]

As a tip of the hat to his naval background, he designed the interior in the fashion of a captain's cabin, using applewood dismantled from the interior of retired ships for the paneling, crown molding, and the fireplace mantle. Leaded windows with diamond patterns were installed. He brought in local stone masters to craft the exterior, complete with a paved stone pathway that extended around the circumference of the house.

Daisy was spending time at Botts almost as soon as Henry finished building the house and, if she wasn't helping him with the initial construction, she was certainly helping him with projects around the house after its completion. She helped him clear brush and land around the house and worked on a broken heater that had Henry flummoxed.

Alice had no interest in roughing it in the New Jersey woods. It was a well-known fact that she preferred the city, so much so that it was mentioned in an extensive profile of her that appeared in *The New Yorker* the year before, in which she was "philosophically contemptuous" of the rural life.[2] It was an attitude that, she claimed,

Henry at the house he built in western New Jersey, on the property that was given the nickname "Botts." He may have built the house, or portions of it, himself. The tree from which the hammock is hung is one of two trees he planted out front and dedicated to his wife Alice. Date unknown (Daisy Bacon collection).

stemmed from a painful time in her childhood when her family lived in Weehawken, New Jersey. Her parents had moved there in humiliation after it was discovered that Alice's father's fortune had been depleted.

But one of the grandest purchases Henry made for the cottage were two elm trees he imported from England at the rumored price of $750 each. He planted one on each side of the front walkway and dedicated them to Alice.

Daisy's thoughts on infidelity were never clearly stated in any of her diaries. She was in many ways like a sphinx, someone who doled out her feelings sparingly within her pages. But a few years later, Daisy jotted down some notes in a journal, possibly to use in the novel she was writing at the time. The heroine, Doan, is engaged in a love affair with a man named Michael, who is older than her, sophisticated, and married. Much of it seems to have been set at the Botts house. These snippets are in many ways the closest we get to knowing how Daisy felt about her relationship with Henry.

> This storm really broke in the middle of the night. Doan wakened and set up in bed and in the flashes of lightning her slim figure [was] outlined in sculpted by the sheet. Michael, she said sharply, did this room belong to Hortense. Did she sleep in this bed?
>
> No, Doan. You needn't worry about that. Hortense never cared for this place and she never even spent a night here. It was too isolated for her. And even though it was father's—mother never cared much for it. I guess I liked it even better than my father did.
>
> And where do you sleep at home now. Does your room join hers?
>
> I sleep on the third floor in the rear and her rooms are on the second floor in the front. What are you getting at? You're the woman I love and always will love. Come here to me. Do you believe me?
>
> Comforted, she fell asleep again despite the storm, but not Michael. As on the night at St. James the actual duration of the storm was short. He got up and sat by the window and watched it strike down in the valley.[3]

When it came to the magazine, however, she treated the successes and failures of matrimony from a strictly pragmatic approach. It was the story and the author's intent that counted, a philosophy that came to bear dramatically in Daisy's first years as editor and working with a serial written by Ruby Ayres.

The story centered around a married hero who is falling in love with his secretary. His wife, who had only married him for his money and prestigious career, continually feigns illnesses to gain attention. But the serial was in serious trouble, because Daisy had let the first installments of the story run in the magazine without having the final installment in hand, a decision that most editors would conclude was a very bad one. Ruby, in the meantime, was traveling in South Africa. As the weeks continued, the final installment failed to appear.

As the deadline approached, Daisy took matters into her own hand and wrote the final installment herself. In the penultimate installment, Ruby had the wife check herself into a nursing home with two nurses at her disposal. Now, Daisy had to solve the issue of what to do with the wife. The plan was to have the hero go to the nursing home and ask for a divorce. But just having the wife, the villain in this story, agree to the divorce was not the way a love story ended, at least not in 1929. Wife needed to act according to how the reader viewed her, which was in a selfish, vindictive way. According to Daisy, the only resolution was to have the wife, in the heat of the argument with her husband, get tangled up in her negligee and billowing curtains and eventually fall out of a window.

And that's how she wrote it.

Daisy was roundly criticized for this decision. But, she argued, she wrote it as she thought the author would have written it.

> Everyone said it was not logical that the two young people should find themselves able to marry so easily and without any guilty feelings about it and that the wife as the type who would have done everything in her power to prevent it. Of course, it was not logical but it was the way this particular author would bring it about.[4]

Sure enough, when Ruby's final installment did appear in the mail, the problem of the wife was solved by having the wife fall out of a window.

During office hours, Daisy was a business woman and she was able to separate her own life choices from her professional decisions. Still, the Ruby Ayres serial stuck with her for decades; she brought it up again in *Love Story Writer*, more than twenty years later.

The summer of 1929 was a mild season for New York City weather. Yet the economy and the public's confidence in the future were anything but blasé. Manhattan was in a frenzied state of skyscraper envy. In the first nine months of 1929, plans were filed for 709 new buildings in the city, and builders began a contest as to who could build the highest structure. Workers began construction on the Chrysler Building, with plans on it being the tallest building in New York. But construction on the Empire State building would begin the next year.

The entire country was still embroiled in the stock market craze with everyone in a stock-buying frenzy. The market had begun to experience heart-stopping drops since 1927, but it had always managed to rally back within a few months with enough of a rebound to keep public confidence from cratering. Herbert Hoover was sworn in as president that spring, right on the tail of Calvin Coolidge's declaration that the economy was "absolutely sound."[5]

In somewhat of a declaration as to their robust financial health, the three big pulp publishers continually took out ads in the trade magazines promoting their stable of magazines. In September of that year, Street & Smith bragged that they had fifteen magazines in circulation, while Fiction House declared they had ten, and the Hersey Magazines twelve. They all were, as always, clamoring for stories, stories, and more stories. They needed content—all and any content. New writers, established writers, has-been writers: If they could string words together, they had a good chance of getting a story printed in a pulp magazine.

While some of the demand can be credited to the public's seemingly insatiable appetite for adventure, detective, western, romance and a myriad of other genre stories, the glut of magazines that catered to that market can be partially credited to a war between Street & Smith and a distribution company. Until 1926, the distribution of pulp fiction magazines had been controlled by one single company, American News Company, which was responsible for shipping and placing most of the nation's magazines in to around one hundred thousand stores, train stations, and newsstands. Tired of being controlled by the company and thinking they could benefit from forming their own distribution company, Street & Smith cut ties with American News in 1926. The distribution company retaliated by sending out the message to other pulp fiction publishers to "fill in the hole" created by Street & Smith. "Bring out other magazines," they exhorted.

Publishers heeded the call. By 1929, approximately one hundred and twenty pulp fiction magazines could be seen on newsstands at any given point. So many magazines appeared that newsstands were unable to hold them all, and many dealers resorted to shoving bundles of them under their counters.[6]

All this growth in the pulp fiction segment created angst within literary circles. Many thought the pulp magazine was a scourge on society. Fanny Hurst criticized the flood of titles that had appeared over the previous years, saying "The 'success story,' the 'true story,' the 'adventure story,' the 'snappy story,' in cheap multiplicity in cheap-minded magazines, have cast over the picture of the American short-story a sorry pall."[7]

However, Willard Hawkins countered that "newsprint" and the confession magazines hadn't replaced good literature, but instead provided another form of reading for those who wanted it. "The latter have not supplanted literature, any more than the photoplay

The November 17, 1928, cover of *Love Story*. Masquerade balls were a very popular setting for stories in the magazine. A heroine could arrive incognito and meet her hero but not know his real identity, or witness unsettling scenes between her hero and another woman (*Love Story Magazine* © Condé Nast).

or the radio have supplanted it. There have merely opened up a new type of entertainment, to which a large share of the public is responsive."[8]

No less than thirty-three brand new pulp magazines were launched between the first of January and the end of October of 1929. Some were short-lived, such as the ones that featured more obscure themes, such as *Wall Street Stories, Scientific Detective Monthly, Submarine Stories*, and *Zeppelin Stories*. Others, such as *Sky Birds* and *Science Wonder Stories* (soon to be renamed *Wonder Stories*) were to last much longer and become quite successful, despite the financial storm around the corner.

The romance genre within the industry was seeing some major changes. One magazine that had been released a few years prior had even spawned a new cottage industry. In 1926, flamboyant editor Harold Hersey, who had at one point been an editor at Street & Smith and then Clayton Magazines, had launched *Ranch Romances*, which contained stories that were a blend of the romance and western genres. Hersey soon discovered that the words "love" and "Western" seemed to go together like beans and cornbread. Edited first by Bina Flynn and then by Fanny Ellsworth, *Ranch Romances* became a home for many solid and well-known western writers such as S. Omar Barker, Clee Woods, Frank Robertson, and Franklin Richardson Pierce. Other publishers soon caught on and began to release western romance pulps, which would end up being the most successful of the "super-specialized" pulp fiction magazines, and *Ranch Romances* would eventually become the longest-lasting pulp fiction title in history. There's nothing to show that the romance western magazine pulled readers away from the general romance magazines like *Love Story*, at least in the beginning. In another ten years, it would be another story.

As publishers increased the number of pulps on the market, more and more of them took the opportunity to jump into the romance genre. Dell Publishing had jumped in as early as 1924 with *Cupid's Diary* and *Sweetheart Stories*, both of which were selling solidly. Other publishers tried the market with *Love Romances, Love Affairs, Love Stories, Love Secrets, Marriage Stories*, and *Miss 1929*. A few new magazines were jumping on the super-specialized genre phenomenon that was taking off in the pulps, such as *Love and War Stories* and *Flying Romances*. Some of these titles came and went within a month or two, their cheap cover art betraying their shoddy production that barely gave them a chance on the newsstand. None of them presented anything close to competition for *Love Story*. Still, they opened a new market for the hungry writer. Joseph Lichtblau wrote in *Writer's Digest* that "The proportion of sentimental love magazines to other periodicals is so good, that any writer must be delighted at the field for his talent presented by this one market."[9]

One more magazine emerged in the middle of the year. *All-Story Love Stories* emerged from the Munsey Corporation after a decades-long, complicated maneuvering of mergers and decoupling between two giants of the pulp magazine industry: *Argosy* and *All-Story Weekly*. *Argosy*, the magazine that had inspired the creation of the pulp fiction magazine back before the turn of the century, and *All-Story*, a magazine that had been launched by Munsey in 1905, had spent the past decade as a merged title, the *Argosy All-Story*. Now, the Munsey corporation decided a change was needed again, and *Argosy All-Story* would be split into two magazines. *Argosy* would once again become a separate magazine with its own title and would continue as a general fiction magazine that featured stories of all genres. *All-Story*, on the other hand, would become *All-Story Love Stories* that would be dedicated to romance fiction. Munsey Corporation was ready to take on the romance genre.

Much like *Love Story*, *All-Story Love Stories* had the advantage of a large corporation and a historic title to help it along. With the Munsey Corporation behind it, *All-Story Love Stories* had the money to produce a quality product with attractive cover art and polished stories and columns.

The Munsey Corporation assigned Madeline Heath as its new editor, but within a few years another woman would be named editor who would become one of Daisy's chief rivals: None other than the first editor for *Love Story*, Amita Fairgrieve.[10]

As Daisy and Esther dug themselves out from beneath the piles of manuscripts that arrived in the office every day, Ralston and the Smiths were slowly introducing Daisy to the media. Their new editor—a woman barely in her thirties and in charge of the biggest selling pulp magazine in the country—was certainly worth a few inches of press. This article began a long tradition of interviews for traditional press, writer's magazines, gossip columns, and radio shows, and the beginning of the Daisy Bacon legend.

The *Author & Journalist* had a long-standing history with interviewing editors in the magazine business, including the pulp fiction segment. The September 1929 issue includes Daisy's first interview and introduction to the world.

> What do you think of a girl who doesn't like caviar, pâté de foie gras, candy, or pie, but eats sugar on lettuce? What is your mental picture of a person who works 12 hours a day, runs her office like a slave driver, but has no personal secretary? How would you rate the ability of one who does all the reading for a weekly magazine and attends to the correspondence which it entails? Would you picture her as blonde, slight, with a low, indistinct voice and a face that should launch at least a hundred ships?
>
> Such, at any rate, is a partial description of Daisy Bacon, editor of *Love Story Magazine*. She is under thirty and sold the first thing she ever wrote to the *Saturday Evening Post*. She was quite successful with popular fiction before she took up editorial work. After a time, she went to work for Street & Smith and became editor of a weekly.
>
> She is a keen businesswoman and has a mind that works like lightning. In fact, Miss Bacon has made her living in three other businesses besides that of author and editor. One of her boasts is that she can make her living at anything.[11]

With this first article, several inaccuracies were born that would reappear in articles for the next twenty years. "Under thirty" was false; by the time this article appeared, Daisy was not under thirty—she was thirty-one. Daisy herself would embrace this error, never asking for retractions when her age was fudged in articles. She even used the wrong birth year, 1899, in her passport application that year. The statement that she was "quite successful with popular fiction" is based on her writing that handful of short stories for *Love Story*, and her articles in the *Saturday Evening Post* should be classified as more non-fiction than fiction. And Daisy may well have felt she could make her living at anything, but there's no indication she worked in three other businesses, much less made enough to live on. She also was not, nor ever would be, a blonde, something that would be obvious from looking at any photographs of her.

Professional journalists would normally fact-check statements before printing them. The puzzle of why this writer allowed falsehoods to appear is perhaps because of who she was. Joa Humphrey was a pseudonym that was used frequently by her sister Esther, with "Joa" the name of a female relative. Making note that her sister ran the office "like a slave driver," could have been a dig by Esther, but more than likely was one approved for the article. Other fibs could have been used for "color."

Shortly after the *Author & Journalist* article appeared, Daisy embarked on an ocean liner for an excursion to France and England, a nice reward for surviving her first year and a half as editor of *Love Story*. This is the trip that is commemorated in Daisy's 1929

Top: Daisy in front of the Notre Dame Cathedral during a vacation through England and France in the fall of 1929. *Bottom:* Henry in the exact same spot, with the same object held by Daisy in her photograph in his pocket (both photographs Daisy Bacon collection).

passport that she saved for the rest of her life. Stamps showed she arrived in Southampton, England on September 19. After five days, she sailed to France on September 24. Ship manifests and photos in Daisy's belongings reveal that Henry was her companion.

Even though Charles Lindbergh had flown across the Atlantic three years before, traveling on ocean liners was still the only mode of viable transportation across the Atlantic. To meet the demand, shippers were offering liners with more and more amenities for passengers. Daisy's trip on the *RMS Majestic (II)* out of New York was no different. A liner that began life as the German liner *SS Bismarck* (not to be confused with the famous Bismarck during World War II), she was handed over to the allies after World War I as war reparation and was renamed the *Majestic (II)*. At 956 feet long, she was the largest ocean liner in the world when Daisy stepped aboard in 1929. The *Majestic* was the epitome of luxury and excess. A palm-lined dining room, thick carpeting, walls and ceiling moldings, tapestries, a swimming pool, Turkish baths, a reading and writing room, a salon with a carved wood and crystal ceiling, a grand staircase, and murals were just some of the amenities. Suites had sun verandahs and flower gardens.

Henry arrived in Southampton two days ahead of Daisy, aboard the *Aquitania*. Both stated on the ships' manifests that their contact in England would be Banker's Trust in London. They spent several days in England before crossing the Channel to France, where eventually they would end up posing for their traditional "twin" photographs on the sidewalk outside the Notre Dame Cathedral.

Sometime later, Daisy jotted down more thoughts into her writing journal for her novel:

> Four years of companionship, openings, supper dances, exhibitions, races and the hundred and one things there are to amuse one in and about New York. Four years of intimacies however brief—four crowded years not without quarrels for since Doan's success in the business world she is apt to be ugly at times and jam the telephone receiver down hastily if Michael broke an engagement with her.
>
> Four years of intimacies—however brief. And one whole week (alone) absolutely together (in France).... They motored down to Dover where even the crossing was made for them smooth as glass. And then Calle—France. Michael had a friend's apartment in Paris.
>
> And from there they motored somewhere each day and dinner and dancing etc. each night.... Isn't she much younger than he? But does she make him happy? Apparently she did and he did and waiters were no longer curious and more satisfied to leave it at that.[12]

When it was time to return to New York, Daisy left Cherbourg on October 4, 1929, on the *Leviathan* and Henry left Cherbourg the very next day on the *Mauretania*. They returned to New York three weeks before the stock market crash. For many people, the wild ride was coming to an end. But for Daisy, it was just beginning. *Love Story Magazine* was soon to become the best-selling pulp fiction magazine of all time, and be the most powerful income-earner for Street & Smith. Whether or not the company would give the magazine and its editor the respect it deserved remained to be seen. After all, it was just a "love pulp."

10

Correspondence School

It appears that Henry and Daisy had a falling out shortly after their romantic trip to Europe. Tucked inside the mysterious black box in Daisy's personal possessions is a telegram dated January 5, 1930, sent from London. In it, Henry, using his nickname Harry, pleads forgiveness for an unknown transgression.

Whatever the source of friction was between them, it must have been quickly resolved, because after Henry returned to America, the two saw each other frequently. According to her mother's diary entries, Henry came over for dinner or came to pick up Daisy for nights out on the town and was frequently there for breakfast as well. He came over for tea. And almost every weekend, Daisy and "HWM," as Jessie would mark in her journal, would head out to "the country."

Later, Daisy would jot down thoughts of illicit rendezvous:

That is why people go to hotels because there they can have each other just the person…. Four bare walls in a hotel can be more truly a lover's paradise than the most beautiful full home where there are pitfalls lurking in every nook and cranny.

Cable found in Daisy's personal papers, apparently from Henry, pleading for forgiveness (Daisy Bacon collection).

77

> In a hotel what have you more than a nightgown and toothbrush a snowy bed (even in the most humble inn) and each other to live in each other's arms with no telephone or tradesmen to break into your ecstasy.[1]

Henry and Alice were still leading practically separate lives, with Alice spending most of her time abroad or in Hollywood and Henry hiding out at Botts every weekend—many times with Daisy. Henry would receive affectionate and breezy notes from Alice from abroad that detailed her trips and updates on their friends, but occasionally they hinted at the distance that had settled down between them. She bought and sold property without discussing it with him ahead of time, mentioning it like she had bought a new dress.

> "This Sunday I am going down to May Ladenburg at Southampton. We have sold the Fondey house there for twenty-thousand."

Alice then chastises Henry for keeping her in the dark as to goings-on in *his* life.

> "I have heard nothing from your affairs, financial, real estate or cats."

Alice signs off with an acknowledgment that is comfortable yet stiff.

> "Affectionately yours, ADM."[2]

With receiving almost a million manuscripts every year, the Street & Smith building had, for a long time, been a well-known address to the New York Post Office. Even if the envelope had the wrong address or no address at all, if it said "Street & Smith," Station O of the New York Post Office knew exactly where to deliver it, turning Street & Smith into the Santa Claus and the building on 7th Avenue the North Pole of pulp fiction publishers. Bags of mail were dropped in the *Love Story* office every day and, according to Daisy, "out of the mess came *Love Story*."[3] "I believe she could separate a stack of manuscripts into two piles with her eyes shut and in one pile would be the only copy worth her reading," Jane Littell commented later.[4]

The workers in the mailroom kidded that Daisy must be running a correspondence course. This sentiment wasn't that far from the truth. By 1939 one journalist estimated that three-fourths of romance writers who wrote for the pulp magazines had their first stories published in *Love Story*.[5]

As for her being able to read a million words a week, the figure that was most attributed to Daisy's reading skills as an editor, that figure isn't unreasonable. Divided over a five-day work week, a million words would have been split into 200,000 words a day. Speed reading would have been an asset for this task, and after being on the

Daisy about the time that the circulation of *Love Story* was at its peak (photograph by Joseph Captaine).

job a few years, most editors worth their salt and wanting to survive in the pulp world would have been able to skim stories quickly and ascertain their general quality. Jack Smalley, who edited *Battle Stories*, reported that he was taught a trick by another pulp editor, John Jensen: Give up trying to read the entire story and just quickly skim your eye down the middle of every page. "[A] few words down the middle tell you all you need to know," Jensen told him.[6]

Over the previous years, Daisy had been able to hone her editing skills and work effectively with writers, but she still relied on the seasoned writers to write the serials and perhaps one or two of the short stories. She then pulled the remaining five to seven short stories out of that "mess" of mail bags and worked with the writers if needed to fine tune them before publication.

While there is no way to fully verify each author's publication history with only surviving Street & Smith bookkeeping records and Internet searches as sources, it appears that a good percentage of the magazine's issues were made up of either new authors, or at least authors new to *Love Story*. The September 6, 1930, issue has six out of ten stories written by writers who were relatively unknown or new to the pulp fiction world.

An article written by agent August Lenninger that appeared in the May 1930 issue of *Writer's Digest,* added another stamp to her public image: That of the Helpful Editor.

> Never too busy to give a serious young writer a friendly and helpful bit of advice, rendering perhaps the quickest decisions of any magazine, and even prompter checks, Street & Smith's Daisy Bacon has first place in many a writer's heart. For she has given more scribblers their first chance than any other editor in recent years.[7]

This doesn't mean that she was the only editor who was open to mentoring new writers. The record is full of editors that enjoyed working with new authors in training them in the how-to of writing a pulp fiction story. The pulp fiction story had very exact requirements that were very different from the standard short story and it wasn't necessarily picked up on the first try. Just a few examples are Henry Maule, with Doubleday, who was known for his helpfulness, encouraging letters, and taking writers under his wing for nurturing. Ronald Oliphant, editor of Street & Smith's *Wild West Weekly*, patiently taught this author's grandfather in the do's and don'ts of writing a juvenile western story in the early 1930s.

Daisy herself knew that she could be opinionated and insular. "From a child, she has always been a very autocratic person. She never asks any one's opinion about the stories she buys, nor, for that matter, about anything she does. She knows what she wants and she gets it, even if her authors do go mad rewriting their material," she wrote later.[8] As the years went on, she became much blunter about her opinion of editorial feedback.

> I *am* the editorial conference. If you ask someone else's opinion, you only get what he thinks you expect.[9]

One writer, grateful for the attention Daisy paid her, sent her some rayon underwear as a thank you, apparently assuming that women editors must always appreciate lingerie as a professional gift. Daisy was amused and probably embarrassed by the gift, but vividly remembered it for years afterwards:

> Asked why she didn't wear them, she said, "It may be smart to be thrifty, and I know rayon is cheaper than silk, but along with some of my other likings I still like handmade undies along with my great liking for big beds, cats and dogs, and rocking in a chair."[10]

Daisy also noticed that some writers were not necessarily asking for publication tips, but craved attention.

> The people who think they can write ... mostly what they want is somebody to take an interest in 'em. They're lonely....

Daisy and Esther regularly invited authors to dinner at the apartment, took visiting writer out to lunch, and hosted book launch parties for others. Maysie Grieg was one such author, although she had already experienced quite a bit of success before meeting and becoming friends with Daisy; her "Peggy of Beacon Hills" 1920 series was eventually adapted to film. Australian by birth, Maysie wrote no less than 38 serials, most of them between 1927 and 1943. After moving to England in the 1930s, she became a prolific novelist, writing 200 popular romantic novels that were published by Pocket, Doubleday, and Triangle. A woman who practically wrote in her sleep, she was writing novels while concurrently writing serials for *Love Story*.

Another who became a friend was Gertrude Schalk, an African-American woman who was 24 when her first story appeared in *Love Story* in 1930. Schalk, who was born as Lillian Schalk in 1906, in Boston, was also known as Toki Schalk Johnson. Before submitting stories to *Love Story*, she wrote several stories, four of which were published in the *Saturday Evening Quill*, a publication that became a hallmark of the Harlem Renaissance. One of her stories, "The Black Madness," was included in *The Best American Short Stories of 1928*.

Shortly after her first story was printed in *Love Story*, Gertrude traveled to New York and made a call on Daisy. In a letter that she wrote to a friend afterwards, she excitedly wrote about the reception that she received.

> And did I have a fine time!—And was she nice to me! Oh, girl! I was so tickled. Took me to lunch at the Hotel Pennsylvania and everything![11]

Gertrude apparently thought a lot of Daisy, so much so that when Daisy mentioned that she would see Gertrude off on a cruise, Gertrude wrote her friends asking that, because Daisy would be there, they show up as well. She thought a large "entourage" to see her off would impress the editor.[12]

On at least one occasion, Daisy and her half-sister and mother opened their doors for artists or writers who need temporary lodging. Douglas Hilliker was an artist who drew many interior illustrations for *All-Story Love Stories* and *Collier's* and would eventually paint covers for *Railroad Stories*. In 1930, Hilliker, his wife, and their daughter were staying with the women temporarily, as they were listed as lodgers at the women's apartment in the 1930 census. This was part of a pattern in which the Bacon/Ford residence became a frequent place for writers and artists to stop by. Literary agents who represented many established pulp fiction writers, such as August Lenninger, would come by to drop off manuscripts for Daisy to peruse. This practice would become a source of grief between Daisy and Street & Smith management a few years later.

As Daisy worked with authors, as she read the million-odd words a week, and as she co-mingled with authors and others outside of the office, she began to fine tune what she felt were some of the most common fallacies and misconceptions she saw from authors who were submitting stories to romance magazines. One was the general stigma around the "Cinderella story." In the late 1920s, an era when sophistication and cynicism in culture was prevalent, a lot of criticism was heaped on the poor girl living with rich-relatives and then "marrying up" storyline.

knowledge on all interesting subjects, with the result that the field is too large for them to stick to any one subject long; yet while engaged upon the acquisi- of knowledge pertaining to that subject, they acquire a great deal of knowledge. The result is that Gemini natives are storehouses of information. Profound in some subjects, they also are well-informed in many others. Their imagination is powerful; and the mind is given to speculative thinking. They build mentally, then make their dreams come true.

The Gemini native is so active mentally that some- times the brain becomes feverish from overwork. Injuries may occur to the head and arms, with pos- sible fractures—often the result of carelessness and unnecessary exposure to danger.

MERCURY is the ruling planet of Gemini. It gives the Gemini native the power to choose between the high and the low. If he chooses the high, he becomes exceedingly refined both spiritually and mentally, and his spirit soars aloft to un- dreamed-of heights. If he chooses the low, he drags himself down and destroys the desire to be otherwise. Thoughts are like seeds; one does not sow tares and bring forth wheat. Then sow thoughts that are winged and the harvest will not be disappointing. Mercury rules the power of sight; Geminians, there- fore, have great perception. The influence of Mer- cury is elevating, and Gemini natives can harness that influence to their bidding.

The Gemini native has a profound understanding of sex, due largely to the influence of Mercury, the ruler of this airy sign. Mercury has no particular sex among the planets, but partakes of the nature of the dominant planet with which it may be configurated. It is this sympathy with all planets which imparts to Gemini natives coming under the influence of Mer- cury the ability to feel as others feel, to see as others see, but also to feel and to see from other angles as well, gaining a comprehensive viewpoint rather than one of restriction—a bird's-eye view, so to speak. Because of the capacity of Mercury to take upon itself the quality of planets which may influence it. Gemini natives who come under its rulership have the ability to make the best of circumstances, which they either change to their own liking or to which they conform if it is the proper thing to do. They weigh life's problems wisely and usually adopt the right course.

Gemini natives like objects of dual blend, stones with alternating colors, cloth material of twin de- signs, colors of red and white shaded one into the other. They like the hills, mountains, and other high places, including the upper floors of sky- scrapers.

While all natives of Gemini have much in com- mon, there are some slight differences between them, according to the portion of the sign wherein the Sun may be at the time of their birth. This difference may take the form of accentuation of certain Gemini traits; or there may be a lessening of their intensity.

For convenience of reference, I will divide the natives of Gemini into six classes, as follows:

Class A—from May 21st to May 26th;
Class B—from May 27th to May 31st;
Class C—from June 1st to June 6th;
Class D—from June 7th to June 11th;
Class E—from June 12th to June 16th;
Class F—from June 17th to June 21st.

The natives of Classes A and B are generous and humane. They have great ability, and can attain great heights by reason of their capabilities; but frequently they stand in their own light and injure themselves by improperly directing the forces of their thoughts. Their intellect is exceedingly strong, but at times their judgment becomes warped and brings misfortune upon them. They should think dispas- sionately and not let personal feeling interfere with logical thought conclusions. By holding the proper thought their difficulties will vanish, no matter how dark they may seem at the time. These natives should learn not to temporize with *themselves*.

They like to make speeches and frequently go in for literature, at which they are gifted. They are inclined to use their reasoning faculties more strongly than their intuitive qualities, thereby creating an un- balance within themselves contrary to their true na- ture which, if properly expressed, gives perfect co- ordination of intuition and reason. If they will use

Gertrude Schalk, popular young writer, possesses the liter- ary ability of the Gemini native.

Gertrude Schalk, one of a group of authors who became friends. Gertrude was considered a member of the Harlem Renaissance literary movement. This photograph appeared in a later Street & Smith issue of *Ainslee's Smart Love Stories* (*Ainslee's Smart Love Stories* © Condé Nast).

Daisy disagreed with that stereotype, writing later that "...every story in which a girl marries above her social circumstances or betters herself financially could be called a Cinderella story. That is simply the traditional American story and the history of the rise of many of our rich and powerful families." But many authors who submitted stories to Daisy apparently hadn't been able to stray far from the fairy tale, much to her consternation. Many writers sent in tales of women living in poverty and living under charitable circumstances and who were always sweet and honorable, while their rich relatives were always snide, conniving, heartless people. "This situation dominates the story instead of the details of how a clever girl can manage to make a good marriage. It can make for pretty boring reading matter."[13]

Instead, she continually reminded would-be authors of the value of looking at other settings, other people, other situations. Look at the most common, least glamorous setting you can imagine, and more than likely, you'll find a story about conflict. Authors who thought that only the rich people were the villains were severely limiting themselves for material, she said, adding that "...anyone who thinks that only those people who do not have to work for a living have the capacity for making other people's lives miserable has just never spent an hour inside of the average factory, hotel, school or department store or around almost any office."[14]

Stories should not just be centered around clichés and stereotypes. "New Yorkers do not stay at the office or take work home with them every night but neither do they necessarily go to the Stork Club when they go out. Yet ten out of every ten out-of-town writers picture them doing just that."[15]

It was a common belief amongst writers, probably not just pulp fiction writers but others as well, that they would have a better chance of getting published if they lived in the Big Apple, where they could haunt the publishing companies and "drop by" on their favorite editors from time to time. As a result, many pulled up roots and moved to New York City. With unemployment skyrocketing across the country in the early months of the Depression, many probably felt they had nothing to lose.

Street & Smith had an open-door policy when it came to authors visiting editors, so many writers dropped by the office to meet Daisy. Many of them would write later of the first impressions of her, and how polite and patient she could be. But one author saw another side of her: that of a more opinionated, outspoken side that appeared occasionally. While he discussed his recent submission with Daisy, Daisy suddenly took a phone call. The visitor was somewhat taken aback as Daisy seemed to be discussing force-feeding someone.

> After several seconds of "yes" and "no," the editor said, "Well, a bit of raw meat ought to be good and be sure and dip it in oil if he won't take it any other way. Of course, the proper thing to do is just pull his lip back and force a spoonful down him."

The writer wondered if he had perhaps had one too many at lunch, until Daisy put down the receiver and blurted, "Mr. C's cat is sick again and the man is such a fool! Doesn't seem to know a thing about cats. The idea of thinking a cat will drink ice cold milk. Now about your heroine. I really think that she ought to...."[16]

Jane Littell was one author who eventually moved to New York City. After first breaking into the love pulps with stories sold to *Sweetheart Stories*, Littell then sold her first stories to *Love Story* in 1928. For the next three years, she was a vagabond, writing stories while living in places like Leland, Michigan, Kendallville, Indiana, El Paso, Texas, two hotels in Hollywood, and four different addresses in New York City. She claimed she had been a circus performer for a time, which would explain her frequent and totally random change in residences.[17]

Jane and Daisy became, if not close friends, colleagues with a mutual affection and trust. There was probably something in Jane's nomadic lifestyle that appealed to the young editor who had been saddled early in life with too many responsibilities. Over the next eight years Littell sold at least fifty-nine stories to *Love Story*. But Littell wasn't completely loyal to Daisy. She also wrote stories for other magazines during the same time, such as for Fairgrieve over at *All-Story Love Stories*, and she also penned stories centered around the character Pussy Fane for the short-lived *Underworld Romances*.

Even with the popularity of the romance genre, *Love Story* writers were still only getting half of what they would get on average writing for other genres featured in the pulp fiction magazines. Most of the editorial offices at Street & Smith followed a procedure in which every story bought was logged onto an 8" × 10" card called a "Manuscript Purchase Card." Each story, poem, and column that was bought by a freelance writer was recorded with the author's real name, the title of the story, when it was bought, the word count, and the dollar amount paid. From these cards, one can determine the word rate an author was given. Oddly, pay rates sometimes could vary as little as four to five hundredth of a percent.

Even in the boom year of 1929, *Love Story* authors received from between a halfpenny a word to a penny a word. A short-short story of 2750 words would earn you only twenty bucks. A five-thousand-word story could vary, from between one-third to one-half cent per word, for a check between $26 and $30. A twelve-thousand-word story would earn a paycheck between $100 and $180. Writers with some experience and who wrote long serials didn't necessarily earn a higher per-word rate. Ruth D'Agostino wrote a 60,000-word serial that appeared in five installments, and earned what seems like whopping compared to other checks: $400. But when broken down to word count, that amounts to a little more than a half-cent per word. Poets were given a perfunctory rate of between one and nine dollars per poem.

Occasionally, in the hectic days of 1930, whoever was responsible for recording information on the *Love Story* manuscript tracers was not even bothering to record the word count, as if they were guessing how much an author should be paid.[18]

Several years later, an article would be printed in *Scribner's Magazine* that would have major repercussions in pulp fiction studies for decades to follow. Author Robert Uzzell claimed the lower rates were due to the "thriftiness" of the women editors; however, publishers had always followed the routine from the 1920s of putting less value on a love pulp story, even though many time the romance pulp magazine was the main breadwinner of the company.

Love Story's circulation continued to be strong during these first few years of the Great Depression. It has been said that figure of 600,000 copies per week were sold, but there is no solid documentation to back up that number. Editors, including Daisy, were rarely privy to exact circulation figures and it was rumored that the only time she did learn of her numbers was at the weekly cocktail parties where she could get them from the distribution company representative. It is possible, however, that Daisy was given that number and passed it along to journalists such as Uzzell, who would put that number in his article in 1938, where it would become part of the *Love Story* legend.

The only circulation figures that survive for Street & Smith are figures in which all

This August 30, 1930, cover of *Love Story* is one of the first instances that an actual kiss was depicted on the cover (*Love Story Magazine* © Condé Nast).

their magazines were lumped together for reporting purposes. In December 1929, that figure was 1,303,052, but that included all nine of their magazines, and was designed to use only magazines issued once a month. Hence, only one issue for each of the weekly magazines was used in the total.[19] While most mainstream magazines submitted to a yearly audit required by their advertisers to report their circulation numbers, most of those advertisers shied away from buying space in pulp magazines. The advertising companies that bought space in these magazines like *Love Story* were not under the same requirements; because Street & Smith bought the space in bulk, Street & Smith had to only report their numbers in bulk.

By this time *Love Story Magazine* was 160 pages, and it could be said that it contained something for everyone. While many heroines were still mired in financial difficulties and an inexplicable amount of them were still orphans, at least most of them had escaped the bedroom in the attic and many of them were occupied in entertaining job situations.

The September 28, 1929, issue that appeared on the newsstand roughly five weeks before the Wall Street crash, is a typical issue for Daisy's first few years as editor. In "Poppy and Her Playtime Girls," Poppy and her girls are a vaudeville team, starting out at a theater where her team is performing. Poppy is engaged to Art Griggs, the owner of the theater, but she meets Barney Burns, the leader of a jazz band, in the first opening scene, and conflict ensues. "Party Girl," a serial by Vivian Grey, opens with Melody arriving at home in a roadster with Kent Mayburn. Her father, furious, locks her out of the house. Melody and Kent banter back and forth as only 1929 rich young people did. "There are always the servants, baby," he said. "Let's get them up. They'll let you in."

In "The Darkest Hour," Dariel, an orphan, lives with her aunt and uncle. She is now marrying a doctor, except she gets left at the altar. In "Fate's Plaything," Janine Grey works in a millinery department in a department store. "Set in Diamonds," opens with Molly-Manette on a ship set for America after having been turned out of a convent in France after thirteen years. Another orphan, her late mother's husband had stopped sending money for her care. Now broke and hopeless, she is rescued from being swept overboard by Ellis Jerrold.

Barbara is broke and alone in "The Gilded Princess," and at a boarding school, where she jumps at the chance of becoming a teacher at the school after graduation. At the end-of-the-school-year party, Barbara gets a chance to play rich when she and friend Winnie, a member of a fabulously rich family, decide to switch roles.

"A Bride by Will" opens with the reading of the will of Henry Schofield. His son, who had been estranged from his father, sits uncomfortably in the room along with other relatives. He and the others are stunned to find out his father had given him everything. Family members, grumbling under their breath, give him their perfunctory congratulations and leave; none of them can understand why this happened. All except one person, who sits behind Henry Jr., and understands everything—Henry Sr.'s secretary Elsie.

Cicely Merrill is a photographer assistant in "Love's Betrayal," who is going about her work touching up portraits when she comes across the photo of "the man she had seen on the most eventful day of her life!"

In "Something Precious," Jordan Symes, an artist and a "regal old Patriarch," approaches the table of Wilsie Gary, whose portrait he had painted. But Wilsie is entranced by the "tall, dark, and handsome" stranger accompanying Jordan.

Intermingled within the stores are six poems, seven pages of "Your Stars Will Tell," an astrology column, the Pen Pal column "The Friendliest Corner," that features forty-five different requests that fill six pages, and finally, "The Friend in Need," which is twelve pages and includes seventeen letters from readers explaining their dilemmas and asking for Mrs. Brown's opinion.

All of the above for the grand total of fifteen cents. And the same amount of entertainment would be on the newsstand the very next Thursday and every single Thursday after that.

Despite the worsening economy, Ormond Smith and Bill Ralston continued to experiment with new magazines. In the year following the stock market crash, the company launched at least eight new or renamed magazines, one of which, *Real Love Magazine*, was given to Daisy to manage.

Real Love was the latest in several titles given to a magazine that had started life in November 1928 as *Live Girl Stories*, featuring tales of adventurous, risk-taking young women. But *Live Girl Stories* sputtered after it was first released, despite eye-catching covers crafted by Modest Stein of women wearing bomber jackets and taming circus lions. The name *Live Girl Stories* was changed four more times in the next four years: to *Modern Girl Stories*, then *Girl Stories*, then *True Love Stories*. When Daisy took over in late 1929, the title was changed yet again to *Real Love Magazine*, possibly because *True Love Stories* was too similar to Bernarr Macfadden's *True Story*. Finally, in April of 1931, the company made a sweeping change to all of the titles in its house, adding the company name to every magazine name. *Real Love Magazine* would become *Street & Smith's Real Love Magazine*.

Some of Daisy's careful crafting of her public image shows up when she writes about the new magazine in her autobiographical notes. "When the "boys" at S & S saw what a success she was making of *Love Story* they gave her a confession magazine—True Love Stories—to do."[20]

While Daisy would claim more than once that *Real Love* was not a confession magazine to compete with *True Story*, the magazine was completely retooled to do just that. It was issued in the larger "bedsheet" format, an 8½ × 11" than the standard pulp size of 7" × 10", to compete with *True Story* on the newsstand. Interior illustrations consist of photographs of staged scenes, the stories are written in the first person as if they are confessionals, and no bylines are used. Daisy claimed later that the magazine's stories were real confessions, "not made up," but her sister wrote five stories for the magazine. If Esther was writing from her real-life experiences, she had a heck of a love life.[21]

Daisy stated in an interview years later that *Real Love* "did not use confession stories where the person sins and atones but concentrated on the strange experiences people have but which are difficult to use in a straight fiction magazine."

For some lucky Manhattan residents, summer was the time to duck out of the city. In a time when air conditioning in office buildings was still a novelty and the city was unbearable, many workers relied on other ways to cool off. Many families would move almost their entire household to a "summer place" where they could escape the concrete buildings, the incessant noise of traffic and construction, and the smells.

On May 30, 1930, Daisy, her mother, and Esther trooped off to western New Jersey. Trunks were sent ahead of time, and then within the next few days the women would follow with cats and Nora in tow. They chose a home near Boonton, New Jersey, about a 15-minute drive from remote Kinnelon where Henry had built his cabin. There they would stay for the entire summer with the two daughters commuting by train into the city, sometimes staying overnight at the apartment in the city while their mother stayed at the rented cabin. "All went back to work today," she noted on June 2, "& I am here in the woods alone."[22]

When Daisy and Esther were in Boonton, Daisy spent many evenings at Henry's while Esther went out with beaus almost every night. As for Jessie, she stayed inside, except for an occasional day trip or drive into town in the evenings.

Henry's cabin at Botts had been completed for a few years by this point. The cottage's stone fireplace and rich wood paneling made for cozy evenings indoors. During the days, Daisy and Henry worked outdoors, clearing areas around the house and planting trees more to their liking. Sometimes Daisy proved to be handier than Henry around the house. "Thinking of the Florence oil heater at Botts. HW of course could do nothing with it. I followed the directions and did," she recalled.[23]

At night she would walk outside, into the pitch black of the woods full of the sound of tree frogs chirping, so she could see the house in the darkness with its windows illuminated with light. The English Copper Beech trees that Henry had planted in 1925 had taken hold and were growing steadily.

Bouts of depression began to afflict Daisy during her stays at Botts. She made notes in her journals years later of her "lost feeling," and remembering that it had affected her at Botts, too. It

Nora, who was more of a member of the family than a maid. She cooked, cleaned, helped with the cats, and was a companion to both Esther and Daisy (Daisy Bacon collection).

probably didn't help that every time that Daisy looked out the windows of the cottage, she would see the two trees dedicated to Alice, reminders that Daisy had devoted most of her spare time over the previous years to a man who would probably never be completely devoted to her.

Over the next several months, people across the country faced layoffs and banks began to fail at record numbers, leaving countless citizens penniless. Breadlines spread around city blocks. People began to view the future with fear; many could see nothing in the future except eviction, hunger, and despair.

Daily life, on the other hand, was quite different for Daisy. At the end of that summer, Daisy and Esther gave their mother some surprising news. They had leased a new apartment at 51 Fifth Avenue. A few years before, the family had moved to East 23rd Street, and while East 23rd was probably a step up from where they were living before, nothing would be close to their next residence.

A 16-story building just built the previous year, 51 Fifth Avenue was a premiere, full-service building situated five and a half blocks north of Washington Square Park and a twelve-minute walk from the Street & Smith building. The neighborhood north on Fifth Avenue was already designated as "the richest shopping district in the world."[24] When they emerged from the building, Daisy and Esther faced a historic Presbyterian Church across the street. Looking to the right, they clearly saw the newly completed Empire State Building towering over midtown. After they moved in, Jessie noted in her diary several times of bumping into one of their neighbors in the tony building, former New York Governor and presidential candidate Al Smith.

Jessie had come a long way from her days as a chambermaid, and the three women had advanced well beyond living above a pet store.

11

Forsaking All Others

By the end of 1930, it was becoming painfully clear that this economic slump was a savage one, and it was severely affecting many writers' abilities to sell stories. Pulp author H. Bedford Jones proclaimed that 1930 had been the "blackest year in the history of American fiction writing." Jones was in for an unpleasant surprise, because 1931 and 1932 would be even worse.[1]

But Daisy, Henry, and Esther and their social circles dined at the best restaurants, shopped regularly at Wanamaker's—a premier department store described as "eleven stories of shopping mecca"—and patronized places like the Stork Club. Later she admitted that she and her family didn't have the same economic problems that others did:

> During the depression I did not have to move my family to a cheaper apartment nor did I have to economize on my clothes. I never knew what it was to turn up at a luncheon in last year's coat and hat or to go out in the evening in a makeshift evening wrap. I had nothing in common with the girls who played bridge and drank cocktails all afternoon and then apologized for the looks of the house by saying that since the depression they had had to let the servants go.[2]

As for the romance fiction industry, roughly ten new love and western romance pulp titles were released between 1929 and 1931. But out of those new titles, only two—*All-Story Love Stories* and *Western Romances*—made it out of 1932 alive. The only other magazines that survived were those that had been in existence before the stock market crash, like *Love Story, Sweetheart Stories,* and *Cupid's Diary.* After 1933, there would not be another growth spurt in the number of romance pulp magazines for another five years.

Love Story's fan base was still solid, and Daisy's efforts to modernize the stories seemed to have paid off. She was, at least, getting press over it. But some credit for the magazine's success should be attributed to the "The Friend in Need" column, the advice column that Daisy had apprenticed on for her first job. Letter writers frequently mentioned that they had been fans of the column for years. Newspaper and magazine accounts reported that the office was receiving roughly ten thousand letters a month. By 1931, the length of the column in each issue ranged from ten to fifteen pages, with sometimes between fifteen and twenty letters and responses.

The Street & Smith bookkeeping records show that Nalia Audreyeff was regularly paid $30 a week for the column from 1931 through at least 1938, but Esther's resume crafted years later listed the column as one of her responsibilities, not Nalia's. Some of the letters to the column read almost like a synopsis of a romance story that appeared in the magazine, and it wasn't uncommon for one letter to fill one or two pages, each page consisting of double columns. In each letter, the writer told of their dilemma with

Daisy and Esther (shown here with an unknown companion) worked long hours at the office, but they managed to spend as much quality time as possible on their social lives (Daisy Bacon collection).

a thorough history of the situation, a great deal of detail, and a deftness in sticking to the storyline. Granted, it was an emotional time for many; people were experiencing economic difficulties so severe that they were affecting relationships and decisions. The depression was even influencing whether or not couples would tie the knot: The number of people marrying during these years dipped by twenty-two percent, an all-time low. For many, writing a letter that recapped their difficulties could easily end up being tomes.

But it's easy to lean towards the suspicion that some of these letters were embellished or even written entirely by Audreyeff, Esther, or other *Love Story* staff or freelance writers. Many a pulp publisher was known to craft "reader's" letters to the editor. Harold Hersey wrote of writing "sample letters" for a new magazine in order to "break down reader timidity" and to stir up interest in a column.[3] But we have Daisy's long 26-page essay on managing letters that came into the *Love Story* office, and she doesn't even hint at the possibility. Minna Bardon, a romance author and journalist, wrote in a 1933 *Writer's Digest* article that no, the letters that appeared in these lovelorn columns were not fake. She had seen plenty of the letters herself. "I've seen stacks of them myself. Pitiful stacks. Scrawls on tinted notepaper from the five-and-ten cent store. Painfully awkward lines on ruled tablet paper."[4] But the letters were, no doubt, edited for readability and who knows, maybe they were embellished.

These descriptions of letters tread dangerously close to the stereotype that romance readers were already subject to: that they were uneducated. As the decade continued, this mindset would be very prevalent in the trade magazines and would be a source of irritation for Daisy, as we shall see.

"The Friend in Need," letters were attributed to a wide range of age groups and marital statuses, education, and sex. The majority were authored by women, but certainly not all. A survey of issues from 1931 showed that an average of at least one and sometimes up to three letters were authored by men in each issue. The age range begins in the late teens and spread into the late twenties and thirties. Letters from married, single, engaged, and divorced people, common-law wives and husbands, widows and widowers all showed up. Topics ranged from the typical teen angst of "why won't the boys dance with me," to much more serious topics such as a husband's excessive drinking that led to domestic violence. But a good portion of topics had less to do with issues with love interests and spouses but with discord between family members and, of course, in-laws.

"Mrs. Brown" wasn't shy about her opinions of letter writers. In the January 24 issue, just one response shows how far the column had come since Daisy took over the magazine.

> What in the world are you, Poor But Proud, a man or a stick? Just because the girl's parents got a little personal in their remarks when they came home and found their pride and joy hadn't consulted them about a husband, you had to leave her in a huff…. Why, you poor prune, you ought to get down on your knees and pray that she'll have you again. And if she does—miracles do happen still—I hope you won't run off again as soon as someone dares to whisper about your wife's money.

In one exchange in the April 11, 1931, issue, a letter writer rambles on for two full double columned pages about her angst about the fact that she doesn't love her husband.

> To-night I'm all alone, and I sit before the window looking down upon the sleeping city. But is it sleeping? Or are there other girls, wide-eyed with fear and remorse, also facing the dark. Girls, more hopeless than I, in trouble? At least, they know what it is to love.

Mrs. Brown answers with disgust, calling the letter writer's misgivings "stupid" and "hysterical" and then throws up another letter from a woman with the same doubts for readers to consider a more "measured" attitude.

> I care for my husband in a quiet, sincere way. Maybe that is a safer way, after all. I am sticking to my home and my baby, and I am getting a lot of quiet pleasure out of knowing I am doing right.

Many letter writers wrote in only to voice their opinion on a topic brought up in a previous letter. In many cases Mrs. Brown encouraged others to write in to share their thoughts on an issue. Readers responded in spades. Their opinions over debated topics could continue for several issues, then disappear, then appear again to string along the topic for several months. The argument over whether flappers deserved respect raged for years.

Another recurring debate was over the theme of whether a girl should tell her love about her flawed past. Men's letters appeared frequently to debate these topics. "Although men sneer openly at all lovelorn letters a huge number of them spend precious hours penning epistles branding the modern girl as a 'Scarlet Sister Mary' or praising to high heaven the little 'home' girl they have found," Daisy wrote.[5]

But some wrote heartbreaking letters. In the July 25, 1931, issue a man, using the tag "Unfortunate," told of his service in the Great War, service that ended at the Battle of the Somme when he was shot in the jaw. While doctors were able to fit him with an artificial jaw, he still was disfigured to such a degree that, according to him, his fiancé broke off their engagement when he returned home.

> I wish her well and hope she is happy. Anybody that can look at my face certainly can't blame her. I'm always embarrassed; people just stare at my ugliness. I am an outcast, forced to shun all social gatherings.... However, my life is still before me. I am only thirty-three years of age.

Mrs. Brown answered in such a way that showed that she could still exude the motherly tone. She gave "Unfortunate" the obvious reminder that if his fiancé had really loved him, she wouldn't have hurt him the way that she did, and that he had no way of knowing what the future had in store for him.

> Take heart and be courageous. Acquire a hobby which will take your mind off your affliction. My heart goes out in sympathy to you, dear boy; don't give up or permit yourself to become too lonely. Let me hear from you again.

Notwithstanding sharp opinions and sometimes nurturing nature, Mrs. Brown's general responses were in step with the norms of the day. Avoid divorce whenever possible. Go back to the husband. Give marriage another chance. There was no cure for emotional depression except to pull up one's bootstraps. In one instance in the same July 25 issue, the letter writer, Flora, fell into such a deep funk after being thrown over that she lost her job and then continued to show signs of depression for months.

> I have nothing to look forward to but routine and the monotony of living from hand to mouth.... Thank goodness, there is no child to make things worse. If that had happened, I think I would have killed myself. Mrs. Brown, what's left in the world for me? Have I any chance for real happiness?

While an advice column in the early 21st century would have swiftly advised her to either seek professional help and/or call a suicide hotline, Mrs. Brown responds in the typical "get tough" attitude of the day.

> Buck up; pull out that lower jaw, and try to stick to new resolutions. Go out and find yourself a job, a job that will keep you busy from morning until night.... Remember, you cannot run away from

yourself, and no matter where you go and what you do, if you don't try to forget the past it will stick closer to you than your shadow. You've got to use your will power.

Mrs. Brown didn't address the fact that "finding a job" might be a bit difficult during the Depression, when twenty-five percent of the country was unemployed.

This lack of mentioning the country's dark economic times was the norm in the column. Readers' financial problems were discussed in occasional letters, but not as often as one would think. Once in a while a letter writer would mention that they had to work because their husband or father had lost his job, or that she had to move in with her spouse's family or, in rarer instances, a reader would mention that she had lost much of her money due to a bank closure.[6]

"The Friend in Need" was so popular that occasionally runaways would show up at the *Love Story* office, looking for the fictitious Mrs. Brown. "Girls leave home and come to New York looking for work (and husbands)," Daisy wrote. The office staff would send the travelers to "suitable places where they are looked after until work is found." A detective from the city's Missing Persons Bureau occasionally called on the office, looking for youngsters who had been reported missing by their families.[7]

The pen pal column, "The Friendliest Corner," was another column that took up a reasonable amount of real estate in each issue. In it, readers requested pen pals, writing their advertising best to show that they would be most worthy of a pen pal's choice. Over fifty requests could appear in one issue. Letters from South Africa, Canada, Panama, and various countries in Europe reflected the international appeal of the magazine and the lure of writing to people in other countries.

Mary Morris, "owner" of the column, was always very clear in her preface of the rules that must be followed. "It must be understood that Miss Morris will undertake to exchange letters only between men and men, boys and boys, women and women, girls and girls."

The isolation of some of those who requested pen pals, along with their economic struggles, was sometimes just as evident in this column as it was in "The Friend in Need."

> Dear Miss Morris: I'm just a modern girl, 18 years old. My mother is dead, and I'm trying to be a mother to my younger brothers and sisters. I have hazel eyes and brown wavy hair, and I'd love to hear from everyone. Linda
>
> Dear Miss Morris: I'm an invalid, and have been in bed for three years, not able to sit up at all. I'm 35 years old and like the company of young folks. I used to be a musician, but have been too ill to enjoy even the radio. I'd like to hear from other settings, and especially from anyone in New York or the West. Helen
>
> Dear Miss Morris: Who wants to write to a nineteen-year-old girl bookkeeper? I can read and write Spanish, and would appreciate the opportunity to correspond in that language. I'm interested in the things that are discussed today, read the best books, see the best plays, and love the opera. Perhaps Pals will help me forget my regret for the college education I never finished and the utter loneliness that comes to me at times. Ex-Collegian

Love Story Magazine was in no way the sole bearer of depressing columns for Street & Smith. Throughout the 1920s and 1930s, Street & Smith's flagship western pulp magazine, *Western Story Magazine*, included a column, "Missing," that printed entreaties from people looking for lost relatives, friends, and loved ones. During the 1930s, when so many people left their families in search of work, dozens, if not hundreds, of requests appeared every week.

In May of 1931, Daisy rented a house on Bromleigh Way in Morris Plains, about a

30-minute drive from Kinnelon. "It had the right atmosphere," she said, for writing her novel about Doan.[8] She was writing her novel about Doan, but she was also writing short stories, one of which, "Wife of Tin Pan Alley," would appear in *Short Shorts* in September of 1932. The story, a two-page romance, focuses on a newlywed's differences of opinions over the husband's servant. The jarring descriptions of the servant, a Japanese man, show Daisy was not above using the stereotypes surrounding people of Asian descent prevalent in the 1930s.

> Kato, coming in with the tea things just then, spoke in his usual naïve fashion. "Mister like song, Kato know Missie like also. Allee samee put him on machine."[9]

Coincidentally, Daisy's friend Elmer Davis had a story, "Unopened by Mistake," in the same issue.

On May 30, she transported her mother and sister to Morris Plains to keep her company. However, the first evening upon their arrival, Daisy didn't stay long. Henry immediately came over and picked up Daisy to take her back to Botts, a pattern that continued through the summer.

There are no personal letters or notes that reveal if Alice Miller knew about Daisy, but there are hints in Daisy's diaries that they may have at least met. Daisy chronicled her dreams regularly, and occasionally she noted that Alice appeared in them, as well as

Left: **Henry and his English setter at what appears to be the exterior of the house at Botts.** *Right:* **Daisy with Henry's dog, possibly around the same time (both photographs Daisy Bacon collection).**

her and Henry's son Denning. Later, Daisy mentions getting a letter from Denning and to have met Alice's sister Caroline.

One of the most intriguing hints that Alice knew of Henry's and Daisy's relationship is revealed in Alice's verse novel, *Forsaking All Others,* which was published in 1931. *Forsaking All Others* is about a married financier who has an affair with a young woman he meets at a dinner party.

The opening scene is of a young woman, Nell, who has asked her friend Lee to a dinner party. Nell describes the man, Jim Wayne, and his wife, Ruth, to Lee:

> "Not that you'll like him," Nell said,
>   "No mystery—no romance,
> A fine, stern, eagle-like head,
>   But he simply reeks of finance,
> Started from nothing-self-made—
>   And rather likes you to know it,
> And now collects porcelain and jade,
>   Or some Seventeenth Century poet."[10]

The poem travels through their meeting at the dinner party. Lee and Jim Wayne are entranced by each other immediately and spend the entire evening in conversation with each other, while Ruth, an older woman who seems quiet and dowdy, watches silently from the sidelines. On the car ride home, she dreads what will happen next, a repeat of "having to compete" with younger women.

Lee is presented as a pushy, insecure woman who eventually throws herself at Jim when he doesn't call her right away. They end up having a torrid affair, but Lee is tormented by the fact that although Jim spends all his spare time with her, he will not leave his wife.

If Alice did know about the affair, and *Forsaking All Others* was her way of voicing her opinion about it, the book does a good job of poking fun at Daisy, having Lee chase after Jim, calling her injured, remote, and self-centered, and who starts a campaign to break up his marriage, while leaving Ruth untarnished for the most part. Jim ponders the fact that while Lee had written him letters every day, Ruth had sent him letters "all his life."

> Leading him back to his alien youth,
> And his love—his first deep love of Ruth.[11]

Through *Forsaking All Others,* Alice championed the idea that marriage should last through infidelities. When discussing the book with her, Henry agreed.

> "Perhaps, Alice, the Victorians were right in making men and women hold fast to matrimony. No easy way out by divorce. With long association, habit and affection will make any marriage a success. Your idea in *Forsaking*."[12]

Henry would later call this poem his wife's "masterpiece," and claimed that Jim Wayne was not modeled after him.[13] The fact, however, that he had to bring it up puts that into question, of course.

Even though Jessie accompanied her daughters many times on outings to Boonton and Kinnelon that summer, she was in chronic pain. She was experiencing several health issues, one of which was diagnosed later as myocardial degeneration, or disease of the heart muscle. She also was suffering from an obstructional hernia that she had tolerated for almost twenty years. Now, as she and her daughters tried to settle in the summer house and tolerate the heat, Jessie came down with a bout of the shingles. Ten days after arriving in Morris Plains, she was fed up.

"This sure is some joint to be in & sick in bed. Wish I was back in N.Y. even if the taxi drivers do fight under my window."[14]

As the summer continued, Daisy and Esther took the train into the city for work. The season was considered the quiet period for many publishers, when both staff and many readers went on vacation. But Daisy had a busy summer, at least when it came to radio and newspaper interviews. Starting in May, her first major appearances in syndicated newspapers gave her opportunities to voice her opinions on the "modern girl," romance, and women in business. On May 31, an article appeared in the *Boston Sunday Globe*, "Modern Miss Doesn't Want the Old Hokum." The headline was the beginning of a tradition of bold eye-catching statements attributed to Daisy.

The up-to-date girl's famous last line is now "'a woman marries and the trouble begins.' And it is the chronicle of these troubles and the solving of them that women want to read about now," continued Miss Bacon. "Before the war editors had green grass under their feet, for women still believed everything they read; especially the hearts and flowers, moonlight and roses sort of stuff. But in the last 10 years girls have been around the block a time or two and you can't hand out the same old hokum and expect them to swallow it."[15]

She then speaks her mind about how stories should reflect the new reality of relationships.

If you must print "happy ever after" stories, you must show clearly how it is done when the girl wants to keep on working after marriage. Or how she is to decide whether to marry or be a bachelor girl. Or whether love can endure when the girl makes more money than her husband.

The same interview was picked up by the *New York Evening Post* on July 9, who posted it with an even bigger headline, above the fold, and with a bigger picture.

MEN MORE DOMESTIC AT HEART THAN WOMEN, SAYS EDITOR OF LOVE STORY MAGAZINE. *But Daisy Bacon Finds Modern Girl Growing More Romantic. And Believes Economic Independence Has Brought It About.*

Esther and Jessie. Jessie, very frail, was housebound by this time. Still, she managed to keep a diary of her and her daughters' daily activities (Daisy Bacon collection).

While the article begins with discussing Daisy's opinions about interior decorating—this was the newspaper's women's section, after all—Daisy manages to bring up her favorite topic: women in business. When asked if women were more domestic of the two sexes, Daisy asked "Women domestic? Why, women are simply in their element in business." The article closes with one last opinion from Daisy on the evolving nature of women and how they can be both businesslike and feminine.

> The fifty-fifty girl of a few years ago was a girl who believed in paying her own way. But there's a new kind of fifty-fifty girl coming into existence today, and that's the girl who knows how to be a business woman in business hours and an alluring feminine thing after 5 o'clock.[16]

As much as she tried to bring to the forefront the subject of women in business, the photo of Daisy that accompanies the two articles stuck to the prevalent attitude that a woman's beauty was just as important as anything else. Daisy is shown with bare shoulders, a comely hair bob, and heavy eye makeup, giving the impression that she is anything but businesslike. It appears that her nose was altered in the photograph.

The photograph was most likely Daisy's call. Daisy was a vain woman, and it was pointed out in almost any article written about her that she was "pretty," "blonde," or "attractive." She also placed a great deal of importance on the role that beauty played in any kind of male/female relationship in business, and could be quite critical of her own gender when it came to how they reacted to unwanted male advances in the business world. It all depended on how pretty you were, she wrote.

This comes into full view in an essay she wrote called "The Sex Complex in Business." It was her opinion that unattractive women couldn't handle a man's advances in the business world.

> All the women who had claimed that their bosses had asked them to step down from the straight and narrow path were pretty much of the same type. Generally built along the lines of a railroad tie and utterly lacking in feminine charm and "it." In fact, your guess would have been that they would be safe even in a Turkish harem.

She then uses the example of when a women of the description above accuses her boss of making unwanted advances. The other "plainer girls" in the department believe her, and even some men did as well, but "every pretty girl in the place dismissed the incident with one of those fascinating looks that pretty women reserve for each other, and "another bedtime story," as if it wasn't true. Daisy herself didn't believe the accusation because she "knew the man well."

But attractive women were not immune to her sharp pen.

> My private opinion why a pretty woman wouldn't tell if such an incident ever happened to her is this: She likes to have the world believe that, no matter how much a man may admire her, she is beautiful enough and charming enough to keep the situation under control.[17]
>
> Being editor of a magazine is as much a business she knew as manufacturing tin cans or making ice boxes.[18]

If there was one thing that Street & Smith was never guilty of, it was forgetting to treat their magazines and the stories in them like commodities. They incessantly and efficiently crossed into other forms of media to milk every single cent that they could out of their most popular magazines. Countless pulp stories were adapted into screenplays for the hungry movie audiences that flocked to the theaters during the 1930s. The company continued to reprint many of its stories that had appeared in its western, detective, and adventure magazines into book form and printed them under their imprint Chelsea

House. Many of its stories would end up in Saalfield Publishing Company's Little Big Books, authors given a flat fee of $50 per story for the privilege. Fan clubs were established and premiums offered for sale. Many Street & Smith magazines were printed in international venues such as in Canada and England, such as its *Wild West Weekly* magazine that was renamed *Wild West* in England and featured some of its standard heroes, but without their original authors' bylines.

Probably the most important cross-over was one that would have dramatic consequences for the entire industry. Radio programs were beginning to show promise as a vehicle to interest audiences into buying pulps. With that, Street & Smith had decided to transfer *Detective Story Magazine* to the world of radio in the previous summer.

Once "The Detective Story Hour" was launched, Bill Ralston and others at the company waited impatiently for the buyers to begin flocking to the newsstands to buy copies of the latest issue of *Detective Story*. But that didn't happen, at least to the degree that Ralston hoped for. Instead, another phenomenon was beginning to build, and it didn't relate to the magazine stories as much as the voice that introduced them every week.

> The Shadow knows ... and you too, shall know if you listen while Street & Smith *Detective Story Magazine* relates for you the story of....

The same voice concluded each show.

> The Shadow knows....

Stories began to filter back to Ralston of what was occurring on the streets at the newsstands. Buyers were asking not for *Detective Story*, but for "that Shadow magazine." Ralston approached Frank Blackwell, editor of *Detective Story*, to come up with a new pulp fiction magazine, one featuring the new star of radio, The Shadow.

Ralston knew he had to move fast, before the name was copyrighted by a competitor and to tap into the popularity of the figure while it was peaking. He needed an actual magazine created which he could use to register the copyright, a procedure called an "ashcan" issue. But Blackwell and his staff were far too busy to write the story for the first issue, even though Ralston was offering them the easier task of just rewriting an old unpublished Nick Carter story.

Almost by providence, and with what one historian called "a masterstroke of destiny," a writer named Walter Gibson appeared in Blackwell's office soon after to discuss ideas for upcoming projects that Gibson had in mind. Gibson, a newspaper and ghost writer, was also a magician with a passionate interest in magic. Blackwell hired Gibson on the spot to write The Shadow stories.[19]

The Shadow, A Detective Magazine appeared for the first time on newsstands in March 1931, a rushed issue with cover art that had, in true Street & Smith style, appeared on one of their earlier *Thrill Book* issues. It was shoved onto newsstands for a heightened, almost fanatical reading public that had listened to The Shadow on "The Detective Story Hour" over the winter.

Gibson folded his magician talents into the stories, including hidden staircases, two-way mirrors, robots, and magician secrets.[20] The first hero pulp initiated another genre for the industry, one which would eventually influence comics as well. It wasn't long before its circulation climbed to 300,000 and became a serious contender for *Love Story's* standing as the biggest selling pulp magazine. And while it would not affect the romance genre specifically, the hero pulp magazine was a phenomenon that would not go away.

These heroes would lead the way to an entire industry of heroes and superheroes, one that would eventually make its mark in the comic book world.

The Shadow and Walter Gibson would eventually cross paths with Daisy Bacon in the distant future, as would the next successful Street & Smith pulp hero, Doc Savage.

Buoyed by the success of *The Shadow*, Street & Smith continued to target radio for circulation boosters, and Daisy's magazine was in the cross-hairs. On July 29, 1931, Street & Smith signed a contract with Ruthrauff & Ryan, an advertising agency, to produce a radio broadcasting program based on stories from *Love Story Magazine*. No scripts survive from that early schedule but, based on a resurrection of the program later in the 1930s, it's safe to conclude that the scripts were based on stories that had appeared in the magazine. The program, one-half hour long, began on October 1, 1931, and ran on Thursday evenings from 9:30 to 10:00 p.m. The original contract between Street & Smith and Ruthrauff & Ryan called for the program to run for 52 weeks, with an option for the publisher to pull out after 26 weeks if they desired. Distributed by Columbia Broadcasting System, the program ran in twenty cities, mainly the large cities on the eastern coast, but also inland to Chicago, Cincinnati, St. Louis and as far west as Kansas City. The show was advertised heavily in various Street & Smith magazines and on *Love Story* covers, with a circular icon declaring the program was "On the Air Every Thursday Night."

Daisy and Esther made frequent trips to the recording studios to attend the airing of episodes. In February, Jessie noted that Daisy went to an event to hear Winston Churchill speak and sat next to a "Mrs. Roosevelt." With this type of exposure to society, going to the recording studios, the Stork Club, attending opera and plays, and running to the country every weekend with her lover, Daisy's life was more hectic than ever.

By the middle of 1932, the number of pulp fiction magazines on newsstands had changed considerably. Directly after the stock market crash, there had been 180 fiction magazines on the stands, of which 100 were pulp magazines. Out of those, a little over half were gone by 1932. Manuscripts that had been accepted but had no place to be published sat in piles on editors' desks. Editors were laid off and writers began taking less money for their work. Writers who had been getting four cents a word in the 1920s found themselves having to accept two cents a word, sometimes even less, in order to be published.[21]

Even some of Street & Smith's most venerable titles were affected. *The Popular Magazine*, the company's very first pulp fiction magazine, had been merged into the title *Complete Stories* at the end of 1931. *Sea Stories Magazine*, which had been launched at the beginning of the Roaring Twenties, had gone through two name and genre changes until it was called *Excitement*, but that wasn't enough to save it. The schedule for *Detective Story* was changed from weekly to semi-monthly. Daisy's new assignment, *Real Love Magazine*, failed to catch fire and its last issue appeared in September 1932.

Still, the magazine market continued to be glutted. In December, Street & Smith competitor Fiction House suspended twelve magazines, and in an announcement they succinctly summed up the situation.

> The influx of lower-priced magazines and the incidental cheapening of product has created a market situation which is unsound and cannot continue.[22]

Bad news did not stem the flow of manuscripts that arrived at publishers' offices and there was still a unrelenting demand for stories. Frank Blackwell summarized it up perfectly in an interview with a writer, saying "What we want is stories. We never have enough of them; never! I need nearly 750,000 words of fiction and fillers a month to fill my three magazines. This matter must conform to our standard, of course. And if you don't think it's a job to select 750,000 words of passable stuff every month, the year around, you ought to come into this office and see for yourself."[23]

Cottage industries were already established and growing, however, around the need of writers to get their stories published in the pulps. One opportunistic man, Wycliffe A. Hill, even invented "The Plot Genie," which was a two-part mechanism for creating any kind of plot you wish for the specific genre you were writing. *The Plot Genie* book listed plot elements, characters, and settings for a genre, and gave each element a number. You use Plot Genie included with the book, a crude cartoonish "genie" complete with a "crystal ball," in the form of a cardboard wheel. You spin the wheel, and then write down the numbers the wheel, or crystal ball, reveals. Then return to the book and use those numbers to find your plot, your heroine, your hero, and your setting. According to Bold Venture Press, which currently produces a reprint library of the Plot Genie books, "… Plot Genie might have seemed like a ray of hope to struggling, unemployed citizens. Purchase a book for five dollars (which was like spending seventy-five in those days), dash off a few lines, and tell the bank to stand by for your deposits."[24] It's questionable as to how many writers actually used the system, but apparently it was enough for Hill to spin off books for the following fields: Action/Adventure, Scientific, Comedy, Detective, Short-short Story and, of course, Romance.

There are no indications that *Love Story* circulation was dropping, nor that authors were getting cuts in pay. Most were still getting the perfunctory $50, $75, and $85 for short stories. Others were getting uncommonly good sums for serials. Later that year, in the height of the Depression, Maysie Grieg was paid what was an astronomical sum at the time, $1,500, for a seven-part serial, "Professional Lover," that was published in early 1933. Because the word count was not specified, only an educated guess can be made on the per-word rate. If the serial was 50,000 words, which would be the limit for a serial, that would mean she was getting at least 3 cents a word. Then, just a few months later, Ruby Ayres was paid $2,200 for her seven-part serial "Always Tomorrow."

The bottom line is that was a still good market for writers who wanted to sell to the romance pulps. Every three or four months the *Author & Journalist, The Writer, Writer's Digest*, and other trade magazines loaded up on advice for writers on how to break into the romance fiction field with articles on every subject, from how to use real-life situations for storylines, to how to write them, submit them, and bother (or not) an editor for an answer.

Regular columns listed publishers that were buying stories and their requirements. All editors wanted to differentiate their magazine from others on the newsstand. Some editors advised writers to stay away from the "Cinderella story" but, within a few years, they would do an about-face and say that yes, stories of heroines being rescued by men of a higher social strata were now welcome again. One editor wanted stories of the confession type, but in the third person rather than the standard first person normally used by the confession magazines, which could lead to some interesting reading. Some editors warned writers to stay away from sordidness, but others wanted heroines that "lived vividly and loved dangerously." But in the same breath, they would warn, "The action should be emotionally daring, but must not approach the indecent."[25] Writers would have to twist themselves into pretzels to accommodate some of these editors' guidelines.

Some editors stressed that setting was all-important, because everyone knew that the basic romance storyline—girl meets boy, followed by tension, misunderstandings, and obstacles that prevent their union, with a final admission and declaration of love—could not be tinkered with. In the early 1930s, the aviation setting was golden. A female pilot character exuded an air of independence, courage, and adventure. And, as everyone knew, the air field was full of handsome men. "There are always men about—a prerequisite for the good love story—the mechanics, fellow flyers, officials of the airport."[26] But everything, from Broadway theaters to the Saharan desert, was fair game.

When sending in manuscripts, occasionally a writer would send in a cover letter boasting that they were already a published author in other, more respectable publications and that they were doing the editor a favor by sending in their story to a pulp. This was not a recommended practice, to say the least. When Daisy received one of these, the writer was likely to get back their unpublished manuscript marked up heavily, with a polite but pointed letter saying that they had a long way to go before their story would be accepted. "He thinks I am soft … until he gets a letter from me."[27]

If writers wanted to take her advice and were tough enough to handle her sharp pen, they could resubmit their stories. An accompanying letter eating humble pie could help their situation. Daisy was more than happy to work with them after that and give them her philosophy about writing the love story:

> More than any other story type, the love story is looked upon as a freak, which can be turned out without much thought or preparation. It is felt that any set of stock characters will answer the purpose as long as they fall in love and the heroine gets her ideal man or the hero wins the woman of his heart and that no matter how dull the story form, moonlight, white shoulders, and soft music will take care of that. As a matter of fact, the love story is all that any other story is—and a love story, too.[28]

Occasionally Daisy received stories that had been published in other magazines several years before. Daisy responded with a witty letter, telling the writer that "*Love Story* would be glad to have another look at them."

Plagiarism was a continuing problem with most pulp publishers during the Depression. The Munsey company issued a public shaming on one plagiarist who had passed two stories onto them that had been previously published in 1915. This type of wrongdoing was harmful to everyone, the publisher declared, as it made all editors suspicious of any unknown writer. "Newcomers are likely to suffer," the publisher warned.[29]

Other writers attempted to influence Daisy to buy their submissions by using devices in their story that they hoped would appeal to her passion for animals. In the beginning of 1933, Daisy and Esther witnessed a horrific incident in which a cat was hit by a car. The driver didn't bother to stop, so Daisy and Esther rushed the gravely injured animal to a veterinarian. The cat died the next morning. Furious, Daisy placed an ad in the "Notices" section of a local newspaper's classified section.

> To the Motorist Who Ran Over the black cat (12th St.) Wednesday night and left him; I took the cat to a vet, where he died the next morning. D.B.

That act of kindness could have ended there. But the Humane Society of New York was advised of the incident and awarded Daisy and Esther a certificate of appreciation at a ceremony the next week, an event that was covered by the *New York Times*.[30] They were also interviewed for a short *Times* article on the incident, in which Esther defended Daisy's decision to place the ad. Although some people might consider it silly, the sisters felt that if the motorist read it, it would be worth it. "What he did was wrong," she said, "and if he sees it and realizes how wrong it was, perhaps it won't be just a futile gesture."

It wasn't long before the *Love Story* offices were inundated with manuscripts that featured cats in the story lines, much to Daisy's irritation. "The net result was that I began receiving stories in which a cat or cats figured prominently and continued to receive them over the years. Reading these stories, I discovered that many of the authors had never had a cat and knew practically nothing about them."[31]

The early months of 1933 saw lines of people, either waiting outside bank doors that would never open again, or in bread lines for hot soup, or for the rare job opening. Even *Love Story* radio program wasn't immune to cost cutting. While The Shadow continued to thrive as a radio show and a magazine, *Love Story*'s adventures on the wireless were not faring as well. Radio episodes constructed from light and airy romantic stories were no competition against other programs broadcast during the golden age of radio. Even a guest spot by the narrator of "The Shadow" couldn't increase the ratings.[32] By December 1932, the "Love Story Radio Program" had been dropped.

12

What Do You Know About Love?

In the spring of 1933, the country was emerging from the fourth brutal winter of hunger, cold, and unemployment. Bank failures were increasing in what seemed an uncontrollable pace. That year, over 4,000 banks would fail, an average of ten banks closing their doors each and every day.

In April, one month after Franklin Roosevelt gave his first inaugural speech, the Street & Smith company suffered two shocks almost simultaneously. Ormond Smith, who had ruled the company without so much as a hint of retiring, died of a stroke. Eleven days later, his brother, George Campbell Smith, who had managed the financial side of the company, died as well. They had led the company, co-founded by their father, for almost half a century. "The two brothers had seemed indestructible. They had weathered depression, cut-throat competition, and changes in reading and publishing styles. The void left by these wizards of publishing seemed too large ever to be filled," Quentin Reynolds declared 20 years later in *The Fiction Factory*. George's son George Campbell Smith, Jr., was made president, and Ormond's and George's nephew, Ormond Gould, became executive vice-president.

Even though the staff at Street & Smith were facing uncertain times, the company's stable of solid magazines—*Love Story Magazine; The Shadow, A Detective Magazine; Western Story Magazine; Wild West Weekly; Top Notch;* and *Detective Story Magazine*—provided some sense of stability. The company also continued to experiment with new titles that appeared on a regular basis. In 1933, they launched several other magazines, three of which were centered around heroes: *Nick Carter, Pete Rice,* and *Doc Savage* magazines. Doc Savage would rival The Shadow as one of the most famous and enduring heroes to come out of the pulp fiction era. Described by his writer, Lester Dent, as "Sherlock Holmes with his deducting ability, Tarzan of the Apes with his towering physique and muscular ability, Craig Kennedy with his scientific knowledge, and Abraham Lincoln with his Christliness," Doc Savage was a Street & Smith hero for sixteen years. The company also acquired its first science fiction title, *Astounding*, from Clayton Publishers. Launched under Street & Smith ownership in October, the magazine would eventually become the longest-running science fiction periodical in history.

March of 1933 also marked Daisy's five-year anniversary as editor of *Love Story*. According to her own records, by this time she was making $12,000 a year, although there are no surviving Street & Smith records to verify this amount. This is a startling

By this time, the cringing heroine was disappearing from covers. Emancipated young women—heroines who could pursue love without giving up their careers—became more common. She could be alone on the cover, and most likely was positive and happy with her lot in life. A wide gamut of occupations, from a bush pilot, to an elevator operator, to an office executive adorned covers for the next several years (*Love Story Magazine* © Condé Nast).

amount for a woman to make during that period; in 1933, $12,000 a year was almost eight times the national average income of $1,524.

Decades later, Daisy's lawyer would state that she was the highest paid editor—male or female—in New York City during the Depression. But other reported salaries for pulp editors exceeded hers. It was rumored that science-fiction editor Rogers Terrill made $25,000 in 1939 working for Popular Publications. To muddy the historical waters even more, Daisy declared in the 1940 census that she was making $5,000 a year. Did she use that figure in fear of tax collectors or others who could invade her privacy?

Whatever the amount, Daisy, Esther, and Jessie were living in much better conditions than many others in America. In addition to living at 51 Fifth Avenue, they bought a new Packard, the best-selling luxury car of its day. In true high society fashion, they had the salesman deliver the luxurious car to Kinnelon where the women were summering.

Jessie's diary for 1933–34 reveals a household that is constantly humming with activity in the evenings, but the long days in the New York apartment were interminable for her, a woman who, up until a few years before, was a tiny tornado working as a chambermaid and protesting on city streets in her spare time. Bedridden much of the time, she waited all day for her daughters to come home at lunch and at dinner. To their credit, the daughters made sure that their mother was continually entertained by friends and their aspiring beaus who dropped by day and night.

Esther was in no shortage of male company. Bill Reidel dropped by both the apartment in the city and the summer home. One friend in particular, Lionel Houser, showed up frequently as well. Houser would eventually move to Hollywood and become a successful screenwriter with some 34 movies credits, including *The Courage of Lassie*. At least two of the screenplays that he either wrote or adapted featured women in the publishing business: *Third Finger, Left Hand* in 1940 features Myrna Loy as a successful and wealthy New York magazine editor, and 1945's *Christmas in Connecticut* is about a woman who writes an advice column under a pseudonym and has a maid named Nora.

In 1933, it wasn't unusual for Esther would see Reidel one night, Houser the next. One night, both of them showed up for dinner. Jessie doesn't note what the atmosphere was at the dinner table, but it must have been either very tense or very lively.

Yet, at the same time, the two women were dealing with sickness and stress. "[B]oth look like shadows," their mother observed on January 15 when the two arrived home one night after work. Luckily for all the women, doctors were still making house calls at the time and their long-suffering physician, Leo Shifrin, checked on Jessie almost every day at the apartment. Jessie wasn't faring any better, as she noted on the 17th. "Doc here at night to see Es. & he got scared about me, as my heart was bad. Made me go to bed."

The new year of 1934 began inauspiciously. Daisy had spent the entire Christmas season dealing with an ailment. Jessie did not indicate precisely what this injury or illness was, but the month of December revealed that Daisy had spent many days in doctor's offices and at one point received an injection in her leg. On January 2, 1934, Jessie wrote, "D went back to the office after being home for a month. I don't know what to think." On January 15, Jessie noted that Daisy had gone to a Dr. Kelly for "suffering treatments."

But by March she was feeling well enough to board a train bound for New Mexico, with friends joining her at the train station to see her off in grand style. Upon arriving, she called her mother and told her that Henry was there with her.

There, on the bed of a tiny creek with a backdrop of desert mesquite, Daisy and

Left: **Daisy loved the western United States and frequently vacationed there. This shot might have been taken on a 1934 trip to New Mexico and Arizona.** *Right:* **On that same trip, Henry was with her. This photograph, with him sitting across the creek from where Daisy posed, is another example of their twin photograph traditions (both photographs Daisy Bacon collection).**

Henry continued their tradition of taking matching photos of each other. In one photo, Daisy sits at the edge of the tiny creek, stretches her long legs out in front of her, and gazes dreamily across the creek. In the other, Henry sits on the other side, but faces the camera head on, hugging his knees.

Jessie had to be happy for the occasional phone call or telegram from her eldest. On March 19, Daisy sent her mother a telegram.

> Located no place as dust as bad in Arizona as New Mexico. Try have definite word tomorrow. Harry and I seeing lot of country. Love DB.

Despite her complaining, Daisy fell in love with the west. This, she thought, was where she belonged. For years afterwards, she talked about the vastness of the horizons and the wild landscapes. The west would be a frequent destination for her for vacation over the next decade. Out of all the photos she left, there are only a few in which she is broadly smiling and relaxed. These photos were taken when she was on vacation in the west.

Back in New York, a story about Daisy was circulating in gossip columns in several syndicated newspapers.

> Daisy Bacon, vivacious editress of "*Love Story Magazine*," took a stroll in Washington Square the other noon hour. On a bench gloomed a lass of 12 or 13, so obviously blue, with tear-streaked face; and downcast eye, that Miss Bacon was touched and inquired.
> "Oh, nuthin." !
> "Tell me. Trouble at home? "
> "No." A sob.
> "At school?"
> A shake of a curly head.
> "Is it—Er, is it a boy?"
> The youngster turned her face up for the first time and nodded—and then pronounced calmly:
> "Sure. But what on earth could you know about love?"[1]

The story's veracity is unknown, but it's a good metaphor for general assumptions made by both the public and those in the industry about the pulp romance magazine, its readers, and Daisy herself, who was seemed to battling misconceptions on a regular basis.

At one point in that period, the gossip and the criticism all became a bit much for her. She had already been branded a prima donna at the office, a label that would stick with her for the rest of her career. One night, maybe fueled by a little alcohol, Daisy typed nine pages of rambling, error-strewn, and sometimes self-congratulatory notes. Ostensibly they were intended to be used for a future interview in which Lionel Houser was to be the interviewer. It was time to air some grievances and to set the record straight. As far as she was concerned, she was disliked, envied, and unfairly gossiped about in the industry.

> Editors don't like me because I won't be friendly. I won't go to editor parties. They start stuff going that isn't true.

According to her, Amita Fairgrieve considered Daisy a particular thorn in her side, either because of the press that Daisy received or because of *Love Story*'s dominance of the market.

> One time I asked jane Littell why Miss Fairgrieve hated me so, she followed me all the time and did what I did and so on and jane said it's because you're in her air and she can't get u out....

Daisy notes that Fairgrieve passed along untruths about Daisy.

> Miss Fairgrieve is always saying don't take this story to Daisy she wouldn't buy becuz she only buys stories about rich girls....

Daisy was also peeved that her office was frequently the subject of gossip.

> They know in other offices when a pin drops in mine.

She also spills the beans on a few strategies used by other rivals.

> Editors all get together and they say this and they say that for a formula ... they influence each other to get all their magazines alike ... a magazine is a personality that's true.

It is obvious these notes were for the interviewer to follow a script carefully supervised by Daisy.

You've got to tell the picture rite that every time a new publishing house starts they always put out a competitor and they always say I'm gonna have competition at last, and then!!! During depression there was only one left ... we have 10 times the circulation of nearest competitor (All Story)!!!

A few years later she would expand on her bitterness that she was misunderstood:

People like me and hate me and envy me enough to send me anonymous letters (not all of them are from women either) and spread stories about me. Just harmless little things, of course, like stretching the cost of my clothes and exaggerating the number of men I know. If I should have, for instance, a new coat of mink paws, it would be Russian mink by the time the story was well started and people would say "How can she afford that on her salary?" Or if I went into a bar with two men and had two drinks of whiskey, it would be four men and eight whiskies by the time I got out.[2]

By the fall of 1934, Daisy was fed up with the gossip and sniping thrown her way from other editors. The accusation that appeared to push her almost over the edge was that she only used blondes for *Love Story*'s cover art. According to a story that appeared in Walter Winchell's powerful column, "On Broadway," Daisy was so angry that she decided to pose for the cover herself. "...It will be her way of thumbing her shapely nose at her critics and rivals and the front likeness will be of an alluring blonde they all know— Daisy Bacon, herself!"[3]

While Winchell's column was strictly gossip and should be taken with a grain of salt, one part of this story is true. In one of the few times an actual editor appeared on the cover of her own magazine, Daisy appeared on the cover of the *Love Story* December 8, 1934, issue. Wearing a black cocktail dress, she kneels and wields a Japanese fan over her head, smiling broadly.

But that was the only part of the story that can be verified as true. As for Daisy's hair color, it is not blond on the cover: it's jet-black.

It seemed as if romance pulp readers couldn't catch a break, either. Those that picked up a *Love Story* at the local newsstand were likely to be subject to a lot of snickering from bystanders. On one of her vacations out west, Daisy received an earful from other guests at the dude ranch:

... a woman out at the ranch had an idea that taste of everyone who read this mag was very low ... that is another fatal thing ... to judge your audience as morons....[4]

Such an attitude was common in the publishing field towards readers of all pulp magazines. In June of 1933, *Vanity Fair* printed an article: "The Pulps: Day Dream for the Masses," in which Marcus Duffield pulled a figure of twenty million readers, give or take, that read the pulps in 1928. He was curious, he wrote, about "those who move their lips when they read."[5]

Editors of pulp fiction magazines themselves weren't immune to being prejudiced against their readers. Alvin Barclay recalled that on the first day of his job, the managing editor told him, "Always remember that we are getting out a magazine for The Great American Moron!'" The editor that uttered this famous battle cry may have been none other than the inventor of the pulp magazine itself: Frank Munsey.[6]

Those that read the romance pulps were especially subject to this attitude. In articles that catered to fledgling romance pulp writers, trade magazines regaled their readers with ideas on who exactly the romance reader was. Psychoanalysis of the reader received as much coverage as the story requirements, if not more. Contributors opined and pontificated in article after article; but the bottom line was that most thought that pulp romance readers were simple, unimaginative, uneducated. They thought they were

Taken for a later article in *Parade's Weekly*, this photograph shows Daisy "checking in" on artist Modest Stein's work for an upcoming *Love Story* issue. More than likely, however, this was a staged scene for the article; artists like Stein had their own studios (photograph by W. Eugene Smith, reprinted with permission from Black Star).

perpetually poor, narrow minded, and even had then pinned down to being averse to taking risk.

One article in *Writer's Digest* warned that if the new writers didn't like hanging out with the crowd that frequents five-and-dimes, they better stick to writing for *Harper's*. "Write as if you were writing for somebody with little education, but plenty of dreams of romance," wrote Minna Bardon.[7] In soliciting for new stories in the trades, the editor of *Cupid's Diary* explained, as early as 1928, that its readers were "inarticulate, and who look to fiction for romance which they hope to but cannot realize in their own lives.... Our readers are unsophisticated and elemental, and the stories should deal with elemental things: love, jealousy, intrigue, struggle against environment, and against handicaps...."[8]

A few months later after Daisy returned from New Mexico, Amita Fairgrieve declared what she thought readers liked in their romances. *All-Story Love Stories* focused on the physical attraction between the woman and men. Women wanted the cave man type, someone who "would kiss with a sneer on their lips." She added that "Next to the cave man is the maligned hero. If a man is suffering, sympathy is on his side at once. When a story has a maligned cave man as a hero, the whole idea is splendid."[9]

As much as they loved to theorize on why people loved to read the pulps, with words that filled pages and pages of the trade magazines every month, at least a few were much more sensible and yes, egalitarian in their opinions. Will McMorrow sent in a letter to the *New York Times* a few years later, with a simple theory:

> People read woodpulp because they find it interesting. There it is. The mystery is solved.[10]

Street & Smith management assigned another magazine to Daisy's office that summer, a rerelease of their early success, *Ainslee's Magazine*. *Ainslee's* had attracted an impressive stable of authors and poets in the early part of the twentieth century, including Edna St. Vincent Millay, Sir Arthur Conan Doyle, Jack London, Frank Norris, Stephen Crane, P.G. Wodehouse, and Theodore Dreiser. It had even published at least four stories by Alice Duer Miller between 1903 and 1906, when she was still a struggling writer, and had printed many of her sister Caroline's short stories, poems, and plays. *Ainslee's* had also printed a play, "Union and Mr. Thompson," in 1903 that was co-authored by Carolyn Duer and none other than Henry Wise Miller.

Ainslee's had carried Street & Smith a long way on the road towards breaking into the glossy, upper literary market, their long-term goal. But with the burgeoning pulp field and increasing competition from slick magazines, *Ainslee's* was discontinued in 1926, its operations merged into an already-existing western-themed pulp, *Far West Illustrated*. Now the company decided that it was time to try to capitalize on the strength of the romance market by bringing the title of *Ainslee's* back. It would be romance-specific, but with a more urban look. And in a twist, it would have slightly racier themes than what appeared in *Love Story*.

Daisy was excited about the new assignment, writing in her notes to Lionel that she had been assigned "another child to look after, the firm having decided to revive the one-time famous and well-known *Ainslee's*."[11]

James Aswell, gossip columnist on the New York social life, reported on a serendipitous event while announcing the release of the magazine:

> Recently Daisy Bacon, editress of one of the more romantic pulp paper magazines, was presented one evening with a black kitten.... She named the feline Ainslee in commemoration. Next morning at 9 her desk telephone rang and she was informed that the once-famous *Ainslee's Magazine* was to be revived and that she had been picked as pilot.[12]

Many of Daisy's standard stable of writers contributed to stories in *Ainslee's*, including her friends Ruth D'Agostino and Gertrude Schalk. A few first-time writers appeared in the magazine, but they were mixed with pieces from seasoned authors. "The new writer is going to have an even break with the seasoned veteran," she promised.[13]

With a bedsheet-sized format, *Ainslee's* was the company's bridge between the pulp and the slick. Its masthead of large freeform capital letters and cover art that featured women in daring bathing suits projected modernity and maturity. Zoe Mozert, who would later be known for her work in slick magazines and Hollywood studios, painted at least five covers for the magazine that cemented the image of the magazine, promising a dreamy, sophisticated world for its readers. Thirty-year old Mozert was already a well-known and established artist who had created many covers for magazines like *Romantic Story, True Confessions,* and *Love Revels.* Born Alice Adelaide Moser, she was formally trained at LaFrance Art School and the Philadelphia Museum School of Industrial Art. With striking platinum blonde hair and Jean Harlow looks, she first started as a model before branching out into freelance artwork. Some of her cover work hints at Mozert using herself as the model.

Full-page advertisements heralding newly-released movies dominated the ad space, and those notorious ads that pulps were famous for—those that heralded offers to cure piles and baldness—were relegated to the back of the magazine and there only in the margins.

Daisy had developed an intense interest in astrology, numerology, and the supernatural by this time. She was beginning to think that she had a gift of being able to foretell the future. In later articles she would say that she had a "friendly spirit" who would advise her of upcoming events, some affecting the world at large, others having a more personal impact. Daisy's interest in the stars was seen in regular columns in *Love Story,* and she would claim later that including astrology in the magazine was the first of its kind and started the fashion of including horoscopes in magazines.[14] *Ainslee's* would include exhaustive, six-page astrology guides that included features on celebrities and the occasional author, like Schalk.

Stories featured heroines and heroes living in the upper echelons of society and others who struggle in humdrum jobs but brush up against people who were more economically fortunate. Undergarments appeared as part of story lines. More explicit kissing scenes used words such as "sensuous," and "intimate," sprinkled throughout:

> With a cry he had me in his arms. He was kissing me. His lips crushed against mine as though desperately he would make up for all the kisses we had not known.
>
> It was heaven for me again after those two weeks without him. I had never known there could be happiness like that. And as he held me in his arms, I knew at once that I would pay any price for his love. I knew that I would do anything to keep him there in my arms.
>
> I told him then.
>
> "You belong to me," I whispered. "I don't care whether you've promised some one you won't marry or not. It's all the same to me. I love you."[15]

The word "damned" showed up several times in stories, such as Schalk's story "Up the Middle-Aisle" in July 1935. Nudity was openly discussed and in one story, an interior illustration depicted a nude model, who happened to be the heroine (who of course would never pose nude—the story revealed that the painting was done strictly based on the imagination of the hero). Non-fiction articles appeared regularly with provocative titles such as "The Truth About Honeymoons," "Sex for the Modern Girl," and "What Is Chastity?" These could never have appeared in a Street & Smith magazine under the old regime of Ormond G. and George Campbell Smith.

After four issues, the name was changed to *Ainslee's Smart Love Stories.* As for the kitten Ainslee, it disappeared a few days after the announcement of the magazine's rebirth.

The editors of other romance pulps were slowly changing their requirements for stories. Hortense McRaven reported in a *Author & Journalist* article in August of 1935 that readers were becoming more sophisticated and more educated. Now, she declared, more references could be made to foreign words, historical references, and literary quotations, and the modern romance pulp heroine in 1935 was now allowed to think and to reflect on her station in life. Rather than only being able to react to others' relationships, she could ponder her actions, understand the consequences, and make her own decisions. With these changes, McRaven theorized that perhaps "the intelligence and education" of the average reader was increasing."[16]

McRaven didn't explore the idea, at least in this article, that perhaps the intelligence of the reader had always been there and it was the editors and publishers that needed to catch up with them.

Changing attitudes towards even sex and nudity were appearing in the stories. Before, anything hinting at sex, especially premarital sex, was taboo, a policy that was so prevalent that writers were advised in the early 1930s that "You must pretend, in writing for them, that women fall in love with eunuchs."[17] But by 1934, the words "undies" and "nude" could now be used in stories, although only in the context of viewing a woman from afar, such as dispassionately looking at a model. Lastly, the marital status of the heroine, or exploration of being involved with "other than single" men could be flirted with. Before, women were single until the end of the story, which always ended with marriage or the promise of it. Now, heroines could be married, divorced, or widowed. They could even contemplate an affair, but never to the point of action.

But, according to some, *Love Story* was not catching up with these trends as quickly as its competitors. It was still acting like an old maid and Daisy was stuck in the past. According to other editors, her stories were too old-fashioned: the stories always ended with a chaste kiss, and there couldn't be any scenes, dialogue, or settings that remotely hinted that the heroine and hero were engaged in pre-marital sex. After all, it wasn't until 1930 that a cover painting on *Love Story* depicted a man and woman actually kissing.

But this judgment wasn't entirely based on fact. In just one March 1934 issue, there are at least three stories that display a much more racier tone than could be found in pre–1930 issues. In "Worth Possessing," runaway bride Rona meets a charming man who sleeps under a bridge. Rona decides that she needs to stay close to him. But first she must take a bath in the lake.

> Rona, followed by the terrier, ran down to the water's edge. Off came her peach colored pique jacket and dress. Then her peach colored pique shorts and brassiere. Into the water she plunged. After her bath, she returns to where the hero is sleeping with his dog. Cautiously, she laid down beside him, with Boatsun between them. Just as she was dropping off to sleep, Rusty flung out an arm and drew her close.
> "Sheila," he muttered in his sleep. "Sheila, darling."

Daisy was aware that the trends were changing and *Love Story* did not blindly follow the trends. She dwelled on this topic in an article by Virginia Lee, "'Love Stories' Must Mirror Life," that appeared in the *Author & Journalist*.

> "But still," Miss Bacon mused, "when you pin yourself down to facts at the end of a dissertation on love as reflected by modern fiction, one must admit that although the style of love stories has changed, and although settings have changed, and although the problems have changed—and even though the lovers themselves have changed—one finds that only one thing remains the same. That is love."[18]

Daisy finished the manuscript for the Doan novel and sent it to a friend at the William Morrow & Company in the spring of 1935. In April, she received the following letter in return:

Dear Daisy:

I have read the first 153 pages of your novel with the greatest care and there has been another reading.

I am awfully sorry to have to say that I don't think it comes off…. When we come to Doan, I should not have realized her character from these pages, if I had not talked to you…. From the manuscript, Doan seems just insensitive, and so not to be admired for her reserve and nonchalance. Her personality does not come across.

It is with a great regret to me to write you this way, especially when you are not well….[19]

There aren't any records as to how Daisy felt after this rejection. She is silent about it in her journals, only once mentioning her attempt to write a novel. The manuscript is not in her personal papers, nor is there any indication that the manuscript was submitted to any other publisher. Daisy probably handled the rejection by simply putting it away. Someday, she might have thought, she would be able to work on it again.

Daisy must have faced the reality that Alice, by contrast, was enjoying a resurrection of her career. When Daisy and Henry were in the first years of their relationship, Alice's career had cooled off somewhat, and she was thought of as something of a has-been. Yet now, one her latest novels was being adapted to the screen. The movie "Roberta," based on her novel *Gowns by Roberta*, was first produced as a play in 1933, the theater production featuring several songs written by Jerome Kern and Otto Harbach. The movie, starring Irene Dunne, Fred Astaire, Ginger Rogers, and Randolph Scott, was released in 1935 and would propel many of those songs into the national spotlight, especially the immortal "Smoke Gets in Your Eyes." Daisy herself, accompanied by persons unknown, saw the play in late 1933.

A tidal wave of change had arrived in the pulp magazine industry, and not all of it was good. In 1932, Harry Steeger of Popular Publications had introduced *Dime Mystery Book Magazine*, a magazine in the spirit of *Grand Guignol* theater, with the emphasis on horror, shock, amoral acts, and torture. *Dime Mystery* attracted so much attention that Steeger quickly launched two more magazines, *Terror Tales* and *Horror Stories*, and other publishers that were brave enough followed suit with their own titles. These

One of Daisy's few photographs that show her smiling was taken on one of her many vacations out west, maybe at a dude ranch (Daisy Bacon collection).

magazines eventually earned the badge of being known as "weird menace" magazines or "shudder pulps." The covers of these magazines, which almost always featured women in various stages of bondage and torture, became more graphic and shocking until public outrage led to campaigns to censor the publishers.

Other experimentations would push boundaries of censorship. In 1934, Culture Publications would push the genre-specific magazine to another level. *Spicy Detective Stories* came first, then *Spicy Mystery Stories* and *Spicy Western Stories,* all featuring your standard fiction stories but with racy (at least what the 1930s considered racy) sex scenes tossed in. Then Snappy magazines appeared, a sibling of the Spicy titles. All of these gave the concerned good citizen more reason to hate the pulps, but not enough to keep them from buying a copy or two from their local seller, who kept them under the counter.

Still, there were enough hero, sports, flight, horror, and a fledging new genre called science fiction to keep readers entertained without turning their stomachs or making them blush. Western pulp magazines were selling just as well, if not better, than romance magazines as a whole, and were instrumental in the churning out of countless serials and B-movies that kept Depression readers and movie-goers entertained for years.

Street & Smith had never budged past their strict policy regarding decency. They knew that many of their readers were young and impressionable. Yes, they were letting the occasional "undie" show up in a *Love Story* novelette, and their western pulps like *Western Story* and *Wild West Weekly* were becoming more and more violent (even though the word "blood" was forbidden in the latter). But they would never move into the territory of a weird menace or a spicy pulp.

Even with the success of *Love Story, The Shadow, Doc Savage,* and *Detective Story,* the Street & Smith owners wanted to push beyond the tarnished reputation of pulp paper magazines. Bill Ralston's daughter had suggested the year before that the company attempt—one more time—a non-pulp magazine. It would be a fashion magazine catering to young women, but cheaper than the expensive *Vogue* and *Harper's Bazaar.* Even though they were dubious at first, the executives decided to give it a try. No one could come up with a title for the new magazine, until editor Desmond Hall's wife came up a name: *Mademoiselle.*

While the company was willing to give the magazine a try, they still held back in determining its composition. Fiction, not fashion, was the company's forte. Playing it safe, they ended up filling up the entire issue with fiction, and the final version only had one page devoted to fashion and one "Beauty for Mademoiselle" department.

The result, the first issue released in February 1935, was a confusing muck of a magazine that no one liked. News dealers didn't know how to sell it and men, thinking it was a "girlie" magazine because of its name, were disappointed to say the least. The company retreated, skipping one month and then releasing the second issue two months later that had less fiction, more articles, and more emphasis on fashion. While the sales were still slow, they at least improved over its dismal debut. The magazine was spared the axe and continued to grow in circulation. In 1935, few people inside the Street & Smith building would have guessed that this minor aberration in the company's repertoire would, one day, dictate the company's entire future.

13

Codes and Symbols

Jessie Holbrook Bacon Ford died on July 30, 1936, an event that would affect Daisy's outlook, work, habits, and relationships for years. She would mark the anniversary date of her mother's death in her diaries for the remainder of her life.

If Jessie recorded anything in diaries in the last two years of life, those diaries have not been found. But she did collect clippings, poems, various news events, articles about horses, and Daisy's various interviews from newspapers. We only know from Jessie's death certificate that by 1936 the family had moved to 40 Fifth Avenue, just one block south of their old address. Daisy would eventually decorate the apartment fitting for a romance magazine editor: the walls were painted a rich red and the apartment filled with antiques and books.

If Daisy wrote in diaries in the 1930s, they have not survived, but Esther's diaries did. Starting in 1937, she wrote in a perfunctory manner, sometimes only noting the weather for the day and one activity or event that encapsulated her day. It could be something as mundane as getting her hair shampooed—during a time when women only washed their hair once a week—or as glamorous as going to the Stork Club, Sardi's, or the Longchamps Restaurant. Esther took over in chronicling the goings on of both Daisy and Henry from her mother and, like her, she used "HWM" in her notes to refer to Henry and either "DB" or "B" for Daisy. Her diaries show that Henry was still very much in the picture, with entries like "HW returned from Hollywood—here for dinner" and "DB & HW to farm."[1]

Jessie Holbrook Ford in an undated photograph (Daisy Bacon collection).

115

By this time, Daisy had developed a drinking problem, confessing in some later notes that she had become "seriously entangled" in the habit of drinking what she called the "Demon Rum." Later, her entries from the late 1940s and 1950s reveal that her drinking started during Prohibition, when going to speakeasies and glamorous nightclubs were the thing to do for everyone who was anyone in Manhattan.

Scattered amongst Daisy's journals, address books, scrapbooks, and photographs are four small notepads with "Enjoy 1936" embossed on the covers. While some of the notes are written with the intent of using in a novel, with the character Doan from her now-rejected novel appearing once, Daisy's previous writings make it a good bet that these notes were based on her own experiences.

> In Prohibition, drinking was sort of a defiant childish gesture—carried on with carefully planned secrecy to show that we would have our fun anyway. After repeal, the secrecy was no longer part of the game and with legalized drinking, there was [no] longer any necessity of the defiant gesture. We became deeper & deeper involved as the days & nights [went] by until it looked doubtful whether or not we could ever pull out of it.

But eventually Daisy began to see a problem in her association with this tradition.

> Before Mother died, we hardly knew what the inside of a night club looked but we certainly ought to have known that winter, although we were perhaps not always in the exact condition, let us say, to be sure of our own surroundings....

She documents when she and her group made scenes in the restaurants and nightclubs they frequented.

> ... In shocked and horrified silence as brandy after brandy & whisky after whisky was consumed a highly conservative eating place (east side) where everything you wanted for dinner had to be ordered the day before.... Don't touch those bottles, we kept shouting at the waiters who came past. There were four of us at the table & four bottles on the table & two of brandy—one of rye & one of scotch.[2]

It is in Esther's journals that the frequency of Daisy's drinking really becomes evident. On March 30, 1937, Esther begins to use a symbol in her diary notations in relationship to Daisy. It appears to be shorthand, a necessary skill for secretaries who needed to take dictation. The symbol doesn't come close to resembling the Gregg shorthand symbols for "drunk," "intoxicated," or "smashed," or "high," nor does it resemble adjectives that might fit the situation, like "tired," "cranky," "moody," "happy," or even "depressed."

But it does exactly match the *Gregg Dictionary* use for the word "tight," a common slang word then for being drunk.[3]

From around this time until the mid–1940s, this symbol dotted Esther's journals on a regular basis. Every few weeks the symbol for "tight" pops up, and it frequently reoccurs several days in a row, and it almost always is used in conjunction with Daisy's name. Occasionally, Esther adds the words "no sleep" or "no sleep all night" afterward. When using the word in relation to other people, Esther spells the word out. For some reason she felt the need to hide Daisy's condition from whoever would look at her diaries.

The competition in the romance pulp market had intensified, almost doubling over a one-year period, and the number of magazines was making a serious dent in *Love Story's* leadership. Some records point to *Love Story's* circulation dropping to around 350,000 at this point. Still, Minna Bardon noted in the *Writer's Digest* that "the circulation of *Love Story* is today, and has been for years, the wonder of the pulp-paper industry."[4] *Love Story's* biggest competitor was not a single title but the sheer number of titles and the tack that many publishers took with sleek, modern logos and sophisticated cover art. *Thrilling Love*, one of Standard Publications' line of magazines with the word "Thrilling" in the name, had been launched in 1931 and was now doing well enough that the company released another romance, *Popular Love.*

Popular Love is not to be confused with Popular Publications, another company that launched not one but two romance pulps of its own, *Love Book Monthly* and *Four Star Love*, in 1936. With most publishers working on extremely narrow profit margins for all their magazines—one historian estimated that a pulp magazine with an issue of 100,000 could net as little as between $460 and $730—most worked under the theory that the more magazines they could churn out, the better.[5] By issuing love pulps, a publisher like Popular could hedge their bets by one, issuing more magazines and two, entering them in a popular genre like romance.

Daisy's friend Jane Littell, now a seasoned writer of romance stories, was wooed by Popular Publications to become the editor of *Love Book Magazine*, and later of *Four Star Love* as well. Jane confided in an interview that "she feels weak in the knees when she

A playful pose at an unknown location (Daisy Bacon collection).

realizes how many capable, efficient editors of love magazines there are in New York and how she is trying the job new."[6]

With these new magazines and a new army of women in charge of them, publishers were playing both sides of their hands. They resorted to stereotypes that dictated that women were the best bet for managing a romance magazine. Very few women were managing magazines that focused on other genres like detective, horror, and westerns. The one most famous exception was Fanny Ellsworth, who managed western magazines before becoming the chief editor of hard-boiled detective pulp *Black Mask* in 1936 while keeping her job managing *Ranch Romances.*

In the publishers' defense, by putting women in charge, they were acknowledging that women could be capable managers of extremely profitable components of their companies. But it's questionable as to whether these companies ever publicly recognized their value.

But for Daisy, it was no mystery. She would voice her opinion in a very public manner at least twice that year. In a bizarre newspaper article called "Go West, Young Woman," written by someone using the byline "Vivien Grey"—a Street & Smith house name used by any number of *Love Story* writers—Daisy talks about what she wants in a man. According to "Go West, Young Woman, If You Want a Man," she believes that the only men worth marrying are those that live west of the 98th Meridian.

> I've promised myself on the most solemn oath I can swear that when I marry I won't sentence myself to a life of boredom by marrying an Eastern "yes man." I want a little excitement and interest along with my matrimony, so the bride groom I middle-aisle it with will have to be Western. And with typical Western ideas of his own.

But she also used the opportunity to make her point about what she felt were injustices to the business woman.

> Business is a woman's game only up to a certain point. She can go just so far and then she finds herself faced with ground marked most definitely "strictly masculine." She prepares herself for a seat at the show which she can never occupy, because she's a woman with woman's mental and physical equipment and men to compete with. In other words, except in marriage, she's all dressed up with the well known nowhere to go![7]

But Daisy would have to continue to wait and see whether her value at the company would ever be acknowledged.

Love Story wasn't breaking any

Esther at the Botts house. Esther would occasionally go out to the house, and Henry made frequent stops at the women's' apartment, indicating that Henry's relationship with Daisy was an accepted part of their lives (Daisy Bacon collection).

barriers at this point when it came to the heroine's roles or their occupations. The June 20, 1936, issue is a standard fare of rich girl, working class girl, and ambitious girl. A nurse wants to be promoted in "Lips of Gold." In "Cupid Writes an Ad," Marjorie Pittman's advertising agency is threatened by an old college-mate, Bill Crosley, who opens another agency across from hers. Some stories painfully remind us that we are still in the 1930s. In "Hungry Hearts," the first installment of a serial, six-foot-two All-American hero David Gray is on a mission to rescue a missionary and his daughter in deep Ethiopia. It's a story not only threaded with the African native/white woman attitudes of the day ("The woman is of some fairness,"—David smiled a trifle grimly at the old chief's naïve frankness—"the Great White Lord who rules from across the seas, has no understanding of the desires of men.") but also a pre-war animosity towards Germans with an "oily" villain named Hans Schmidt.

The issue includes an installment of "What Type Are You," which attempts to place women into distinct personality types based on their physical attributes. This installment looks at the "Oval-faced Brunette," who, according to this unnamed author, are more sympathetic than fair women and are loyal and delightful to her friends, but arrogant and difficult to others. In a sidebar, the column describes the other physical types who are featured in this series, most notably the "large-limbed, square-headed and muscular woman, who has a distinct mental and physical make-up." Thankfully, this series is takes up only one and a half pages.

But the issue also includes a story that shows that the magazine was becoming much more open to more openly sexually suggestive stories. In "Fascination," Pennie Lee is attracted to nightclub dancer Dave Garth. When Dave begins to dance,

> Dave fell into the mood it always roused in him. He forgot himself and became part of the beat of the music, at first languidly alluring, mounting higher and higher with the savagely exotic undercurrent of the drums. Its hypnotic repetition stirred him, and his strong, lithe body became whiplike and poised as that of a weaving cobra…. It was like some delicious agony that he wished never to end.

Daisy continued to simmer over what she viewed as Street & Smith management's inability to either recognize her contributions to the company or take her ideas seriously. Her attitude wasn't entirely a figment of her imagination; the struggles of women during the Depression to get hired for any job—much less get promoted to levels in which they had an active role in a company's decision-making process—are well-documented. Most Americans were against women working outside the home in the Depression, with many feeling that if a woman did work, she was taking a job away from an able-bodied man. A 1936 *Fortune* poll showed 48 percent believed that women should not have a full-time job outside the home; a Gallup poll the same year resulted in a whopping 82 percent agreeing in that sentiment.[8]

Daisy was not only working, she was one of the most famous and well-paid in her field. But she felt that she could not move beyond her current position and that her ideas were being discounted. Since the two patriarchs of Street & Smith had died in 1933, their two sons, George and Gerald, had run the company, along with George's brother in law, Armetas "Judge" Holmes." Once a champion tennis player, Judge seemed to have a close relationship with Daisy and Esther. But friendships aside, Daisy was feeling as if she could no longer stay silent. She had to speak out on the slights she was feeling in the office. So, one day in 1936, she sat down and wrote an essay.

Apparently afraid that there would be repercussions if her opinions were known by the Street & Smith management, she wrote the essay behind an anonymous byline, giving it the title of "Women Among Men." She sent the essay off to *The New York Woman*, a new magazine that had just appeared in May. It was, according to one reader, "one of the first efforts at a women's liberation magazine."[9] Described as being in the "manner of

Esquire," it was intended to target the sophisticated, well-educated woman of New York. According to the trade magazines, twenty-four women staffed with newspapers and magazines made up the advisory board. An announcement before its launch in one of the trade magazines noted that most of the articles were going to be staff-written, but exceptions were to be made.

"Women Among Men" appeared in the October 21 issue. Daisy lies about her age again in the essay, and her remarks about the importance of beauty, the figures she quotes, and the complaints she voices are from her perspective. Yet, as a whole, the essay resonates as an example of how women were treated in the business world in the 1930s.

> In the boom year 1929, I was one of 12,000 women in the United States. Now I am probably one of about 8 or 9,000. At the height of the boom, statistics show that there were only 10 or 12,000 women in the country who earned five thousand dollars or more a year. And except for the buyers in department stores and some of the fashion writers, most of them were fairly old, and not many were even good-looking.
>
> … A lot happens to a woman on her way up to a fairly decent salary. To begin with, most women who are making over five thousand a year are getting it because they have something to offer which the men in the business cannot afford to ignore. In my case, it seemed inevitable. I was not trained to make a living but I made money for my firm almost from the first week that I had a job with them. I've worked four times as hard as a man but that, too, was one of those things which seemed impossible to get away from. And I can't even say that I wanted to get away from it. Women love to work themselves to death and men—at least the older ones—expect and demand more from a woman than from a man in the same position. When a man makes a mistake in judgment, the attitude is one of "Oh well, we're all boys together and he was doing his best." But when a woman does the very same thing, she ought to have known better. This applies only to women in responsible positions, however.

At one point, a bit of paranoia and even a little hostility towards her own gender, creeps in to Daisy's opinion as she describes an instance from a vacation out west the previous year.

> This is also a popular belief among women who have never worked for a living: that there is some magic formula for getting a top-notch position. Last year when I tried to get a little rest at a dude ranch, the women there pestered the life out of me as to how I had managed the men. They all wanted to become buyers, editors and customers—women without any previous experience. I hated to disillusion them and they all thought I was lying anyway but it has always been my contention that women could not advance themselves in business by vamping any man. Possibly he might be willing to help the stenographer or reception clerk to a better position if she cast her wiles at him but it has been my experience that after a woman has made money for her firm her bosses have very little personal interest in her. I am no authority on this because if I ever had any wiles to cast, I cast them outside of my business. But I point out the fact that the world is full of pretty women who are not in the business world.

And then Daisy comes to the heart of her unhappiness at work. She has no hope in moving into upper management.

> There are difficulties on the way up for a woman who rises to place of authority and difficulties for her after she gets there. But then the mere business of being a woman is often difficult so this is not surprising. The main thing is that it is possible for her to get there. So far so good but what of that brilliant future? I have raised myself from twenty-five hundred to twelve thousand a year and I have a position which not only other women but men envy me and that is all right as far as it goes. But where am I going from there?
>
> It is only recently that I have realized a fact which has an important bearing on this step. Although I bring a great deal of money into the business and although I control the way that money is made, I have absolutely nothing to say about spending this money. Over a period of years I've had a great many ideas about promoting new business but they have never been taken up. And not only that but

several of them have been accepted later when they were put forward by men. Two of the best plans I ever had (the details of which I cannot tell you without revealing the nature of our business) have been recently accepted and put into operation by men who are almost strangers to us and almost totally without business experience. At the time I advanced my plan, I had had some results from the idea itself working it through our regular channels that the men who put it over had nothing but a plan to offer.

Now I have been in business long enough to know the men are very slow to act upon new ideas but it does seem funny that the same idea will be accepted when presented by man and put down if put forward by a woman. Obviously this means that a man has more confidence in another animal looks thinks and acts like himself. A man friend of mine says that the answer is that women are afraid to take chances about money. But this explanation seems absurd to me. A woman's whole life is a cycle of reoccurring chances she must take, so why should she be afraid of taking a chance with money? I have talked about this to several women executives and they have all been of the opinion that there is nothing in it. In fact I will go so far as to say that women take chances in business as in life which men would be afraid to take. I myself have taken chances which if my chief had known about would have given him cat fits.

At one point, she states that she, and other women, may have placed too much importance on just being grateful to be working, a belief that caused her to discount her ideas on changing her situation, whether it be to make a higher salary or presenting plans to executives.

I believe that part of the trouble is due to the fact that women do not know how to make themselves understood by men. A man rarely stops to analyze the situation so any new departure must present an attractive enough picture to make him want to try it. To be truthful, I am wondering if I have not always worked so hard that I did not allow myself to little time in which to present my plans. Or if I have not always been so thankful to be making a living that I never made myself or my ideas important enough. Men make a great song and dance about the things they do for the firm but have always been pretty matter-of-fact about my accomplishments.

And then she opens a little window into the dynamic between her and her bosses at Street & Smith.

Now anything which is to be done about the situation would have to be done by the women themselves because men regard moneymaking as a male prerogative and they do not like to feel that a woman can do as well at it as they can. Men have always made me conscious of this in little ways. I have never asked for a raise that my chief did not say, "you're getting a good salary for a woman." Whereas I would retort "what is being a woman got to do with it?"[10]

After the essay appeared, the first letter to the editor that appeared in the magazine wasn't positive.

But, please avoid articles like "Women among Men" (Anonymous) in your October 21st issue. They are not even funny—they are a disgrace to every hard working man and woman.[11]

But the next week, other letters were strongly positive.

If I knew you (the writer), and I am just as curious as I suppose every other man is who read your article, I would shake your hand, and if I knew you really intimately, perhaps scramble a few verses together in your honor. It's that ever recurring problem of equality. Before suffrage, women were a static quality. There they were—they would be there when it pleased men to look for them. They were absolutely taken for granted—a chattel to be desired, and possessed, and taken for granted.[12]

Daisy wasn't planning on passing along her essay to anyone in the office. But, according to her, the essay was instrumental enough to sell out the entire issue and generated plenty of talk on the street. At some point, someone "outed" Daisy to Walter Winchell, king of the gossip column, who mentioned it in his column on the fifth of December.

Every Wednesday

THE NEW YORK WOMAN

OCTOBER 21, 1936

15¢

The cover of *The New York Woman* issue, Volume #1, No. 7, October 21, 1936, in which Daisy's essay "Women Among Men" appears. This magazine, which seems to have lasted only 18 months, is not to be confused with *New York Woman* magazine, which was in circulation from 1986 to 1992 (photograph by Ann Parker/author collection).

"The anonymous author of "Women Among Men" in a recent *N.Y. Woman* issue is Daisy Bacon, a love story editor."

Unfortunately for Daisy, practically the entire country was reading Winchell's column during this time.

On the day that the snippet appeared in Winchell's column, Daisy went to work. She had not read Winchell's column yet that day. But apparently many people at Street & Smith had. She walked into an ambush, "blissfully unaware that everyone in the office was lying in wait for me."[13]

She didn't record how the confrontation fared. But chances are that she would have defended her essay in the usual Daisy fashion: defiant, blunt, and unapologetic.

14

Harbinger of Change

"Mr. R used to say that everybody likes to see a piano fall on somebody."[1]

In early 1937, Daisy and Esther were assigned to manage a new magazine, *Pocket Love Magazine*. In a digest-size format, *Pocket Love* was a member of a trio of magazines, the other two being *Pocket Detective* and *Pocket Western,* that seemed to be an attempt by the company to gain some traction in the newly emerging paperback and digest markets. *Pocket Love* had no artwork on the cover, only a list of stories in an attempt to portray the image of a literary magazine.

A novelette by Daisy's friend Marguerite Brener was included in the first issue, along with stories by Philip Johnson, Russell M. Coryell, Constance Foster, Frank Bunce, Thelmar Cox, Elizabeth Booth, Clarke Robinson, and Foley Martin, all of whom had experience writing romance pulp stories. Frank Bunce was already a regular contributor to the *Saturday Evening Post*. Other than advertisements for *Love Story* and *Smart Love Stories* on the inside front and back covers, there are no other ads in the magazine.

Daisy was now managing *Love Story, Ainslee's Smart Love Stories*—the title of which had been shortened to *Smart Love Stories* in October 1936—and now *Pocket Love*. Walter Winchell announced the new magazine in his column, giving Daisy an incorrect job title, by announcing, *Pocket Love* is the tag on a new mag due March 4. Daisy Bacon publishing."[2]

The "Love Story Radio Hour" radio program was resurrected in 1937. In "Two Diamond Bracelet," sweet violins introduce the episode and the narrator sets the scene:

You are about to hear a romantic drama, "Two Diamond Bracelet," from Street & Smith's *Love Story Magazine*, featuring "The Love Story Girl" in the role of Catherine Conyers.
The scene is the Café Rouz, the most popular of society nightclubs. Outside the street is rain swept, but inside the mood is different. The golden glow of suffused light. The soft seduction of Russian music. At a corner table sits a lovely Catherine Conyers, the most photographed girl in the world, and another young woman, basking in the reflective glow of Catherine's popularity. Their escorts, having excused themselves for the moment. Catherine, too bored even to light her cigarette....

Every week, listeners were treated with a fifteen-minute story with titles like "Love on the Sun Deck," "Hostage of Love," "Army Kisses," and "A Prince Arrives," and each one with the heroine branded as "The Love Story Girl."

Smart Love Stories had now been in circulation for two years. Many of Daisy's standard stable of *Love Story* writers made it into the chic magazine: Gertrude Schalk, Ruth D'Agostino, Georgia Maxwell Robinson, Marguerite Brener, and Dorothy Ainsworth all contributed stories over the next year of the magazine. Brener would become one of Daisy's closest friends, with she and her husband continually socializing with Daisy over the next several years, and Marguerite would eventually dedicate her 1939 novel, *My Country Tis of Thee,* to Daisy with the words, "Dedicated with love to Daisy Bacon for the inspiration of her unfailing interest and treasured friendship."

Sometime during this period, Esther met one of the *Smart Love Stories* authors, Clarke Robinson. A burly man of impressive stature, Clarke was confident, gregarious, and not at all afraid to talk about his accomplishments. He had dipped his toe in many ponds: First trained as an opera singer, he made his stage debut at the age of fifteen. After singing as a tenor in vaudeville, light opera, and opera performances in America and abroad, Clarke served as an officer in World War I. According to his own account, he lost his voice during the war and was forced to find another line of work afterwards. For a while, he worked as a sales manager for the Royal Typewriter and Underwood Typewriter companies.

Esther (left) and Daisy in a rare professional shot taken of the two together. Date unknown (Daisy Bacon collection).

Clarke decided that he would try his hand at being an author. By early 1937, he had written three short stories for *Smart Love Stories,* along with his *Pocket Love* story "The Dawn Caravan." His heroines and supporting characters play amongst the fringes of upper society, singing in nightclubs and spending time at the racetracks. He had also published at least two novels, *Fate Is a Woman* and *Behold, This Woman,* and purportedly other pieces of fiction and non-fiction.[3] His fiction writing, at least in the world of *Smart Love Stories,* was heavy on style, light on plot.

Clarke's real area of expertise, however, was in the world of horseracing. The sport was at a peak in its popularity in the 1930s, thanks to the easy access to listening to races on the radio. Many states had taken advantage of this interest and built new racetracks as a way to raise revenue. Seabiscuit was in the first of his highly successful racing years and was already becoming a national obsession.

Daisy and Esther seemed to be bitten by the racing bug as well. *Smart Love Stories* began a long string of articles on horseracing as well as stories using racetracks as a backdrop. Clark's lengthy article for *Smart Love Stories,* "Rainbows in Cellophane," was a long treatise on why the regular working girl should avoid the local bookies when she wanted to bet on the races. Instead, she should go to the racetrack, do her homework, and learn the complexities of handicapping rather than relying on a "tipster." He even encourages them to search out the "respectable women" at the races, women who are there every day and can teach them a few things. "They may be a trifle masculine in their demeanor and frequently have a somewhat hardened exterior but, as a rule, they are honest."[4]

Clarke Robinson, second from left, taken during World War I. Robinson, who was trained in opera before the war, sold typewriters for a living for several years afterwards (Daisy Bacon collection).

It's not known which came first: Clarke writing for *Smart Love Stories* or Esther meeting him and then inviting him to submit stories to the magazine. In any event, Clarke and Esther began to see each other regularly by 1937. They frequented tony restaurants such as Longchamps and attended the races at Belmont Park and Saratoga. In one photograph, Esther, clad in a fur coat, glows as she and Clarke stand in front of the awning at Sardi's. Esther was smitten, and it seems that as soon as Clarke was on the scene, other beaus that had hoped for Esther's attention faded away.

Daisy was still going to Botts on a regular basis. One weekend during this time, Daisy and Henry took several photographs posing around the house. Daisy, by this time in her late thirties, is starting to show her age, and drinking may have caused her face to be puffy. But ever the fashion maven, she poses in a smart pant suit with a colorful scarf casually draped around her shoulders. She leans against the wall next to the entry door and, with hands on hips, looks off into the distance. In another, Henry puffs on a pipe as he lays in a hammock hung in one of Alice's trees. But with one leg firmly on the ground, he doesn't look completely relaxed. In another, Esther stands alone on the stone pathway and, as usual, is relaxed and smiling. In all the photos, the house's stone exterior is not far away.

But the relationship between Henry and Daisy was beginning to show signs of unraveling during this time. Daisy wrote years later that, after her mother died, she began to pull away from Henry.

Thinking about HW & 1946, history repeating itself—I had glimpse in 1937.[5]

The feeling of discontent might have been mutual. In March of that year, a friend of Alice's and Henry's, prolific British novelist Marie Belloc Lowndes, became temporarily homeless due to a fire in her own dwelling. Lowndes had seen enormous success with her 1913 novel *The Lodger*, a psychological thriller that eventually was adapted to screen five times, including a silent film directed by Alfred Hitchcock in 1927. Alice generously invited Marie to stay at the Miller apartment in New York, even though Henry would be the only other person there at the time. Henry and Marie got along well, so well in fact that Alice wrote to Woollcott later that "If Marie is in love with Henry, he is even more with her, so that is quite all right." In a later letter she followed up with "Marie and Henry seem so happy together I should hate to interfere with them."[6]

It's doubtful, however, that Alice was trying to push the two together romantically in an attempt to pull Henry away from Daisy. Alice's breezy references to the two being in love could have been just a remark in the vernacular of the time. Marie was also married to newspaper editor Fredic Sawrey Archibald Lowndes. Finally, unbeknownst to Alice, Marie wasn't as happy living in the apartment as Alice thought. In a letter a few years later to her daughter Elizabeth, Marie confided that she had been uncomfortable in the apartment. "I really hated being in her beautiful flat and longed to leave it. I did so a week earlier than had been arranged." In the same letter she revealed some interesting aspects of Henry.

> I did get fond of Harry Miller, he is in fact very like a certain type of English squire.... Of course he hated spending Alice's money. She had bought him a seat on the Stock Exchange but in partnership, so he could do nothing silly.[7]

Marie didn't mention Henry again in her letters to her daughter, but in a letter to Woollcott years later, she mused that she could not see how Alice and Henry had ever had any kind of connection. "He used to talk to me about her with a queer kind of puzzled admiration, but I felt he did not really know her."[8]

If anything did occur between Henry and Marie, it didn't have a long-lasting effect on his relationship with Daisy. In December of 1937, Daisy was staying at Botts for several days at a time. But she wasn't feeling well at the beginning of 1938, spending so many days in bed that Esther ended up hiring a nurse for her. Daisy was well enough, however, to continue to travel to "the farm," or "the country," as she and Esther called Botts. And *Love Story* churned on as always, no doubt assisted by Esther's capable skills and unwavering dedication.

It had been a long four years since Ormond and George Campbell Smith had died. Daily activity inside the building on Seventh Avenue hummed along as usual, and during lunches and after work, people patronized the nearby businesses like they always did. They congregated at bars and restaurants around the neighborhood, like the Levenback Deli, up the block, or the various luncheonettes or automats scattered across the city. Much of the time, Street & Smith people would gather at the lunch counter at Liggett's Drug Store on 14th Street where, according to Daisy, "more gossip about the state of magazine publishing could be heard than ever appeared in the combined columns of *The News*, *The Mirror* and *The Journal-American*."[9] Those needing something stronger would slink off to Duffy's (which was playfully pronounced Duff-EE's) to get a beer.

Death once again was the instigator for major change within the company. George Campbell Smith, Jr., who had taken over as president after the two founders died four years before, died on April 7, 1937. Armetas "Judge" Holmes, a son-in-law of the original George Campbell Smith, was made president. Frank Blackwell, who had edited *Detective Story Magazine* for twenty years and occasionally reminisced about driving his horse and carriage to the train station in the early days of the twentieth century, was named Editor-in-Chief, and F. Orlin Tremaine, who had overseen *Astounding Stories* and *Mademoiselle,* was assigned Assistant Editor-in-Chief.

Campbell's horse and buggy memory was what many people felt was the theme of most of the company's magazines. There was a great deal of discussion in the hallways over what many felt was the company's failure to keep up with changing times. The magazines were old-fashioned, some complained. Sales were lagging; in response, the company had begun to slash the cover price of many of its magazines. *Love Story* would see the first change in its cover price since it began, from 15 cents to 10 cents in April.

In September, a memorandum signed by both Blackwell and Tremaine spelled out the issues that they thought were wrong with the company.

> The Editorial Department has claimed in the past, and with some justification, that it has been restricted by Company policies from selecting the type of stories which, from the standpoint of plot, character development, and style, were thoroughly attuned to the demands of the modern pulp reader.... We agree that the editorial policies of a number of magazines must be changed substantially, and we are in agreement as to the general character of these changes.

In due course, Blackwell and Tremaine would produce a list of suggested changes in editorial staff "to provide a fresh point of view" that they felt was much needed.

But Daisy, *Love Story*, and *Smart Love Stories* were, at least for now, immune from any changes: "The editorial staff of these magazines will remain as at present: *Mademoiselle, Pic, Love Story*, and *Smart Love Stories*."[10] Daisy's magazines would continue to be under the management of Bill Ralston.

Pocket Love, by this point, was already a fatality; it was not mentioned in the memorandum and was probably already on its way to the dustbin. *Pocket Love* and *Pocket Western* had lasted four issues and *Pocket Detective* eleven.

The slashing of titles continued across the company. The stock market crashed again in October, leading to what many called the "Roosevelt recession." Street & Smith discontinued a number of their pulp titles, including long-term pulps *Top Notch* and *Complete Stories*.

But another, much more drastic, event occurred the next spring. On April 1, 1938, almost exactly five years after the deaths of the Smiths, Allen L. Grammer arrived to take over Street & Smith. For the first time in the history of the company, a person outside of the Smith family was in charge.

Grammer, white haired and just shy of turning 60, had started his career in the steel business before moving over to the prestigious Curtis Publishing Company in 1916, making his mark in the standardization division. His forte was printing, and he had invented several tools to speed up the printing process of four-color prints. Efficiency was his passion, so streamlining the production of the pulp magazines, especially with a company with the print volume that Street & Smith produced, was a job in which he could really shine. What he would do to the magazines themselves—the quality overall and the stories inside—would remain to be seen.

Almost forty years later, Daisy bitterly recalled Grammer's first few days as president. According to her, a few days after his arrival, Grammer arrived at the building one Thursday—the regular weekday when payments were disbursed to writers and artists—only to find scores of people loitering about the building lobby and stairways as they waited for their checks. Grammer didn't take kindly to the crowds and was irritated when he had to cram into the Iron Maiden with several of these ne'er do wells. On that very same day, Grammer implemented a policy that authors and artists would no longer be paid on a set day of the week. Instead, payment would be issued based on another set of criteria.

It was an omen, according to Daisy.

> A small enough change, it might be said, for any new president to make. It was, however, a harbinger of further changes to come, although at the time this was not readily apparent.[11]

When Grammer and his entourage of supporters from the Curtis company showed up, it was, as *Air Trails* editor William Winter described, "as if a volcano blew up." It wasn't long before people were terminated in bulk. "The art department of the old place was thrown out *en masse* on a Friday afternoon. I came back from lunch and God, the north side of the second building, top floor, was empty." Winter reported that his office was moved nine times in one year after Grammer took over.[12]

By this time, the number of romance pulps on the newsstands had ballooned to nineteen. When combined with the romance western titles, there were thirty titles available at one point or another during 1938. Over three million people were reading the romance pulps every month.

Robert Uzzell's article, "The Love Pulps," was printed in the April issue of *Scribner's Magazine*. *Scribner's* wasn't necessarily a high-circulation magazine at the time, so most Americans probably didn't read it or even knew of its existence. Yet the magazine wielded power within the publishing world, and the article's claims of circulation and descriptions of the romance pulp readers and editors would be copied and quoted within the pulp fiction world for years to come.

Uzzell, a seasoned literary agent who frequently advertised himself in writing magazines as someone who could shepherd new writers to publication, singled out four women editors of the most successful love pulps: Daisy of *Love Story*, Amita Fairgrieve of *All-Story*, Jane Littell of *Love Book*, and Rose Wyn of *Love Fiction* and *Ten Story Love*. These did not encompass all of the successful romance pulps; Leo Margulies of Popular Publications also edited *Thrilling Love* and *Popular Love*, two other big sellers.

While Uzzell gave each editor equal footing and went over the mechanics of the business and the reason for each editor's success, he fell into the standard practice of the day of describing the physical attributes and marital status of the female editors: "On an informal inquiry once as to the best-looking editorial staff in New York, Miss Bacon, with her half-sister, Esther Joa Ford, her only editorial assistant, also a spinster, came off with top honors."[13]

According to Uzzell, romance editors pandered to a readership that didn't have the capacity to think critically. "[Daisy] understands the naïve code of conduct which is the only religion left to many of her readers; and finally, she knows what makes a story logical and convincing to a mind without logic and convinced of nothing."[14]

When it came to harsh opinions about romance fiction readers, Uzzell was just getting warmed up.

> These readers possess no fertile imaginations; their dreams must be written out for them. The dreams must not be too complex—motivation must be simplified to merely instinct responses. It is this inviolable rule of simplification which gives the pulp story its mark of triteness. The cliché and the familiar complication are necessities, not lapses....

The July 24, 1937, issue of *Love Story* issue, with an iconic cover by Modest Stein. Exotic locations were popular backgrounds for stories but Daisy always stressed that authors "write what they know" (*Love Story Magazine* © Condé Nast).

... and

> The strongest trait of all in the sub-mass female reader, however, is not sex or even the maternal, but devotion to convention. What her neighbors, her girl friends, will say of her is still her most passionate concern. Tribal mores hold her in a grip firm beyond the comprehension of anyone capable of intelligent behavior.[15]

Uzzell's article also may have been responsible for the theory that *Love Story*'s circulation hit 600,000 in the early 1930s, a figure that has been carried down through the ages. While Uzzell discusses the fact that few editors knew of the exact circulation of their own magazines, he then throws out this supposition:

> In any case, it is well known in the business that *Love Story Magazine*, published for seventeen years by Street & Smith, tops the field by a fairly wide margin. Various estimates place *Love Story*'s circulation at figures varying from 92,000 to 350,000. The latter figure is probably nearer to accuracy, but even that is far below the boom heights. Back in the 1929 era, when the price was fifteen cents rather than ten, *Love Story* sold thirty million a year, close to 600,000 a week—probably the highest circulation ever attained by *any* pulp magazine.[16]

While it's possible that this number was pulled out of the air, it's unlikely. What's more possible is that he attained the thirty million figure from Daisy when he interviewed her. Those cocktail parties she attended in her early years were proving to be quite the treasure chest of information.

Daisy lounging in another pair of twin photographs. The location and dates are unknown. Henry seems to be trying to hide his face in this photograph (both photographs Daisy Bacon collection).

The beginning of the week of May 16 was mundane. Henry left for Europe on May 18, sailing on the *Normandia*. He was accompanied by Alice and daughter-in-law Alison. In an intriguing twist, Esther mentions in her diary that she and Daisy also went to see Henry off at the port. How Daisy, Alice, and Henry managed this intriguing interchange, if there was one, will have to be left to the imagination.

It was five days before Daisy's birthday. It was a critical one: she was going to be turning forty years old.

Esther made her usual perfunctory notes in her journal that week. According to her entries, the days of that week were not much different than other days. On the 19th, Esther noted in her diary "up to see psychiatrist," although it's not clear whether she or her sister was the patient. She finishes that day with "B cranky, neuritis bad." The next day she noted that Daisy was tight again after being out with their maid Nora.

On May 22, the day before Daisy's birthday, Esther's entry started with her usual short notes.

"Cleaned closets. Dinner with C. Tight." But the next sentence is written in shaky hand and in very light pencil, as if Esther could not face the reality of what she was writing. "B—suicide. Up at 5:30."

Daisy never indicates in her later diaries whether there was a specific trigger that drove her to attempt suicide. They do reveal that she was very aware of her depression and that it was cyclical. She wrote frequently about feeling hopeless and how the feeling closed in on her at various times, and she mentions signs of it appearing in 1937. As Daisy describes it, her drinking was beginning to bother her too: not because of the many risks involved with alcoholism, but because she could no longer be in control.

Her later diaries also reveal more about her suicidal tendencies. At the same time, she is ambivalent about her need to kill herself. "[D]idn't really want to die, I guess— 1938. That was when it really began" she reflects twenty years later.[17]

She did not go to the hospital right away. Instead, a physician came to see her in the home. But three days later, on the 25th, Esther wrote that Daisy was admitted to Doctor's Hospital, located on East End Avenue and Eighty-Seventh and Streets on the upper East Side.

Built in 1930 for what was then a fantastic sum of four million dollars, Doctor's Hospital was known as a place for "a rest." An upper-crust hospital, it was owned by doctors and shareholders and had a reputation for exemplary care. Designed with the goal of being more of a spa than a place to treat illness, and "to surround the patient with all the comfort and refinement of a well-to-do home," its motif was home, not institution. Medical equipment was tucked away out of patients' and visitors' sights, and all the patient rooms were supplied with spectacular views. Visitors that wished to stay with their sick relatives had the luxury of their own private rooms, restaurant, and gymnasium located on another floor.[18]

Daisy stayed at Doctor's Hospital for ten days, with Esther, Clarke, and Nora visiting her daily. Knowing the amount of work that Esther could handle and her experience, it's likely that she just took over for her sister at the office. Once again, Esther was there to pick up the pieces. During this absence, Esther was notified by Bill Ralston that *Smart Love Stories* would be discontinued after the October issue. At least two co-workers in the building were fired during that time as well.

Eventually Daisy was discharged. On June 6, fifteen days after her suicide attempt, she was back in the office and facing the stark reality of Allen Grammer's new vision for Street & Smith.

15

Soft Rain at Botts

"Office politics are responsible for half of the nervous crackups in the country and for the taking of those last drinks for the road and the extra sleeping pills that lead people eventually up to the edge of a precipice. Occasionally the web of intrigue leads a man or woman to go quietly out of a twentieth floor window."[1]

Many of Grammer's immediate changes were, at first, just annoying distractions to those who had been with the company for any length of time. It seemed to be a matter of optics more than anything else. He ordered operations to be modernized and the offices spruced up and stripped of their Edwardian furnishings right down to the roll top desks. He then installed a time clock on the floor occupied by the editors ("to bring us *really* up to date," Daisy dryly noted later). He seemed to move through the offices as if he was wielding a sledgehammer. In a way, he was, as it was becoming clear to many that Grammer didn't put as much stock in the pulps as he did with the company's potential for publishing slick magazines.

Eventually Grammer and Daisy began to clash over several policies, such as the management of writers and artists. Grammer thought that her attitude towards them was too benevolent. For example, on occasion a writer's pay could be garnished for unpaid taxes or liens, and Grammer found this to be abhorrent. When it was learned that Daisy's writers carried a higher percentage of wage garnishments than other editors, he took her to task. But even though she explained that she had more publications than other editors with a larger number of writers, and most of the stories were bought on the open market, Grammer was unmoved. "His Nibs was always asking me why I couldn't buy stories from writers who didn't allow themselves to get into financial difficulties," she complained later.[2]

One artist who contributed frequently to Daisy's magazines had a drinking problem that occasionally landed her in a sanitarium. Daisy continued to take work from her and made sure that provisions were made for the artist's daughter while her mother was in difficulty. The next thing Daisy knew, Grammer was asking her why she couldn't find artists who didn't drink.[3]

Then her long standing practice of allowing authors or agents to drop off manuscripts at her apartment fell by the wayside. Even though she considered it good business, it had to stop.

What rankled Daisy was that the changes and complaints about her magazine's policies had nothing to do with the magazine itself. "Changes were designed for easy running

[of] company management and to eliminate all the risks that are associated with printing words on paper. It wasn't magazine publishing but more like playing in magazine publishing."

In the spring of 1939, more people were let go. Esther noted in February, March, and April the firing of four employees she knew on a first-name basis. One of Daisy's closest friends at the company, Ronald Oliphant, who had been with the company since the *Thrill Book* days and had been the well-respected editor of *Wild West Weekly* for the previous ten years, left the company. "These are evil times for pulp writers and editors both," wrote Oliphant's replacement, Francis Stebbins. "The good ol' days are gone."[4]

Daisy and Henry spent a lot of time together at Botts, but Henry spent time apart, too. Henry flew out to Los Angeles that summer to spend time with Alice. Alice was writing scripts at a movie studio, telling Aleck that "It is strange—and I dare say shameful—how much I enjoy a life of leisure at $2000 a week."[5] She was amused that Henry was there.

> Henry has been, and still is, visiting me, visiting Brackett in office hours, attempting to open the window of my air-cooled office which would have cost the company $8000 had he succeeded, doing me endless kindnesses, fascinating the Brackett girls, and in short being very much Henry.[6]

Daisy went on a vacation trip to Utah and Colorado that autumn. While she loved the landscape and she also wanted to escape Grammer's draconian measures, there was a deeper, more personal reason for her trip out west. She wrote in her journals later of the profound loneliness she felt, the deep grief and depression that had taken over after her mother passed away. She was looking for answers to reasons why she felt depressed so frequently. Her travels were symptomatic of what was, as she wrote later, "the endless search and discontent for what was."[7]

And her attitude towards Henry was changing. She felt that he had been uncaring towards her after her suicide attempt. "Thinking about 1939 and some of those awful times—HW never asked me why I did it," she wrote years later in a journal note, one that hints that she possibly may have tried to kill herself again in 1939. She also began to see that Henry at times could be a hypocrite. "Thinking of how HW talked when Dr. Blake divorced and married his nurse." But she continued to see him despite her doubts, to the point that she was there to play wife when his real one was absent. She continued to drink heavily.

It's possible that she began to see other men during this time. In a short-short story she wrote called "He Liked Them Helpless Looking," Daisy writes from a man's point of view who meets a young woman, obviously fashioned after herself, on the beach in front of a resort hotel. The man doesn't seem to be fashioned after Henry, because this character abhorred emancipated woman. "The Lord deliver him from these career women who didn't mind talking a man down on his own ground," he thinks as he eyes the young woman. He is attracted to her because she appears fragile and thus unthreatening, and then is surprised to find out she is the manager of a major magazine, is a prima donna, and is not afraid to drinking anyone under the table.[8]

Love Story had begun to ease its restrictions on how lovemaking could be described in its stories, even though some of the motivations and storylines were inexplicable. More frequently, descriptions of affection were more explicit, and the heroine showed assertiveness in intimate moments. "The Lavender Cat," in the February 24, 1940, issue, is the

The last pair of snapshots of the Daisy and Henry found in Daisy's personal papers. While they don't stand in the exact same spot, the landscape appears to be the same. The body language of both speaks volumes (both photographs Daisy Bacon collection).

story of Timmy, a veterinarian at a large estate owned by a wealthy woman who rescues cats. She is drawn to our hero Jep, who came to the estate looking to buy a kitten. As Jep and Timmy kiss, Timmy's physical desires come to the forefront in a description that would have shocked readers of the magazine five years before.

Timmy, under the exquisite emotion that was blazing in her heart, forgot all the things that wise girls are so carefully taught about "keep him guessing" and "be coy and evasive" and all that. Instead, she crept even a little closer in his arms and lifted her soft mouth for his kisses. "I'm afraid I'm pretty crazy about you too. Isn't that perfectly scandalous?" She whispered shakily.

His arms tightened. "Scandalous? It's perfectly swell! It's as it should be. Gosh, darling, you're sweet!" His voice was husky, shaken, and the touch of his lips on hers was fire and honey. Waves of ecstasy poured over her until she felt that she was drowning and didn't mind in the least.

Hours passed. Perhaps they were moments. Neither Timmy nor Jep were very clear about that. Suddenly Jep stood up, his face white and set. His eyes blazed with dark fires that seem to scorch and terrify Timmy, even while she was thrilled as she had never been before in her life. He pulled her to her feet and said huskily, "now I'm taking you home."

In April 1940, Henry came down with appendicitis and was rushed to Roosevelt Hospital. While the surgery was a success, he remained in the hospital with inflammation of the bowel. Alice was in Los Angeles and decided it wasn't necessary to fly back to New York; instead, she made arrangements to visit Aleck at the summer house in Vermont. But Henry wasn't left totally alone in his hospital room. Daisy and Esther went to the hospital every day to visit him.

Daisy was beginning to experience more physical ailments. Stomach troubles caused her to spend a lot of time at home. But she still managed to go to a dinner on June 22 to honor those who had worked for the Finnish Relief Fund, a humanitarian program to help the people of Finland during the Winter War between the Soviet Union and Finland. It was a cause in which Henry was very closely involved, and he had received an award of recognition for his efforts. A photo in Daisy's collection is of Henry standing near Eleanor Roosevelt as they pose in front of a Finnish Relief Fund poster at an event, but Daisy is not in the picture.

Even when she was well, Daisy was working from home, much of it from her bed, a workplace that eventually became her famous trademark. She sat in bed for hours, reading manuscripts and taking phone calls as her cats relaxed nearby. She could avoid Grammer that way, whose management directives continued unabated. In 1940, he implemented several changes to the physical appearances of the company's entire line of magazines. The masthead for all magazines was changed to an ugly block letter font. Then, after forty years of tradition in the pulp industry, he discontinued the ragged edges that all pulp magazines were famous for. The result were magazines with a more modern look with clean edges, but they had lost some of the original appeal of the pulp magazine, that of a rogue publication with messy edges that had become a symbol of rebellion and independence.

On July 19, 1940, Grammer told Daisy and Esther that they were to be given another magazine, *Romantic Range,* a monthly western romance pulp, to manage. Launched in 1935 under the original title of *Romance Range, Romantic Range* hit the market when there were at least six other western romance pulps, and there were at least eight others when Daisy and Esther took over the leadership in July. And that was in addition to the eighteen general romance titles in circulation.

One of the more interesting differences between *Love Story* and *Romantic Range* was, surprisingly, in the pen pal columns. *Love Story* had adhered to a strict same-sex policy when it came to connections between letter requestors and writers. *Romantic Range* was quite the opposite. Both men and women could request pen pals of the opposite sex, and some were "looking for romance." In the April 1940 issues, two young men in Panama were looking for pen pals, and blondes and brunettes were preferred.

Murder mysteries were used regularly, but also simple stories with zero plot. In "Punch and Judy," in the April 1940 issue, Judy falls in love with Hank, top ranch hand, but her father disapproves. Judy goes away, brings home Rod, who seems perfect at first, until he goes to the local bar, picks up a girl, drinks too much and boasts to Hank that he doesn't give a whit about Judy, and ends up with a sock to the jaw. The next morning Judy's father gets a phone call telling him that Rod isn't who he says he is. It was all a ruse. Judy had asked Rod to come and to be on his worst behavior to prove that Hank is a good guy. Judy rewards Rod with a thousand dollars and a car.

Daisy drove out to Botts the last weekend in July. The summer temperature could reach 90 degrees on any July day in the area, the heat and humidity only relieved by the shade of the dense thickets of trees. The trees dedicated to Alice had grown considerably over the past ten years and were now big enough that their canopy drifted over the front pathway. On Sunday afternoon, Daisy got in her car and drove back to the city.

> There in late sunshine I saw the last Sunday ... I ever spent at Botts. I knew then that I was never going back.[9]

Alice had been busy writing. The war in Europe was already raging by this point, and England was just entering the long three-month Battle of Britain. Alice and Henry had both lived through the First World War, and both had developed a long-lasting love of the British Isles. Now the country they loved was at war again. Emotional over the activities in Europe, Alice quickly wrote a verse novel, *The White Cliffs,* some time that spring.

Daisy outside the front door of the Botts house in an undated photograph (Daisy Bacon collection).

The White Cliffs is a verse novel that tells the story of Sue, an American who meets Englishman John at the eve of the Great War. While Sue loves John, she has a harder time adjusting to his family, who are gentry rooted in British tradition and a suspicion of Americans. Sue's American upbringing and her father's hatred of anything English color her viewpoint. Sue marries John, but then the Great War arrives. John dies in combat just as the armistice is announced. Her son, born shortly after his death, is the heir to John's family estate, and while Sue contemplates the state of the upper class and the fact that the family estate is not much more than a money drain, she decides to stay in England. The end of the book has Sue facing some of the same terrible conflicts and dangers she endured in the Great War. Throughout the story, Alice's honest depiction of England, through Sue's American eyes, is a love-hate relationship.

Alice was so enthusiastic about the book that she visited her friend, actress Lynn Fontanne, and read it to her one evening. Lynn reported back to Aleck:

> Alice read her poem to me, I think it beautiful and very touching. I cried. I wonder, if cut down considerably, and accompanied by music, it mightn't make an unusual radio program. It seems to me, it might have some audience, as everyone complains bitterly of most of the muck we get.[10]

On September 13, 1940, NBC radio ran a special broadcast of *The White Cliffs* on their stations across the country. For the first time ever, a radio broadcast aired the live reading of a poem. The program began with soft music, followed by actor Lynn Fontanne's soft, elevated voice.

I have loved England, dearly and deeply,
Since that first morning, shining and pure,
The white cliffs of Dover, I saw rising steeply
Out of the sea that once made her secure.

I had no thought then of husband or lover,
I was a traveler, the guest of a week;
Yet when they pointed "the white cliffs of Dover,"
Startled I found there were tears on my cheek.[11]

There's no record of whether Daisy listened to that historical first reading of *The White Cliffs*. However, there's no way she could have avoided hearing about it afterwards. The book had been selling well before Lynn's narration, but afterwards it became a sensation. Lynn's reading of the poem was repeated a week later, and then read again in Canada. A live reading was performed, and then read again on the BBC later that year. A phonograph recording was released. Movie rights were quickly acquired.

By the end of December, roughly four months after its initial release, *The White Cliffs* was already into its eleventh printing. Alice's life was pulled into a whirlwind of publicity, speaking engagements, and mobs of adoring fans. Henry would be sucked into the vortex as well.

16

Cobbler's Child

"What is love. Just something that burns itself out in the fires of its own creating."[1]

Daisy sat for a glut of interviews for a wide variety of media during 1941, from newspaper articles that focused on her own romantic life, to magazine articles written by journalists with an agenda, to the how-to-write-the-romance-story instructions in the trade magazines, to milk-toast radio interviews that kept to the script. Among the busy schedule of interviews, she and Esther also took on an increased workload that would make Daisy the only woman editor in the country that would manage magazines of three different genres: Romance, western, and detective.

Pulp publishers were experiencing another upheaval in their industry. Many were hampered by an avalanche of magazines that were in the format of pulps but contained nothing but stories that had already been published in other magazines. These reprint magazines delivered a serious blow to the early 1940s industry. Writers took only a quarter of a cent per word for reprints of their stories, but many probably felt they had little choice. With the country focused on what was happening in Europe, and war with Japan a real possibility, declining pulp sales reflected the uncertainty of the period.

A few articles printed during this time reported that *Love Story* was continuing to dominate the romance pulp field, but the overall record is confusing. *Writer's Digest* in 1941 reported that out of the top 33 selling magazines sold in 1941, only one pulp showed up: *Ranch Romances*, which reportedly had a circulation of 165,000 copies. But, as the article pointed out, the figures could be skewed, as the large pulp houses were reporting the sales of all their magazines, not just one.[2] *Lady Editor*, a book published in 1941 that focused on the different fields in which a woman could find a career in journalism, reported that *Love Story's* circulation in 1941 was as high as 350,000.[3]

Despite her economic power at the company, newspaper articles were more interested in Daisy's love life. One interview, immortalized in an article with the headline, "Editor Sells Romance to Lonely Wives, but Has No Love Herself," was seen in syndicated newspapers across the country. The article is riddled with errors, such as stating that Daisy had never attended school and was only at *Love Story* for six months before being made editor. But in between chatting up her hair color ("dark blonde") and declaring that her perfect man would be "one who asks no questions," and "who isn't narrow and who isn't impressed by who people are," Daisy manages to interject a few statements on how women should be perceived in her magazine. "I won't publish anything which puts

139

women in a bad light. Women must always rise above a situation and emerge victorious in the end."

She also pushed her belief that romance magazines needed to reflect modern times if they were to be successful. Daisy declares "America faces a renaissance of romance, a romance that considers economics and will be based on [joint] earnings of husbands and wives."[4]

Smart Love Stories had been pulled from the market in October of 1938. With the addition of *Romantic Range* in 1940, Daisy and Esther were back to managing two magazines. But that changed on May 20, when Grammer told Daisy and Esther that he would be adding *Detective Story*, Street & Smith's first genre-specific magazine that had sparked the detective magazine craze, to their assignments.

Taking over *Detective Story* brought Daisy a new set of challenges. The magazine had carried many popular series characters over the previous twenty-five years.[5] *Detective Story* never evolved into a hard-boiled magazine like *Black Mask* and *Dime Detective*, but its editors had never tried to reach those heights. They had considered it to be more of a slick magazine. *Detective Story* had, for many years, courted another audience, its editors focusing on stories that used less action and centered more around sophisticated characters and wealthy settings. Beginning in 1938, it had emphasized characterization and atmosphere, which were anathema in the average pulp story.

But it had suffered from a turnstile of editors ever since long-time editor Frank Blackwell was kicked upstairs to management. He was replaced by Anthony Rud in 1937, who was replaced by Hazlett Kessler in 1939. Then in late 1940, the magazine was put under the management of Ruth Miller, whose only previous experience at the company was as Allen Grammer's secretary. Introduced in *Writer's Digest* in January of 1941, she glibly announced that, "I'm riding easy in the saddle, until I find out what the horse under me is like."[6] It wasn't long before the magazine shrunk from having five to seven stories in every issue down to only four per issue, and in some cases, two out the four were installments of serials. Miller was taken off of the magazine, and Daisy was brought in to rescue it.[7]

Still, judging from the contents of the magazine from 1941 through 1945, quite a few heavy-hitting writers continued to contribute to *Detective Story*. Raymond Chandler, Hugh Cave, D.L. Champion, George Thomas Roberts, Carroll John Daly, Norbert Davis, Paul Ernst, Lawrence Treat, Johnston McCulley, and Roger Torrey were among many experienced and gifted writers who appeared in *Detective Story* during Daisy's tenure.

A few long-timers experienced difficult encounters with Daisy. She was never one to genuflect in front of a famous writer. In a letter to Lester Dent, William Bogart wrote that, more than likely, Frank Gruber wouldn't pass the sniff test with her. "Boy, I bet Gruber is hot," he wrote. "Daisy thinks his stuff stinks!"[8] Bogart would come up against Daisy himself later in the year. After submitting his story "Hell on Friday," to her, she reported back to him, telling him she was reading it, but "she did not think she would use anything with a publishing background, no matter whether the story pictured the racket in a favorable or unfavorable light!"[9]

Daisy had inherited what Bogart called a "big inventory of crap" from Ruth Miller, and Daisy had to first let the serials run their courses.[10] She then put a stop to the serials and put a call out for shorter stories between 5,000 and 25,000 words. She hoped that she would be able to bring in some new blood into its stable of writers. "A woman may be the central character, the slant may quite definitely appeal to women and the author

Daisy looking through the usual pile of manuscripts that awaited her approval or rejection (photograph by W. Eugene Smith; reprinted with permission of Black Star).

may be a woman," *Writer's Digest* reported of her requirements in May of 1942. She handed out orders for stories, both for *Detective Story* and *Love Story*, feeling optimistic about the future. The change in scenery seemed to have breathed new life into her outlook on the job—for a while.

On June 13, 1941, Daisy sat down for a radio interview on station WNYZ. Called

"The Writer and Your Life," the program was, according to the announcer, "aimed at a better understanding between you and the writer." Daisy wasn't the only one being interviewed; Esther's fiancé Clarke was also a guest, most likely pulled in by Daisy to give him some publicity for his writing career. The interview was recorded, and Daisy kept the records for the remainder of her life. The recording, now scratchy and almost inaudible, still manages to relay the glamour of the golden days of radio.

MR. ATMOND: When Mr. Robinson agreed to appear, I was happy. But when Daisy Bacon accepted, I positively gloated. Here at last was my opportunity for a classic revenge. Here was a chance to edit an editor. I could just visualize myself getting over the sheet that was written what she expected to say and gleefully slashing away with a blue pencil. But somehow it didn't quite work out that way.

I've been acquainted with editor Bacon for some years. I've even sold her stories. But I don't know any more about her now than when I first met her. So far she has refused to talk about herself and it's only my faith in these magnetic powers of the microphone that makes me hope that we may get to do so tonight.

"Daisy, what about it? Just why have you been so reluctant to talk about yourself or your work?"

In her soft, high voice, Daisy answers:

"As for the first, I believe a person's private life should be private. About the second, you can find the answer in almost any magazine. You will find prominently displayed the names of the stories and the articles, and the authors' names. But the editor's name remains in the background."

The interviewer teases Daisy.

"They say that editors are disappointed writers."

"Oh pooh."

"And why do you say that?"

"I can only speak for myself and frankly I just don't know how that ... how well ... that would apply to me."

The interview doesn't delve into any new information that Daisy hadn't already covered in interviews before. She is obviously speaking from a script; there is nothing spontaneous about her voice, and her tone is flat. The most intriguing question is a simple one, and her answer speaks volumes:

"Do you plan on going back to writing?"

"I honestly don't know, and I don't know how good of a writer I am. I ask so much of my writers I couldn't ask them myself."

Daisy's relationship with Henry had ended but everywhere she went, she was faced with reminders of his wife. *The White Cliffs* continued to be on an upward trajectory that didn't seem to have an end in sight, and the publicity surrounding the book continued. Some newspaper articles claimed that it was the "first book of poetry ever to hit the best-selling lists." By the middle of June, the book has sold a hundred thousand copies, with profits going to the British Relief Society.[11]

But Alice was apparently beginning to feel the effects of the hectic schedule. She was not feeling well, struggling with colds and at one point having pneumonia. Still, she insisted on traveling to Hollywood for a length of time to work.

Daisy was having mixed results with her own encounters with newspapers. In November she was interviewed for the "Modern Woman" column in the *Trenton Evening Times,* in which she was given much more real estate to discuss her passion of women in business. But she turned the tables in this interview, to criticize fellow business women on what she thought was a lack of solidarity.

Women haven't made good their threat or their promise in business. There are no female Henry Fords in business. This will continue to be a man's world until women learn the meaning of the phrase, "United we stand." The lack of loyalty among women who work is alarming.

Left: **While most of Daisy's social and romantic life were centered around Henry Wise Miller, she did see other men. Here on a cruise with an unknown companion.** *Right:* **This same man is shown in a photograph on Daisy's desk around 1940 (both photographs Daisy Bacon collection).**

According to Daisy, women were still resorting to petty jealousies and back-stabbing each other.

> Women consider a large salary a man's divine right, but they look sourly at another woman and ask, "Why should she make so much money?" Cattishness?—my apologies to my favorite animals. Jealousy? Envy? I don't know. But women always seem to have a long sharp pin ready to jab into another woman, verbally at least.[12]

Daisy went on to claim that these were observations of hers, not her own experience. But given how she felt about other editors, her historical attitude towards other women editors can only shed some doubt on that claim.

The onslaught of articles displaying Daisy as perpetually single and lonely continued. An article in the *Writer's Year Book* hit a new low. In "The Cobbler's Child," Aaron Mathieu begins with a description of a previous interview in which the photographer asked Daisy to pose in front of her fireplace and "show some leg," Daisy snapped back, "You'll snap me standing in front of the mantel in an evening dress, or don't unpack."

Off to a less than auspicious start, the photographer pressed on. "Who do you date?" he asked her. With the composure of one who had endured hundreds of these questions, she responded with a smile. "I'm like the cobbler's children." Mathieu went on to declare that Daisy had a "poison stiletto ready," to jab at any of her competitors.[13]

Perhaps to make up for the vicious words of Mathieu, the *Writer's Year Book* invited Daisy to write a piece herself that appeared in the same issue. An instruction on how to write for the romance pulps, much of it was repetitive of what she had been telling writers for the previous dozen years. "Should a successful love story have any underlying message? To tell a good story and hold your audience should be your first concern and it is certainly enough."[14]

The Last Real Year

After the Japanese attacked Pearl Harbor, many fiction magazine editors began to call for stories to meet the sudden demand for tales of a Nipponese-American war, spies, possible attempts at invasion by an Asian adversary, fifth column efforts, and so on. But according to a snippet that appeared in the February 1942 issue of *Writer's Journal*, Daisy had been ready for this change even before Pearl Harbor.

> But the tall, slender, blonde fashion plate who edits *Love Story*, *Romantic Range* and *Detective Story* magazines, was ready. Her "familiar spirit" told her weeks before that a war crisis was coming in the Far East, and like a prudent, far-seeing army or navy chief, she was prepared for the requirements of her great number of readers.
> For some time she had been buying fiction the plots of which linked Japan to a treacherous attack; she had a long serial about sabotage in the American northwest. There were many other stories in her possession directly built around such a war as is now going on across the Pacific.[1]

The United States had been grappling with the threat of war for years beforehand, so Daisy didn't necessarily have the scoop on the war starting. Many fiction editors had started to use war-themed covers for a few months, especially editors of magazines that leaned towards action stories. *Argosy* was releasing covers centered around the "Yellow Peril" as early as May 1939, *Adventure* in 1940, and in *Blue Book*, U.S. soldiers were in Europe in 1941. Romance pulps were a little slow to follow, but *Love Book Magazine* carried a woman in the WAVES on the December 1941 cover.

The cover on the *Love Story* issue dated December 6, 1941—the day before Pearl Harbor—depicts a woman holding a letter, contemplating the names of forts and bases that swirl around her head. Covers aside, there isn't any mention of the new war in the magazine until the February 21, 1942, issue, and it is only briefly mentioned in the "*Love Story* Notes" column that focused on fashion. This is a logical delay, however, considering that the magazine was on a six- to seven-week lead time between conception and appearance on the newsstands.

> Wars may come and wars may go, but the busy women of this country are not going to forgo new clothes or the latest fashion for any such reason. Now, more than ever, are they determined to look their best, their gayest, for their own sakes as well as others.

Daisy told the *Writer's Journal* reporter that it was her opinion that eventually things would "settle down," and most magazines would return to their normal line-up of story lines. But, as Daisy and the rest of the country would find out, things would not calm down for a very long time.

During that first year, Daisy usually limited the number of stories centered around

By the early 1940s, romance pulp titles dominated the newsstands. These two women contemplate a wealth of reading material in May of 1942 (photograph by Office of War Information).

the military to just one per issue. Occasionally a cover had a military theme. Later in the year, a regular column, "War Time Recipes," appeared, and in the October 31 issue, the "Love Story Notes" column included a plea for nurses to join the Red Cross or the National Nursing Council for War Service.

The slow response to the war effort may have also been a management decision at Street & Smith. Editors may have been told to hold off on a full-fledged war effort in the magazines until more was known about the progress of the war.

Many editors and writers left civilian life to join the military, and by the end of the year, approximately twenty percent of publishing staff had either been drafted or had been recruited by the Office of War Information (OWI).[2] Elmer Davis, the writer who had reminisced that being with Daisy was one of the "greatest experiences" of his life back in her early days as an editor, was now head of the OWI. With so many entering military service, publishers desperately needed able people—including editors—to fill staff positions, and they began to move women into those positions.

Another shift, albeit small at first, was the worry that most publishers experienced over paper shortages. Concern over the scarcity of pulp materials and paper had started as early as the winter of 1940, when Scandinavian countries, which supplied most of England's paper, became involved in the European war. Almost overnight Great Britain's paper supply was cut off, and they began rationing paper in February of 1940. By 1941, Britain was working with less than 30 percent of its earlier supplies. Newspaper sizes shrunk down from hefty volumes of reading material to a few pages with tiny headlines, no margins, and advertisements that were barely noticeable.

By early 1942, the American paper industry braced for the impact to their productions, and many speculated how long it would be before paper was rationed in the United States and by how much. Even though the War Production Board commented in early January that publishers should not expect a lack of paper, rumors were likely persisting, because special interests began to make their opinions known as to who should feel the pinch first. Pulp fiction magazines should be the first to go, the International Council of Religious Education told the government, stating that "in the event of an acute paper shortage that churches receive paper priority for Sunday school pamphlets, but that publication of pulp magazines be banned. "Americans can do without a flood of cheap and tawdry 'crime,' 'wild West,' and 'love' story magazines."[3]

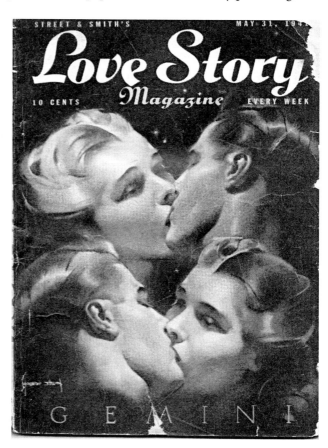

By the middle of 1942, photographs were used frequently on *Love Story* and *Romantic Range* covers. *Love Story* featured happy, smiling women, sometimes even in bathing suits, sometimes in poses suggesting they were pining for their romance to write them, other times in more active scenes such as playing baseball or with tennis racket in hand. By 1943, the majority of covers featured women alone, without a male in the picture. This could have been following the conventions of the day, or an attempt to emulate the glamorous slick magazines of the day or, because so many men were overseas in the armed forces, an expression

By this time, photography had become the most commonly-used form of cover art for *Love Story*. The astrology feature had become a strong member of the magazine's columns, and this issue highlights Daisy's sun sign of Gemini (*Love Story Magazine* © Condé Nast).

of solidarity for the millions of women fighting the war on the home front without their male counterparts.

As soon as Daisy and Esther had taken over *Romantic Range*, changes almost immediately became evident with more content, more pages, and more variety, and these were in full effect by the middle of 1942. Serials were used almost the minute Daisy took over. But by far, the biggest change was in the amount of content and number of pages, with the magazine moving from 128 pages to 160 by middle of 1942. The May 1940 issue has two novellas and five short stories. By contrast, the August 1942 issue was reminiscent of the early *Love Story* issues: It had nine short stories, one novelette, one serial installment, five poems, four columns, and a cover by Modest Stein.

Romantic Range, like so many other western romance and general romance pulps, gave plenty of women authors a steady paycheck. Anita Allen was one of the biggest contributors. She wrote steadily under both her own name and her pseudonym Marian O'Hearn, and appeared almost every month in the magazine, while still contributing to other western romance magazines such as *Western Romances, Romance Round-Up, Rangeland Romances* and *Rangeland Sweethearts* from the late 1930s through the early 1950s.

Muriel Newhall, writing under her own pen name Mona Farnsworth and the house name Muriel Ives, was probably the biggest contributor to *Romantic Range*. Like Allen, she diversified and wrote for other western romance pulps. One of her most regular characters in *Romantic Range* was Sherriff Minnie, who solves murders while spurning the daily wedding proposals from Peter Whittlesey.

More male western writers appeared, some of whom wrote for the general western pulps. Writers such as Wayne D. Overholser, Ed Earl Repp, George Cory Franklin, and Kingsley Moses, who wrote earlier in his career in the late 1920s for *Wild West Weekly*—appeared in the magazine, and under their own names. According to John Dinan in his seminal book *The Pulp Western: A Popular History of the Western Fiction Magazine in America*, Daisy informed him that 55 percent of romance western writers were men.[4]

The sisters had changed the magazine's front column, "Grapevine Whispers," to something friskier, "Party Line," that contained travel reports, mainly on dude ranches in New York state. The December 1941 column has Esther's fingerprints all over it.

> If we break out and use expressions like "Howdy, waddy," and "That ornery hombre"—well, forgive us, for we feel in a very Western mood after a visit to Boulder Greens, one of America's most famous dude ranches. And one of the most "Western" ones, too, although it's not out where the coyotes howl. As a matter of fact, it's right in the heart of the Adirondacks, about eight miles from Warrensburg, N.Y.

Later the column would discontinue with the on-the-road travel reports and would instead provide overviews on the national parks ("Why don't you visit Yellowstone?"). Later it would become a standard "about the authors" column.

Daisy received yet another new assignment around this time, one that would bring her a challenging and yet satisfying diversion. She began to work part-time for the Special Services Division, a branch of the military whose goal was to disseminate entertainment materials to the armed forces overseas to boost morale. Daisy's assignment was to prepare *Detective Story* to be distributed overseas. She said later that "many of the boys wrote us that they had never before realized how much of an escape fiction stories could be. And civilians as well wrote that while traveling they had discovered fiction for the first time."[5] Early articles misrepresented the department for which she worked, saying that she was working for the OWI, but there is nothing documented showing that she worked for the office headed by Elmer Davis.

Even though the assignment may have been a good diversion for her, it was only temporary. She lamented later in her typical dramatic and hyperbolic fashion that the early 1940s were some of the worst years of her life. She was drinking regularly, according to Esther's diary, who on several days wrote only one or two words: "Daisy" and the shorthand for "tight." Daisy wrote in her journal years later that she spent New Year's Day of 1942 in the hospital recovering from "blood poisoning in her foot." Blood poisoning was a term commonly used during that time for what was probably septicemia, or sepsis.

Alice had also spent the New Year in a hospital around the same time for what was initially believed would be exploratory surgery. She awoke from the surgery to find out that most of her reproductive organs had been removed to remove a cancer. A letter her son wrote to Aleck after the surgery reveals an estrangement between Denning and his father.

> How and why H.W.M. came to broadcast his first drastic reports of her condition I don't understand and don't much care to. I am satisfied that there is positively no further threat hanging over her and that's all I care about.[6]

Henry stayed close to Alice during this time, but he kept in touch with Daisy and stopped by the apartment to see her in April. Daisy was most likely seeing other men during this time. A photograph of another man adorned her desk top and photos of the group of her and friends on a cruise show the same man, with he and Daisy holding hands. Daisy, for all intents and purposes, was moving on.

On August 22, a reporter and photographer from *Parade Weekly* arrived at the *Love Story* office. They were assigned to interview and photograph Daisy Bacon for a "day in the life" feature, which would include her workday, her home, and her social life. As the reporter asked questions, the photographer, W. Eugene Smith (who would later become a famous Vietnam War photojournalist) took photographs of Daisy behind her roll top desk, of her sorting through manuscripts, of her looking pensive in front of a wall of *Love Story* issues. He climbed up a ladder and took a shot of Daisy at her desk, feet up, as she looked out at her realm, as her ceramic cats, collected from all points of the globe and given to her by friends, perched on top of the desk. Unbeknownst to many, the days of that roll top desk were numbered.

Writer and photographer followed her around the entire building. Smith snapped photos of Daisy consulting with the men in shirt sleeves in the printing and linotype departments. He perched Daisy and Esther on a stack of *Love Story* issues in the mail room, wrapped and ready to be shipped, amongst a sea of other parcels ready for shipment. He had her "drop in" on Modest Stein's "studio" and watch as he painted a cover for *Love Story*. Stein, with grey hair now but with eyes still as dreamy as Emma Goldman found them, poses in the typical artist pose, holding his paint brush out to "frame" his subjects.

Later in the day the *Parade* crew joined Daisy at the Fifth Avenue apartment. In probably one of the few times in his life, Smith took photos of his subject in bed. Smith snapped his camera as Daisy, wearing a frilly bed jacket and cradling a phone receiver, sat up in bed and looked at a manuscript with one hand and pretended to talk on the phone with the other. One of her cats lounged on other papers strewn about the satin bedspread. Nora stood next the bed, writing pad in hand, waiting for Daisy's instructions for the day. The reporter made a point to take a tour of Daisy's closets—all three of them—with one strictly for hats and coats, including a mink, and another full of original frocks from designers in her signature color of black.

Daisy regularly worked from her bed in the mornings, a habit that helped her image as a pur-veyor of romance. This photograph, taken for the *Parade Weekly* "Love Story Editor" article, was probably one of the few times that a business woman was photographed in bed for a feature (photograph by W. Eugene Smith, reprinted with permission from Black Star).

They wanted to show Daisy out on the town. They posed a model, a handsome man in uniform, waiting patiently inside Daisy's apartment as she prepares for their "date." As her "escort" pays the check at dinner that night, Daisy is shown checking her watch. "Even here, Miss Bacon must watch the time. Tomorrow will be another very busy day!" the caption says.

Later that evening, Esther began to fill in the entry in her diary with her usual notes on happenings at the office. "Boys from Parade here." She then chronicled what she and Clarke Robinson did that evening—they went to the movies and saw "This Is the Army"—and then she finished her notes about the day.

Alice Miller died today.

Alice's funeral was held on August 24 in Morristown, New Jersey. In a quiet corner of Evergreen Cemetery, she was buried under an imposing headstone designed for two; Alice's name and birth and death dates were the only notations. The left side was blank, reserved for Henry. Daisy did not attend, a decision that she would later regret. But Esther did, noting in her typical brevity of the weather that it was a "lovely day."

Two weeks after Alice died, Daisy had dinner with Henry. But, whether it was his attempt to circle back with Daisy with the hope of a reconciliation, or a simple dinner so he could decompress after the past year, was never disclosed. Regardless of the motivation, the relationship between the two was now colored by Alice's death. Now the question was what would happen now that Henry was free from marital bonds.

18

Hanging On

By the end of 1942, rationing in the United States was in full effect across the country. All types of food—sugar, meats, cheeses, canned milk—and petrol, rubber, and nylon were being rationed. For publishing companies, paper and ink were the materials that concerned them the most. Reports from the government competed with word on the street as to when new requirements would be implemented, which resulted in growing uncertainty as to how the publishing industry would weather the paper shortage crisis looming on the horizon. In September of 1942, the War Production Board had turned an about-face from its earlier announcement and declared that printers and publishers needed to begin cutting their consumption of paper, rolling their output back to 1940 or 1939 levels. Metals used in color-printing was given notice as well.[1]

Now these restrictions were starting to be felt by pulp publishers, and many magazines' schedules were modified or they disappeared completely. In a baffling move, Street & Smith decided to temporarily curtail the production of three of its storied magazines: *Love Story*, *Wild West Weekly*, and *Western Story*. The executives may have been trying to comply with the paper shortage mandate. Or it may have been Grammer's attempt to change the schedule of its weekly magazines. No one really knows. Whatever the reason, the move would eventually cause chaos in the building.

The problem was that someone might have forgotten to check with the Post Office before Grammer put a stop to the presses. The ruling that harkened back to the very early days of pulp magazines required that if periodicals wanted to be granted second-class postage, they must be issued on a regular, scheduled basis.

The February 13 issue of *Love Story* appeared on the newsstand. Four weeks went by, and no new *Love Story* appeared on the newsstands or on the shipping docks.

On March 20, *Love Story* was banned by the Post Office.

Daisy immediately began to phone all her contacts, but to no avail. Grammer and Ralston sent executives to Washington, but nothing transpired, and Ralston eventually threw up his hands and said it was "all politics." Esther even asked Clarke, who by this time was a captain and stationed in Washington, to interfere and try to garner some favors amongst his cronies in the capital. Finally, two weeks later, the ban was lifted, and the magazines commenced publication. But *Love Story*, along with *Western Story* and *Wild West Weekly*, were changed to appear every other week rather than weekly.

But the fun wasn't over yet that year. On May 10, 1943, yet another ban took place, this one issued by the City of New York License Commissioner Paul Moss. Moss had been appointed to the New York Society for the Prevention of Vice, a department created by Mayor Fiorello LaGuardia that had been striking fear into the hearts of pulp, confession, and marginal publishers since the early 1930s. An article in the November 1934 issue of the *Author & Journalist*, "Arbiter of Smut," features John Sumner, a secretary for the department. A serious bespectacled man, he works in a small office on West Twenty-second Street at a desk buried under a paper explosion. The article reports that "the patient gentleman looks at every line of every page, at every engraving and cartoon and advertisement."[2]

Street & Smith wasn't the only pulp publisher targeted in this event. Moss banned the sale of eleven pulp magazines at licensed newsstands across the city. The other ten were a sampler of magazines produced by publishers across the city: *Judge, Close-Up, Speed Adventure Stories, Speed Detective, All-Story Love, Uncensored Detective, Best Love Magazine, Dan Turner Hollywood Detective, Rare Detective Cases,* and *Spotlight Detective Cases.* According to a *New York Times* newspaper article, Moss said the act was "merely a routine step taken in keeping with the city's policy laid down by Mayor LaGuardia to forbid the sale on newsstands of periodicals deemed nonmailable." Why these magazines were considered "nonmailable" wasn't elaborated on.[3]

Esther noted that this time around, the action was lifted quickly. "*Love Story* banned by newsstand," she said, but Hatton, the plant manager, "got union after Moss; everything ok." No other notes on this incident were recorded.

All in all, the paper shortage ended up having an ironic effect on the pulp industry: the magazines that remained on the stands were handed a market that hadn't been theirs before. Companies like Street & Smith and Popular Publications saw an enormous boost in sales, and returns to the publishers hovered around a very low five percent. "We sold everything we put out," Henry Steeger of Popular Publications remembered.[4]

Grammer's vision of pulling back on pulp fiction publications was looking awfully short-sighted at this point.

The number of war-themed stories in *Love Story* had increased notably. In the February 6, 1943, issue, three out of six stories are centered around soldiers or how the war had affected domestic living. In "Firelee Goes to War," by Jeanne Ceres Wing, Firelee Gibson, a young and inexperienced young woman, has inherited from her grandfather a metals production business in her home town. She goes back to town, knowing that the new large propeller plant in town is threatening to take away the aluminum that Gibson Factories needs to operate. In "Marietta Rose" by David William Moore, a waitress named Annie Dolan tells her story of meeting a soldier, Jess, on her shift, who asks her to play "Marietta Rose" on the jukebox. In "You Can Be Sure of Me," Tanis Gorham's family takes in a beautiful French refugee. Tanis takes an immediate dislike to the young woman and it doesn't help that the refugee, Clarice du Le, has eyes for Tanis's sweetheart Steve Farnsworth. In the serial "Professional Hero," written by Maysie Grieg, David Frenshaw secretly takes the place of his brother, Lieutenant Colonel Daniel Frenshaw, who is believed to have been killed in action.

A continuing non-fiction series, "Women and War-Time Living," began, in which readers could learn how to help on the domestic front. The May 18, 1943, issue featured the need for farm workers to fill the United States Crop Corps, either through year-round workers, seasonal workers, or emergency harvest workers. Later that year, the column would encourage readers on how to "make do" with the clothing they had and avoid buying new clothing to ward off textile shortages (December 14), enlighten them on the training that the U.S. Government was providing to soldiers above and beyond battlefield training (December 28), and educate them on the role of the Military Police. (January 11).

Daisy continued to recruit female authors for *Detective Story*. "And, so far, I have found that women handle detective stories very well, and I hope to help develop many feminine writers in this field. There is not space to go into it in this article, but there never was a time when there was room for so many new writers of detective fiction," she wrote in *Writer's Market*.[5]

Not that she was turning *Detective Story* into amateur hour. Stories by many well-known detective and mystery authors continued to show up between its covers over the next few years. Hugh Cave, who contributed stories to all genres and all titles, regularly showed up in *Detective Story* in the early 1940s. Julius Long, long contributor to *Black Mask, Clues, Detective Fiction Weekly* and *Dime Detective*, showed up occasionally as did Bruno Fischer, Frederic Brown, and Cornell Woolrich. Roger Torrey contributed at least thirteen stories. Carroll John Daly, creator of Race Williams, which up until 1940 had been exclusively seen in *Black Mask* and *Dime Detective*, showed up at least three times in *Detective Story* in the 1940s. Seasoned editors also contributed stories, including Ronald Oliphant, who had been the editor of *Wild West Weekly* until 1940 when he re-emerged to write stories as a freelancer, and John Nanovic, long-time editor of *The Shadow* magazine.

Daisy published several writers in *Detective Story* who had first been published in her romance magazines: Emma Forster, Camilla Jordan, Maud McCurdy Welch, and Ethel Donoher Smith all wrote several stories for *Love Story* before taking the leap into the detective genre. Katherine Metcalf Roof had written in many genres before appearing in *Detective Story*. Isabel Stewart Way wrote over a hundred stories for *Rangeland Romances* and *Romantic Range* before writing at least one story for *Detective Story* in January 1942. She then probably decided it wasn't for her and she went back to what she knew best: writing the western romance. Inez Sabastian jumped back and forth between *Love Story* and *Detective Story*.

In May, the government was forecasting that paper shortages were expected to not only continue but increase in severity. On May 27, Grammer notified the staff that all pulps would be cut down to 128 pages. Then, the very next day, Esther noted that *Detective Story* was going to the "small size," which meant it was going to the digest size. This change was implemented across the board for all Street & Smith pulps. As a final note on that day, Esther noted that "Grammer and Johnson both tight."

On July 12, 1943, Esther and Clarke got married. All Esther noted was that it was "the hottest day of the year." Clarke could only get a one-day leave from his post in Washington, so any kind of honeymoon was put on hold.

By the spring of 1944, Street & Smith had moved out of its storied building at 79 Seventh Avenue. The Seventh Avenue building with its Edwardian motif, narrow stairwells, and paper in every crevice was left behind to history. The company moved to the Chanin Building, a smart art deco skyscraper located at the corner of 42nd Street and Lexington Avenue. The waiting room, adorned with up-to-date décor, made visiting writer H. Wolff Salz think that it looked more like a modern advertising agency.[6]

Daisy, noted Salz, was a person who did not like coarseness—both in her life and in the stories she printed. Salz asked Daisy for some examples of what she did not want to see in her stories. She answered that she was not a fan of unwarranted violence. "For example, there's the standby cliché in characterizing the villain, having him kick at a dog.

Clarke received only one day off for their wedding and had to hurry back to Washington, D.C., afterwards. Here Esther and Clarke pose in front of one of their favorite restaurants (Daisy Bacon collection).

It's not only oversimplified characterization, and hackneyed to boot, but presents unnecessary meanness to animals."[7]

Grammer used the move to the new offices as an opportunity to modernize the furniture. The famous roll top desks, including Daisy's, that had been an institution since before the turn of the century were discarded. Daisy was moved into what she called a "tiny, bandbox office" with a desk that was big enough to hold her typewriter, a phone, and not much else.[8]

Daisy had another setback. She and Gertrude Schalk had, for many years, been discussing collaborating on a book that would be an instruction on how to write the romance short story. In the move to the new building, many of Daisy's notes and correspondence disappeared, including the paperwork that was going to be the basis of her book with Schalk. The project was never resurrected, but Daisy would take a different route later, without Schalk.

On March 2, 1944, Grammer informed Daisy and Esther that *Love Story's* frequency would be changed to a monthly schedule. With its shortened page count, photographic covers, and a masthead of modern font, the magazine was unrecognizable from those released in the early 1930s. "The Friend in Need," the advice column that had brought Daisy Bacon to the front doors of Street & Smith in 1926, was dropped.

Esther's journal entries during this time are as matter-of-fact as usual, and there

One of the apartments on Fifth Avenue. A journalist said at this point that Daisy was suspicious of attention and preferred to stay single. Her main interest, he wrote, was her clothes (Daisy Bacon collection).

is no indication that Daisy was feeling depressed or suicidal. Marguerite Brener came to the office frequently and the two socialized at lunch and in the evenings. But Daisy would later note that 1944 was when she was having great difficulty in "hanging on to my life."[9]

One of the reasons for her difficulty could have been because of news from Henry. He was writing a book. A biography of Alice.

19

Between the Lines

"When to tell the truth and how much of it I leave to wiser men."[1]

Henry's book about Alice, *All Our Lives,* was released in 1945. He doesn't mention Daisy outright, or any other women with who he may have had affairs. But he does hint at his and Alice's open marriage and alludes to outside relationships. Even though Henry and Alice understood each other when it came to their dalliances with other people (and Alice may have had her own), Henry still had doubts on whether Alice ever came to terms with his affairs.

> Not long ago she said, "You know, it takes a good deal to stand up to you." As she was referring to my relationship with someone else I was not much concerned. What I would have dearly liked to know was how much of a score was marked up against me in her own books, how much she felt that she had to pay for the pleasure of my society. The question would have seemed to her in the worst spiritual taste and she would not, or could not, have answered it.[2]

He defends any thoughts or deeds of infidelity in the book, saying that long periods apart created opportunities. "Lovers must be careful, absence does not always make the heart grow fonder. Too long a separation is dangerous."[3] Alice's long trips abroad justified his actions—at least in his mind.

Henry accurately portrays Alice as someone who was much loved and respected across the world. But his opinions on how Alice contributed to her generation border on the hyperbole. According to Henry, Alice's column from the suffragette years, "Are Women People," and her speeches on the subject influenced the suffragette movement so much that she was instrumental in women finally getting the vote. He later claims that Alice was paid more per word for her magazine fiction than any other American author, and that her simple and unaffected style influenced the modern writing movement.[4]

When the book was released, many critics were kind but some were not. The *New York Times* review stated that Henry wrote *All Our Lives* with a "rapt fervor…. In consequence, his wife stands out with the definition and conspicuousness of a statue on a mountain top. The background is pretty much of a void."[5]

There is nothing in Daisy's records of what she thought of Henry's book. She still saw Henry on occasion in 1945, mentioning later that they would go to the movies. Whatever Henry said, or omitted, in *All Our Lives* didn't seem to create any kind of breach in the current status of their relationship.

After the book was published, Audrey Frazier, a professor at a small college in Missouri, became intrigued with Henry after reading his book. She apparently knew of his connection to the Kinnelon area because, while visiting friends in the Boonton area, Audrey managed to arrange a meeting with Henry at a dinner party. When she made her admiration for both his book and Alice's career very clear, Henry was intrigued. A romance began.

In May of the next year, Henry's cat, Buzzie, who had been living with Daisy and Esther, died. Knowing that Henry would want the cat buried at Botts, Nora and Esther took Buzzie's body to Henry's apartment the next day. They had not told him in advance that they were coming. When they arrived, they were in for a surprise. "Miller surprised to see me," Esther wrote. "He had woman living with him."[6]

After the end of the war, paper rationing came to an end, and publishers responded by releasing the flood gates. *Love Story* saw the competition from other romance and western romance pulp magazines rise to the point of incredulity. In 1946, there were 24 other romance pulps on the market and another 8 western romance magazines. Most, if not all, of these new love pulp magazines were in the traditional seven by ten-inch pulp magazine size, dwarfing the digest-sized *Love Story* on the newsstands. *Love Story*'s circulation undoubtedly suffered due to these changes.

By this time, the Street & Smith company had moved their main offices uptown to the Chanin Building. Daisy's office was much smaller than the past, and the beloved roll top desk was disposed of. This photograph, taken in 1954, shows Daisy in a similar type of setting (Daisy Bacon collection).

Street & Smith management came to a decision. On September 26, 1946, in what could be called a Thursday Afternoon Massacre, Grammer advised Daisy and Esther that *Love Story* and *Romantic Range* were to be shelved after the new year.[7] Daisy does not mention how she felt about the demise of *Love Story*. Still, it must have been a tremendous disappointment to see the magazine she had nurtured for so many years, that had been such a part of her identity, be shut down.

But the ceasing of *Love Story* and *Romantic Range* did not leave her and her sister without anything to do. They still had *Detective Story* to manage. In addition, since the early 1940s, they had been saddled with also issuing annual anthologies, stories that had been printed earlier in the year in their magazines. Some of these were published under what Street & Smith was calling the "All-Fiction" annuals. *Love Story* was only granted their own exclusive annual twice in this series, in 1942 and 1943. But *Detective Story* saw many of its stories reprinted, and many love stories and western romance stories from *Romantic Range* were included in the All-Fiction annuals. The end of 1946 must have been a dizzying time for the two women, as they juggled three different anthologies with very similar titles: *Detective Story Annual, All-Fiction Detective Stories,* and *All-Fiction Stories*.

Love Story Magazine, the romance magazine that would fuel an entire industry and countless imitators, would see its last days in the February 1947 issue. The cover is a photograph of a rosy-cheeked redhead with a stylish 1940s hairstyle and, in homage to the editor's favorite animal, holding a grey Persian cat. But there is nothing unusual in the issue: no good-bye announcement from the editor, no farewell notice sidebar. After twenty-six years and 1,158 issues containing over 8,000 novelettes, serials, and short stories, and countless letters appealing for advice, the final issue is a run-of-the-mill, rather dreary good-bye for a magazine that had been queen of the romance publishing industry.[8]

Grammer didn't waste any time filling the void. He forged ahead with his ongoing plan of encroaching on the women's slick magazine market. It wasn't long after *Love Story* disappeared that Street & Smith launched *Mademoiselle's Living*.

After the two romance magazines were retired, Daisy and the rest of the pulp editors were moved back to the old building on Seventh Avenue, which might have been a treat for the old stalwarts like her who preferred the good old days. But the building had been changed during the company's absence and they were now in unceremonious offices, by themselves, and isolated from the rest of the company.

Henry Wise Miller married Audrey Frazier on July 12, 1947. But Daisy was not far from Henry's mind. She noted in a diary years letter that he sent her a letter on his wedding day.

Daisy was uprooted by another change. Manhattan was experiencing a wave of housing co-op conversions on Fifth Avenue. Rent stabilization in New York was resulting in the renting of properties becoming unprofitable for landlords. Condominiums were as yet still not legal in New York State. As a result, landlords turned to converting the properties to co-ops. Long term renters who did not wish to join the "co-operative racket," as Daisy called it, were evicted. Daisy was forced to leave her beloved apartment on Fifth Avenue.

Daisy moved to Stewart Manor, a small enclave on Long Island, about five miles west of Garden City. There she experienced a winter of "big snow," in which she had to deal with the inconveniences of shoveling the driveway and bringing in the wood to heat the place.

Henry "Bill" Ralston was with the company for almost fifty years and would be there until the bitter end. Here he is in a photograph taken around 1945 (Daisy Bacon collection).

She was so incensed over being pushed out of Manhattan that she pitched the idea of writing an article about her experiences as a "Fifth Avenue Apartment Dweller," who decided to rough it in the 'burbs.' She approached Gerard Chapman of the International Press Bureau to see if he would be interested in shopping her article to the national magazines. She would write it from the viewpoint of the displaced urban dweller, having to now deal with the hardships of suburban life. While Chapman was mildly encouraging, he had his reservations, thinking that most magazine readers wouldn't be able to empathize with her plight and might think "'Piffle! Too bad about the poor rich people, having to do with three baths instead of six!' etc. etc." The two corresponded over the idea and Daisy ended up writing an article that Chapman shopped around to eleven different publications before it was dropped.[9]

Then Street & Smith moved their magazine production units, including the remaining pulp editors, to 775 Lidgerwood Avenue in Elizabeth, New Jersey. If Street & Smith staff stationed at the old building felt isolated before, this new location must have felt like Siberia.

In a letter to Chapman, Daisy complained that the commute was "killing me." She revealed that "after my R.R. fares and taxis and Income Tax, it might prove as cheap to stay home and try to write."

It seemed that the pulps that remained with the company were being, almost literally, pushed away. There were now three high-profile slick magazines targeted to women: *Mademoiselle*, *Charm*, and now *Mademoiselle's Living*. In a letter, Lester Dent wrote of meeting with Daisy in May of 1948. She was depressed over the state of the company.[10] The pulp list seemed endangered, yet she elected to remain at Street & Smith.

Saving the Superheroes

> Have you ever stopped to think what this country would be like without
> our magazines? I have often wondered and I simply cannot picture it in
> my mind for they are part of our national life.... When they were down-
> town at 27th St. and Fifth Avenue, I used to go out of my way to look at
> the cover paintings of all the magazines displayed in their many big win-
> dows. It never ceased to thrill me to see our *Love Story* covers by Modest
> Stein, W.C. Scott's famous *Western Story* covers, Coughlin's distinctive
> paintings for *Detective Story*, and those for *Sea Stories* by well-known
> marine artists.... Even when I am hurrying for a train, I never fail to take
> a quick look at the newsstands as I fly past.[1]

In June 1948, Daisy and Esther were notified that they were to be the editors of the
magazines that hosted two of the most famous heroes to come out of the pulp era: The
Shadow and Doc Savage. Both magazines had continued strongly through the 1930s and
early 1940s during the period they were edited by John Nanovic, but since his departure,
they had been subjected to a revolving door of editors. Daisy and Esther were now taking
over from William De Grouchy, who had filled in when editor Babette Rosamond was
out on maternity leave, then called in again when Rosamond came back from leave, but
only to quit very shortly afterwards. Then De Grouchy was fired; it was rumored that he
had been caught stealing from the company.[2]

All three of Daisy's charges—*Detective Story*, *Doc Savage*, and *The Shadow*—were
now digest-sized. They had limped through the war and post-war years. Daisy and Esther
were now in charge of three non-romance magazines, all of which had tremendous lega-
cies but were now on life-support.

Ever the traditionalist, Daisy lobbied Ralston to ditch the digest format for all three
of her magazines and return them to the old format most comfortable for pulp readers
with dimensions of seven inches by ten inches. In a letter that Daisy wrote to Gerard
Chapman later that year, she claimed that after the first *Shadow* issue was released in the
old format, circulation jumped twenty-five percent.[3]

The relationship between she and Lester Dent, the author of most of the Doc Savage
stories, was less than amicable. It was, as Lester Dent biographer Will Murray wrote, "the
most difficult writer/editor relationship Lester Dent ever enjoyed." Lester's wife later told
Murray that Lester believed that a woman had no place editing an adventure magazine.

Daisy herself was probably not enjoying the exchange either. The correspondence
between Lester and Daisy is a remarkable and revealing window into how she worked
with her authors. They show that Daisy was not about to pull any punches with the

author, despite his successful track record of writing stories about one of the most famous superheroes of the previous twenty years.

On July 23, 1948, Daisy sent Lester a letter notifying him of the change in editorship, and to let him know what she thought of his latest story submitted.

> Dear Les:
>
> Evidently the firm has not notified you that we have had some changes here and that Ford and I are supposed to edit *The Shadow* and *Doc Savage*. As we are returning to the pre-war size on these magazines, and has been quite a little extra work for both of us considering also the traveling. I have now been able to read "The Green Master" and although there are other things I would rather have changed, I am only going to ask you to make one change for us. In my opinion, the story is not satisfactory from about page 3 on through the hotel scene because the threads of the story do not begin to tie together there. I realize however that you can't make this change without almost doing the story over and since I presume the story was approved in outline form I will let this go. I have always tried to accept what another editor has contracted for.

She invited Lester to come and meet with her if he should happen to be in New York for the summer.[4]

Lester made the changes to "The Green Master." He then sent her an outline for the next Doc Savage story, "Miracle by Williams," but it was promptly shot back by her, accompanied by the following critique:

> Thank you for the speed on the Doc Savage outline. I am sorry not to ask you to go ahead with the story as it now stands but I don't think you have given us much to go on and tying it to the European situation is just too easy. The firm wishes to give the European situation a miss and I would rule it out myself anyway because the public is thoroughly fed up with politics and propaganda in fiction.... As long as we are dropping the science detective and returning to just Doc Savage, I think that we should return to a real adventure story....

Daisy tried to soften her message somewhat next, but somehow may have made matters worse:

> ... After saying these destructive things, I ought to come through with something more constructive but I still have not had time to get a full picture of Doc. I read the first six numbers over the week end but perhaps that was a mistake as they seem to me somewhat immature. However, I have read many character books which have been going for years and I have the idea that perhaps you feel that no editorial direction or thought has been coming your way.[5]

Daisy ended the letter with a more conciliatory tone and at the same time managed to throw in some complaints about the publisher.

> I believe we could help you in this matter but I know that letters are not very satisfactory. I also hesitate to ask for a special background because you know so much better than I do where your enthusiasm lies. We are not terrifically pressed for this story but we haven't got a lot of time either as everything was late when we got it and we have terrific production problems.

Meanwhile, Daisy was struggling with what to do with the story currently on the books to make up the Fall 1948 issue. Lester's story "In Hell, Madonna," which Daisy had inherited from De Grouchy, was on the line to be published. Lester had already run afoul of De Grouchy with respect to the title, De Grouchy telling him that it "stank a little."[6] The previous *Doc Savage* story, "Terror Wears No Shoes," had not been well received by fans, who were tired of the Red Scare theme and wanted to return to the early days of *Doc Savage*, in which realism was usurped by escapism and the imaginative fantasy of hidden worlds.

The decision was made to kill "In Hell, Madonna."

Pulp scholar Will Murray wrote later, "In Daisy Bacon's defense, she was simply being responsive to the general mood at that time. With Eastern Europe transferring into the so-called Communist Bloc, and another wartime ally, China, turning to Communism, the reading public was averse to stories focusing on the Red Scare."[7]

Rather than scramble to replace "In Hell, Madonna" for the Fall 1948 issue of *Doc Savage*, the decision was made to skip the issue altogether, and there was no Fall 1948 issue. Thirty years later, the carbon copy of the manuscript of "In Hell Madonna" would be found in Lester's papers by his widow, and Bantam Books would release it as *The Red Spider* in 1979.

Over the next several months, Lester would continually send Daisy stories, outlines and synopses for future stories, only to have most of them rejected. He sent in the reworked "Miracle by Williams," only to have her respond curtly.

> My feeling is that you certainly spread the butter too thin in "Miracle by Williams." We are doing what we can with the editing but that will not bring out something which isn't there. To get right down to brass tacks, you are turning these stories out too hurriedly and without thinking them beforehand. I am supposed to try to get these magazines back on their feet and I can't do it unless the stories are at least as good as others in the same field. If you are not prepared to spend sufficient time on one of these novels to do a good job, I want you to let me know. If you [have] prepared time to think out the story in advance and then devote time to writing it, I suggest that you start on the new one at once as you mentioned in your letter.[8]

Starting in the winter of 1949, Daisy's wish that all the pulps would return to their standard pulp size was granted, and the magazines—*Doc Savage, The Shadow*, and *Detective Story*—were all released in the prewar size.

Daisy's and Lester's relations apparently didn't improve. Lester was excited about writing Cold-War themed stories, and Daisy wanted to return to the nostalgic 1930s. They also debated story length and style of presentation. Lester, in a conciliatory attempt to appease Daisy, wrote her a long letter on December 19, 1948.

Lester Dent, author of *Doc Savage* stories that appeared in the magazine under the pseudonym Kenneth Robeson. Dent's and Daisy's professional relationship never moved much beyond "cordial at best" (photograph courtesy Will Murray).

> Dear Miss Bacon:
>
> When I was well into the outline for the Doc, I reread our correspondence concerning the previous story, and suddenly it seemed to me that I should put the outline aside and submit some story germs concisely in order to get a better conception of your feeling about what the stories should now have.[9]

He followed with three ideas for themes for the future Doc Savage, which he wanted Daisy to approve or reject based on her "experienced reactions and very good opinions." Daisy responded with her usual approach, in which she complained that Lester did not give her much to go on, but she reluctantly agreed to try with the second idea, a center-of-the-earth adventure. This story, which would end up being "Up from Earth's Center," appeared in the Summer 1949 issue and hit the newsstands on June 7, 1949.

After Lester sent his next synopsis to Daisy, she responded in a surprisingly friendlier tone that also revealed some disturbing news.

> I think you have an interesting idea for the sea story you mention in your letter although I wish I knew more about the plot. It does not matter at the minute, however, because last week we received an order to stop buying stories and art for our fiction magazines.... Naturally, we are all very much concerned ourselves and would like to know what it means.[10]

The reason would become crystal clear five days later. On April 9, 1949, the decision was made to kill four of the remaining Street & Smith pulp fiction magazines: *The Shadow, Doc Savage, Detective Story*, and *Western Story*. The only magazine that survived was the science fiction magazine *Astounding Stories*. Neither Daisy nor Esther marked anything in that specific day in their diaries, but Daisy would later mark each anniversary of the date in her diaries for years to come.

Daisy was fired, two months shy of her 52nd birthday. Even though she had twenty-three years of editing the most profitable magazine of its type and being the engineer of the veritable gravy train for the company, her experience and business acumen were not valued. She was no longer wanted. Before she left the building, she had to do the unpleasant task of notifying her authors that their pulps were discontinued.

Walter Gibson said later that he had been working steadily with Daisy on stories for *The Shadow* magazine the previous year, and the working schedule had continued without interruption. Then, he recalled, Daisy called him.

> ... she called me one day and says, "Don't start the next one; they're not going to ahead with it." Just like that.[11]

Lester Dent was in the hospital, recuperating from a suspected heart attack, when his wife Norma brought him a telegram from Daisy, telling him of the cancellation of the magazines. Lester dryly remarked, "Well, at least they waited until I was flat on my back before they broke the news." His wife never forgave Daisy for sending Lester the telegram while he was still in the hospital; Norma thought it terribly insensitive. But there's nothing to prove that Daisy did it with malice. Lester had already been notified of the company's decision to stop buying stories. Besides, Daisy may very well not have known that Lester was in the hospital.

Walter Gibson, author of *The Shadow* magazine stories, using the pseudonym Maxwell Grant. The last story appearing in *The Shadow* magazine features a Persian cat named "Washington Mews" (photograph courtesy Will Murray).

As she would remember later, it seems that the public knew about the shutting down of the pulps before anybody in the building knew:

> The *New York Times* ran a story on page 1 and a good many people who normally bought the *Herald Tribune* picked up the *Times* that morning. Thus everyone knew early in the day that we had been fired from our jobs, and with radio and television picking up the story it was pretty well established by 11 o'clock that night that our magazines have folded because they were outmoded and the publishing business had passed its peak of popularity.[12]

The *New York Times* quoted Grammer as saying that the type of fiction that Street & Smith was selling was no longer popular with readers, and television was mainly to blame. But he also hinted that the stories themselves weren't the issue; instead, it was the reprint business that drove down prices and making it hard to compete. "There has been a great change in the material offered at newsstands throughout the country," he said. "Picture books and reprints of books that normally would sell for $1.50 to $3.50 are now being made available in the millions and at low prices."[13] In addition, he thought that readers had grown tired of the pulp fiction format and were moving on. In a nutshell, Grammer threw any reason that would stick to the wall to defend the decision.

Daisy would later disagree vehemently. According to her, television wasn't the culprit—the publishers were. She thought that television was a scapegoat, and those members of the public that read magazines were certainly going to continue to do so. To her it was the management with little or no publishing experience and little "feel" for the publishing business that was to blame.

> These people—business managers, sales managers, financial analysts and whatever—were perhaps good in their own line of work, but they were not publishers nor likely candidates ever to be. They took the magazines off course into alien and uncharted waters and in the process they killed the goose that laid the golden egg.[14]

As for readers' tastes, romance magazines were not losing popularity at all. In fact, the late 1940s and early 1950s saw a proliferation of titles in circulation, more so than in the early 1940s. This proliferation could have been in response to the grand dame, *Love Story*, being discontinued in 1947. Suddenly there was a vacuum to be filled. In 1949, there were 20 romance magazines and 10 western romance magazines. In 1950, the number of western romances would jump to 13, making the grand total of 33 titles for buyers to choose from. Not until 1951 would the numbers drop drastically, and many of the leaders would hang on until 1954 and 1955. *Ranch Romances*, which started the western romance phenomenon, would last until 1971.

Daisy wasn't given the opportunity to finish out the last of *The Shadow*, *Doc Savage*, and *Detective Story* issues, which would be released in the summer of that year. That was given to Esther, who was not fired but given the task of giving the three pulps their last rites.

Esther had applied for another job at another publisher the year before, indicating that she may have known of rumblings in the office of big changes coming. But when the day finally came, Esther was the one that stayed. She would remain with the company for over another decade, working on copyrights, permissions, and other administrative tasks.

The last issue of *The Shadow* under Street & Smith was issued in the summer of 1949. The feature story, "The Whispering Eyes," was accompanied by six short stories, including "Big Boss" by Carroll John Daly. The letters column, "The Shadow Readers

Write," was full of letters from readers rejoicing the return of the "old" Shadow. The feature story, "The Whispering Eyes," features a "magnificent white half–Persian cat." Lamont Cranston gives a quick lesson in cat behavior:

> "'Intelligent creatures, cats,'" remarked Cranston. "'Less responsive in some ways than certain other animals, but far ahead in matters that concern their own world or disturb their habits. They seldom display the imitative traits that cause people to consider animals clever. You might call it indifference, but that in itself is something akin to wisdom.'"

This Persian, "eventually given the name of 'Washington Mews,'" plays a definitive role in helping The Shadow solve the crime.

> The cat began to stalk about. From the way it paused, turned to Cranston with expressive meows.... Step-by-step, the cat was retracing the course of Maresca's murderer, at the same time explaining its inability to deal with the human menace that had tried these premises. Pausing beside Maresca's body, the cat looked up, tensed for a spring, then relaxed. This time its meows were more plaintiff than before.

And, like the last issue of *Love Story*, the cover featured a cat, this one a glorious white Persian.

Daisy was a strong believer in capitalism and free markets. It wasn't too many years before, in the "stiletto heel" interview she gave to Aaron Mathieu for the "Cobbler's Child" article, that she had declared her worth was only as good as the money that she made for the company.

> "Long ago I trained myself to believe that there is no gratitude in business. If *Love Story* sold a million copies a week, a thousand weeks straight, and then dropped to 200,000 a week, do you know what my publishers would say?"
> Daisy arranged some gardenias in long green stems in a slender blue vase. "Do you think they'd say: 'Well, we're still outselling the field three to one'?"
> Daisy grinned.
> "Shucks, no. They'd say: 'Damn that Bacon woman. She lost us 800,000 sales a week. Get her out in a hurry.'"
> "Do you think that's right?" I asked.
> "If they worked any other way, somebody else would be in this building. Street & Smith would have failed years ago."
> "That's a pretty grim philosophy to carry around."
> Daisy looked at me queerly. "I don't know anyone worth his salt, who cares for his independence, who would have it any other way. I make every issue of *Love Story* the finest magazine I know how to turn out. I must, or I'm out."[15]

Daisy applied for at least one job after being fired. She interviewed for a job at the birthplace of the confession magazine, Macfadden Publications, on May 11.[16] Macfadden had ventured into the pulp field with *Ghost Stories* in the 1930s, underwriting Harold Hersey's pulp company The Good Story Magazine Company. But by the end of the 1930s Macfadden had left the pulp industry entirely. He didn't need the pulps: the confession magazine market was doing just fine and would soon enter their "Golden Age."

But Daisy either didn't take the job or she wasn't offered it. She needn't have worried about money, however (although she worried about paying taxes for the rest of her life). There's little doubt that she was given a generous severance package. She also had carefully invested her earnings through the 1930s and 1940s in the stock market, more than likely guided by a certain stockbroker named Henry Wise Miller. The value of her investments when she left Street & Smith lasted well to the end of her life: In the 1970s, her dividends alone were paying her $22,000 a year, more than double the amount the average worker was earning in wages at the time. Despite all this income, Daisy would never feel financially secure, and would continually complain about having to pay income tax.

On May 15, Esther received a late-night phone call from Daisy. Their long-time housekeeper Nora had suffered a heart attack. Nora recovered quickly, but the incident was the beginning of a ten-year deterioration in the Irish woman's health, and her relationship with Daisy began to suffer as well.

In August of 1950, Daisy wrote a check for $3,689.93 as a down payment on a house in the small province of Port Washington, Long Island, not far from the mansions on Oyster Bay, such as the Theodore Roosevelt estate. She signed a mortgage for a loan of $15,000 on the property. A few days later, she packed up her belongings and moved ten miles north to her new home.

She had plans to write a novel again. This one, which she called "Love Story Diary," would be a scandalous tell-all of the publishing firm in which she worked. She looked forward to writing about the years in which she was "Queen of the Pulps," and telling the world about the era of Street & Smith, when the company spewed out the most popular fiction magazines of its time.

Small Tributes

For the first few months in the new house, Daisy's mood was almost euphoric. The excitement of owning a new home and decorating it gave her a new purpose in life, and adding to the exhilaration was the realization that her time was her own. "If I had just 10 years left to live, I could write 5 books," she wrote on August 15, 1950. "Must do publishing, as Jerry Siegel suggested."

This last little note could have been derived from an encounter Daisy had with Jerry Siegel, one of the creators of Superman. In a separate undated memo, Daisy wrote that "In January 1950, Jerry Siegel asked me why I didn't write it all up as fiction, disguising it thinly like the [h]ucksters and get it out of my system as well as a fine job of getting even."[1]

Daisy began to keep a diary in earnest.[2] The first Christmas in the new house was so serene that she wrote that it "seemed almost too good to be true."[3] But her feelings of goodwill began to wear off after the New Year, replaced with more days of depression and hopelessness. Being out of the business world, the publishing industry with its small world of gossip and trading secrets, and the limelight of the social scene was an adjustment, even though she commented many times that she was happy to be out of that "scene."

But now she didn't have a job to go to that could keep her from dwelling on her darkest thoughts.

Daisy relaxing with two of her cats. She struggled after retiring, trying to find some kind of gratification in her writing, but depression crippled her on a regular basis (Daisy Bacon collection).

It didn't help that the dead of winter, with the cold temperatures and snow storms, limited her time outdoors. Nora, who had now been her maid since the early 1930s, stayed with her, but that relationship was deteriorating quickly.

Daisy got up, worked sometimes on "Love Story Diary," and painted the house and did odd jobs. But other days she felt overwhelmed, both by depression and by physical ailments. Pains in her stomach and headaches set her back entire days. Insomnia, nightmares, and stomach pains caused many sleepless nights. She knew that they were related to her depression, but she was unable to crawl out of the hole. She thought of Henry at "the farm," and on that day her opinion of her ex-lover was that he had married solely because of his "need to have a companion anyway."

Occasionally, she went back into Manhattan to shop, dressing in her best hat, coat, and gloves. But she couldn't go into the city without feeling a rush of confused feelings afterwards. "I had to go in to NY but it was worse than I thought it would be. Just because I managed to get along ok in Dec. I thought would be all right. What can I do? I cannot cut myself off absolutely if only I could get some solution."[4]

What she wished for, more than anything, was to be relieved of her chronic mental anguish, of being stuck between not seeing anything of value in life but powerless in being able to do anything about it. "A little better today but oh what a life to come to after my great ambitions & expectations," she wrote on March 3, 1951.

Daisy had quit drinking by this time, and she had finally become aware of how much she had suppressed her depressive state with alcohol.

[N]ot so bad until afternoon when I started to unravel knitting ... oh these awful feelings—that are what I used to try to drown in C_2H_5OH. What am I to do? Made worse listening to Hamlet.[5]

The idea of alcoholism was very much on her mind as she clipped out articles on the subject, such as "No One is Born an Alcoholic," "Does Alcohol Make You Show Your True Self?" and "Only 6% Become Alcoholics," and shoved them into her journals.

Things began to unravel in March, with see-saw days of feeling that she was on a good path, followed by days of resignation and regret. "Everything in my life is over and done with. When I had my health I thought and worked for other people & waited too long to try to work for myself."[6] Something as mundane as unraveling a knitting project could trigger despair. She marked her days with wondering why she bothered to even live, but she was still hesitant. "Suicide seems the only way out but that is what I have been doing slowly for years. So why do I hesitate to do it quickly."[7]

The depression was doing what it does best: It was closing in on her, slowly eliminating all other productive thought, turning every experience into monumental tasks until they become impossible and convincing the brain that the only cure for the crushing bleakness is for the person to end her life.

April 30, 1951, seemed to be mundane day according to her diary. She only noted that she had dreamt of "EJ and the Duke of Windsor," with "EJ" most likely the initials for Esther.

Then her diary went silent for ten days.

On May 11, she noted that it was the first time in five days that she had eaten solid food.

The next day, she noted in her diary that she "would have been dead nearly a week."

Daisy never elaborated in her diary as to exactly what happened to cause her to stop writing in her diary for ten days and to not be able to eat solid food for five. She may have been suffering from a severe stomach illness, such as a bleeding ulcer. But she never discussed having to treat any type of physical illness, and later that year she wrote, "I have had thoughts of death all day. Decided to write a note for Ford in case I have another spell so she would not be thinking of having an autopsy."[8] These notes lead to the opinion that she had attempted suicide in May.

After the incident in May, Daisy stopped writing almost completely, with only occasionally jotting down notes of bitterness and recriminations and noting that she needed to start writing "Love Story Diary" again. But she didn't act on the thought. By the end of June, she was tearing out chunks of her hair.

She felt like she couldn't even confide her troubles to the closest friend she had: her sister Esther. In November, Daisy mentioned in a phone call to Esther the troubles she was experiencing.

> … like a fool mentioned myself and how I feel which I swore I would never discuss with anyone. She made me furious when she said I had a beautiful house to live in.[9]

Esther had resorted to an all-too-common philosophy held during that time: A depressed person just needed to start counting her blessings and stop being so ungrateful.

Daisy doesn't mention seeing a psychiatrist for her depression. After a second suicide attempt, it would be hard to imagine her not seeing one. She does speak of seeing a therapist or counselor in the past, who gave her some wise advice on how drinking and depression are irrevocably entangled with each other. Later, in 1976, she was prescribed what she described as Elavel, which may have been Elavil, a medication that was approved by the FDA in 1961 to treat depression and mood disorders. She also may have been attending Alcoholics Anonymous meetings, because she mentions an "AA" convention in the Poconos.

She heard bits and pieces of Henry's life from others. He separated from his old brokerage account in the city, and later news arrived that he had converted to Catholicism, his new wife's religion. He had completely cut off ties with many in the city, but there are hints that he and Daisy kept in touch by letter.

Daisy's salvation arrived in 1952. She sat down at the typewriter one day and returned to work on "Love Story Diary," which she thought would be her opus. Her mood brightened almost immediately. She wrote daily and found satisfaction at the end of her productive days. Even when she struggled with the characters and the settings and found herself stalled, she still found the process productive and interesting. Yet she understood she needed to be mindful of the hopelessness that could descend and prevent her from working. "Now that I have started LSD I hope I can live long enough to finish."[10]

But she continued to have trouble moving forward with the story. "I should know LSD have thought these people over for 14 years," she lamented, yet still could not move forward with the book. Memory being what it is, she might have been starting to forget some of the details of her life at 79 Seventh Avenue.

At some point, Daisy made a crucial decision, and it may have saved her life. She switched gears and started on another book. This one would be nonfiction and would be called *Love Story Writer*. It would be in the spirit of the book that she and Gertrude Schalk were going to write, a simple and small how-to instruction on how to write romance short stories. She doesn't leave records on whether she consulted or reached out to Gertrude to see if she wanted to continue in the partnership with her.

After she made that decision to write *Love Story Writer*, it was as if the book wrote itself. In many ways, it did, because many passages are repeated, almost word for word, from what she had authored for some trade magazines in the 1930s and 1940s. In addition, other passages might have been derived from the work she and Gertrude were going to publish in the early 1940s.

> Love is not a part of living that can be shut off from the rest of the world. You can't split up your life and say, "this is my love life, this is my business life, this is my social life," and so on. They are all too thoroughly bound up together and depend so much on each other.[11]

Esther and Daisy's relationship was strained at this point; Daisy writes in her journals of tense phone conversations with Esther and of her sister's lack of sympathy over Daisy's depression. Esther did not know that Daisy had even written her book, *Love Story Writer,* **until it was completed (Daisy Bacon collection).**

Love Story Writer is a book that is both dated in some areas and timeless in others. The first three chapters are introduction and the relationships between writers and editors, dotted with various vignettes from Daisy's life. The last chapters give practical advice on the appearance of a manuscript and making sure margins are correct—information that may or may not be of use to the writer today. Sandwiched between the first and third parts are three chapters on the actual writing of a love story. In the chapter "Of Love, Geography, and Characters," Daisy writes sage advice on human behavior during a breakup, sounding as if she had personal experience.

> No matter what their status in the world, when an engagement is broken and there is a fuss over the diamond or emerald or ruby ring, the principals are no longer interested in good form in the polite life. All they want to know is what their rights are and what they can do—and what they must do according to law. If a wedding fails to take place at the last minute, otherwise well-bred girls and boys fail to have any regard for Emily Post about the wedding presents.[12]

Even with writing the book, depression would take over occasionally, and she was still stubbornly trying to write "Love Story Diary." On the 27th anniversary of her first day at Street & Smith, she made note of the anniversary and Henry's role in her life at that time. "Looking out dining room window thinking how HW & I used to go out at Botts at night."[13] But she kept writing, even when her stomach and back ailments bothered her.

Through the spring of 1953, she worked almost every day on *Love Story Writer*. She wrote repeatedly in her diary that she knew it was a good book and that it stood a good chance of being published. Before it was finished, she hired an agent to begin to market it to publishers. On the 11th of December, she received notice that Hermitage Press was interested in *Love Story Writer*.

Henry had become fully entrenched in retirement in the house at Botts. Eventually he donated all of the eighty acres at Kinnelon to the Catholic Church, an event that was not lost on Daisy. "I never had the chance, reading that the place was a joint gift made me realize that it was just transient—never any of it mine," she noted years later.

Henry had a stipulation though: he wanted to build on the property: A church that would be similar to the early medieval church of St. John the Baptist in Harescombe, England; a church that had captivated him while serving in World War I. At his second wife's suggestion, he would build the chapel in honor of his first wife, Alice.

Henry, by this time in his early seventies, threw himself into the design and supervising the building of the chapel. He drew up the plans himself, using his memory, books and photographs to guide him. By 1954, the chapel was completed. When Henry was given the honor of naming the chapel, he named it Our Lady of the Magnificat after Mary's Canticle in Luke 1:46–55: "My soul does magnify the Lord and my spirit rejoices in God my Savior for he who is mighty, has done great things for me."[14]

Daisy was elated when she finished the manuscript right after the new year. "Finished back of book—what a relief" she noted on January 13. The manuscript was mailed shortly afterwards and, for the next five weeks, she suffered through the painful period that all writers experience as they wait to hear from publishers as to whether the manuscript was satisfactory. For once her self-confidence wavered, as she waited for the publisher to respond to the manuscript. By February 18 she couldn't stand it any longer and phoned her agent. "No word. Trying not to worry, but 5 weeks yesterday," she wrote.

Daisy's life at this point had been one of quiet solitude. If she ever went out in the evenings, she didn't make note of it. Most of her time was spent listening to radio programs, reading, and writing. Her relationship with Esther had cooled to the point that Esther didn't know that Daisy had written a book until January 13, when the book was practically completed. Still, Daisy would dedicate *Love Story Writer* to her sister. But she used the name "Esther Joa Ford," leaving out Esther's new surname of "Robinson."

As she waited for her book to be released, Daisy was feeling more positive about her life. She arrived at the conclusion that she needed to shift her habits if she was going to be able to survive, writing on March 15, that she had "thought how much I have to do in changing to a positive attitude." Eight days later, she noted that there was "something decidedly wrong with my head." But, for the most part, the first eight months of 1954 proved to be positive for Daisy. She had a few low spots during the year, but they did not last.

The second quarter of 1954 was a flurry of activity. By August she was traveling to the city frequently to meet with her publisher and her publicity agent. Then, on August 26, 1954, her book was released, an event that she marked in her diary with a simple "My book out today."

As she waited for reviews, she noted that she had thought of nothing but the book for a long time. She felt hopeful and excited over the release of her book. Her life was productive again. Good reviews began to arrive in September, and she read every single one. They were good reviews, and she noted that one in *Newsday* was, to her, "an example of believing." She sat for several interviews. Her name was in the papers again.

Hurricane Edna approached Manhattan on September 10, and the weather was threatening to stall daily life on the east coast. Still, Daisy ventured out to the city. As the wind began to blow and rain pour, she walked past Macy's in Manhattan and was thrilled to see her book displayed in the window. She hurried home, floating, despite the pounding rain.

The morning of September 16 began like any other day. Daisy arose and, without much thought, went outside to pick up the *New York Times* that was delivered every morning. She began to leaf through the news, scanning the headlines. At twenty minutes to eight, she noticed an obituary.

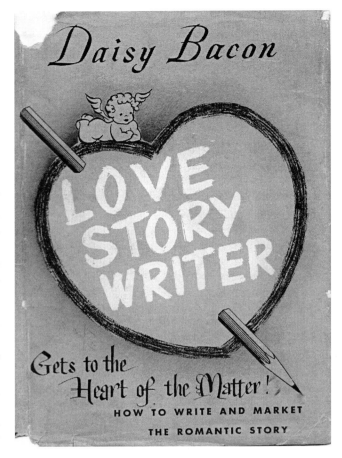

Love Story Writer was released in August of 1954. By staying occupied with writing the book, Daisy managed to keep her suicidal thoughts at bay (author's collection).

HENRY W. MILLER, STOCKBROKER, 78
Retired Senior Partner of Miller & Dodger is Dead—Decorated by Finland[15]

For the next several weeks, Daisy thought of Henry every day. When she sat down in front of the typewriter, all she could think of their evenings out on the town, when she was the top editor in the country, when writers waited on her every word, and when newspapers clamored for her opinion on the state of the "modern girl." And when she heard a familiar bird, when the autumn moon would appear, or an autumn rain softly moistened her garden, she was reminded of Kinnelon where, on a property they called Botts, her lover had built a stone house to share with her.

22

Good Enough

In all of Daisy's journals, she never mentions the word "love." Not in respects to her relationship to Henry, not towards her sister, her mother, or other friends. But she does write about her dreams, many of which featured people close to her. She writes of continually seeing Esther, her mother, and Henry in her dreams. She even dreamt of bumping into Alice in which "she bumps into my chair and then I into hers—she says 'wondered when I was going to find that (about HW?) out'."[1] She dreamt of Bill Ralston, Allen Grammer, and other characters from the building at 79 Seventh Avenue. She chronicled those dreams diligently almost every day of her retired life, and then thought of them during the day while working in the garden, painting the house, going for drives.

After *Love Story Writer* was published, Daisy struggled between days of what could be called serenity—usually when she was appreciating the nature that surrounded her neighborhood—to days when she felt as if there was no hope whatsoever. Stomach and back ailments, which she astutely attributed to her depressive moods, plagued her.

> Could not get up today. Thoughts of HW and the moonlight at Botts running through my head. Even in the worst years and on a day I couldn't move, I always had some hope. Today I have none. I am dead.[2]

Nora, who had been with her and her mother and sister since the late 1920s, became ill and, as her health deteriorated, very hostile. It didn't help that when after her health bills began to mount, Daisy contacted Nora's family and said that they should be responsible. With that, the relationship completely broke down. The last few years of Nora's life were spent arguing with Daisy, to the point that, according to Daisy on April 13, 1957, Nora threatened her with a knife, screaming because Daisy had confided in a neighbor over their difficult relationship. Still, Nora continued to live with her.

If her journals are any indication, Daisy became more depressed and more insular as the years went on. When her beloved cat Pearl died in 1958 after suffering from either an accident or a horrific attack in which her back was broken, Daisy grieved intensely for months, and her depressive nature seems to have completely taken over. Yet, one more time, she made it through, and there were even times when she could look at her life more rationally.

> All those years I courted death I didn't care and now when I have nothing left, I don't want to lose my life—can you beat it?[3]

In August of 1959, another chapter in her life ended when Street & Smith announced that all its assets were sold to the Condé Nast Publications for three and a half million dollars. In addition to some of its slick magazines, the company had developed a solid line of sports journals and yearbooks and, under the Condé Nast umbrella, would continue with that media for decades to follow. The one surviving pulp magazine, the science fiction publication *Astounding*, had been converted to a digest in 1943 and continued as a Condé Nast magazine, with several changes in format, under the name *Analog* until 1980, when it was sold to Davis Publications. John W. Campbell, Jr., who had edited the magazine since 1937, stayed as its editor until the end of 1971. *Analog* continues as a science fiction magazine today.

The shutting up of the Street & Smith shop took many months. Esther sent Daisy a letter in October 1961, in the form of a thank you note after Daisy had given her stock for her birthday. Esther took the opportunity to give her sister a summary of what was happening during the last of the Street & Smith days, including layoffs of long-time employees.

> … Mrs. Cronin, the telephone operator, called me Friday to say goodbye and she said that Dick Burns (he works as an accountant for Kaiser) told her he & the rest of them would be through by the [end of the] year or the early part of next, and, then, of course, he is finished too.
>
> They closed the 57 St office at 2 o'clock Friday and started moving then & all week end. Today was a mess with the phones. The telephone man was at 45 St. Friday + changed all the phones over to

Ever the social butterfly, Esther mingles in the foreground at an office dinner while sister Daisy watches from the right. Street & Smith would turn over all of their offices to Condé Nast in 1961 (Daisy Bacon collection).

Condé Nast & changed all the extensions, too. When you want to call anyone in the office, you don't tell the operator, you dial their extension. The only thing, at 45 St. we don't know anyone's extension number. That, of course, does away with having phone operators.

... Nobody's said a word to me, yet, so I don't know where I stand. I suppose after they are settled at 420, Campbell will begin on 45th St.[4]

"Love Story Diary," the work that would be the tell-all, the work that she had dedicated most of the early 1950s to and was to be her "opus," would remain a work in progress for the rest of her life and would never be published. In a publicity interview, Daisy admitted that she was still working on it. The manuscript was eventually lost or destroyed.

In the same interview, Daisy once again used the opportunity to voice her opinions of the state of women in society.

For the past years, men have more or less continued with their own work whereas the women have had to do everybody's work—and like it. They have to be chauffeurs and cooks besides holding down a paying job and through it all, they have to keep their sense of humor.[5]

But despite her ill health and depressive moods, Daisy managed to take control of her affairs in ways that many women during that time would not have attempted. In 1963, Daisy regained the copyrights to *Love Story Writer*. She then established her own publishing business, Gemini Books, and under that business name, republished it as a paperback under the more apt title, *Love Story Editor*.

She also took on the University of Chicago Press in 1965 when it was discovered that they were using an imprint named Gemini Books. Daisy and her attorney successfully pounced on the press, and a few months later, UCP agreed to stop using the name.

In their later years, Daisy and Esther became close again. Sometime after Clark died in 1962, Esther moved in with Daisy. Nora died in 1964. Afterwards, two women managed with help that came in, rather than a live-in maid.

Daisy still thought of Henry frequently and wrote in her journals when certain incidents would trigger memories, such as when she wrote in 1957 that she "found an old pocketbook which had a

Daisy still went into New York on a regular basis, always dressing up with mink coat, hat, and gloves before venturing out. Bus drivers, not used to seeing such formality get on board their coaches, would ask her if she was going to church (Daisy Bacon collection).

lipstick HW bought me—I didn't even use lipstick when I met him." As late as 1972, she still had "[i]mages of Botts on and off all day." She picked up and read *All Our Lives* a few times over the next several years.

Daisy and Esther spent the next several years in obscurity. New neighbors on one side, William and Nora Haagenson, kept a close eye on the two women. Nora would see Daisy venture outside occasionally, but she would hide behind her trees rather than having to interact with neighbors. One year they received a Christmas card from Daisy. In her usual sunshine-be-damned outlook, she comments in the card of how terrible it was that neighbors were cutting down their lovely trees.

At the age of 77, thirty-seven years after her arguments with Allen Grammer began, Daisy finally got in the last word. Grammer had died in 1969. Seven years later, Daisy wrote "The Golden Age of the Iron Maiden," which was printed in *Roundup Magazine*, the official publication of the Western Writers of America, in 1975. She uses the article to look back when Grammer arrived at the company, the changes he made, and the reasons behind why Street & Smith ceased the publication of fiction magazines. She also hints at why she never finished "Love Story Diary," saying she was "foolishly dissuaded" from finishing it. But she doesn't mention the guilty party who suggested she stop writing.

Two years later, Daisy wrote a few letters to John Dinan, who was collecting material for his yet-to-be published book, *The Pulp Western*. Apparently, he was looking for material or information from Daisy on her days as editor of *Romantic Range*. "I still have copies of *Romantic Range* and since you wrote to me I have read a few issues. I was surprised how well the stories read after so many years." She also proudly noted that not long before, she had judged a western novel contest. "It was a very big contest," she reported, "and I felt that the writers in the western field were doing a much better job than in the detective line."[6] Two years later, Daisy wrote to Dinan again. She had broken her hip and was unable to do much in her recuperation.

The pulps had been long gone by then. Slowly a resurgence in interest in the history of the pulp fiction magazines began, with a few publications of memoirs such as Frank Gruber's *The Pulp Jungle* and histories such as Tony Goodstone's *The Pulps*. In addition, several universities and libraries began concerted efforts to build collections of the magazines. Yet, the romance pulp which were, along with the westerns, the most popular of the magazines, would be overshadowed in almost every study of pulp fiction magazines.

In 1986, Elaine Knowlden answered an ad for work as a live-in aid. Her first assignment was to look after two women in the Baxter Estates neighborhood in Port Washington. Caretakers had come and gone since Nora died, so for the most part the two women were taken care of. But no one had been seen going in and out of the house for a while, and neighbors had called Home Health Care Services when they hadn't seen either of the two elderly sisters for many days, and Elaine was sent to be their new caretaker

Elaine opened the front door and found that she had to find a pathway through a house in which was packed from floor to ceiling with paperwork, boxes, sacks full of mail, and piles of books. She found Esther, the younger of the two sisters, living on the main floor, unable to move much because of her bad knees.

After Elaine checked on Esther, she asked her about the other woman who supposedly lived in the house. Her half-sister lived upstairs, Esther told her, and had been bedridden for many years. Esther proceeded to tell Elaine something incredible: Because of Esther's inability to climb the stairs, and her sister's bedridden condition that could only be tended to by trained caretakers, the two hadn't seen each other in five years.

On her way to the staircase, Elaine noticed that the stairwell had an odd-looking wallpaper. She looked closely. The wallpaper wasn't wallpaper *per se*; rather, it consisted of *Love Story Magazine* covers pasted on the wall.

In the main bedroom upstairs at the right of the top of the stairs, Elaine found Esther's sister in her room, lying in bed. Elaine took inventory. The woman had bed sores, cradle cap, and probably didn't weigh over 80 pounds. The woman didn't speak to Elaine; she simply looked at her with large luminous eyes that had remained unchanged for eighty-eight years.

Once Elaine got settled, she concentrated on getting the elderly woman to the bath tub. The woman stiffened when Elaine gently picked her up and carried to the bathroom. When the warm water began to fill the tub, the woman looked at Elaine and her eyes softened. She began to relax.

Over the next few months, Elaine began to get to know the story behind these two sisters. Esther loved to talk, so learning of their history was easy. Elaine was regaled of stories of a glamorous time of living on Fifth Avenue, fur coats, days at Saratoga race track and nights at Sardis restaurant and theaters.

And she loved to talk about her sister.

Daisy Bacon had been the editor, and Esther her associate, of a famous magazine during the 1930s and 1940s, *Love Story Magazine*, she told her. It was the biggest selling magazine of its kind. Every single week, from 1921 until 1947, *Love Story* was shipped to every corner of the country, promising 160 pages of romance and happy endings to hundreds of thousands of readers for a dime. It was known for its quality of stories, unlike other pulp magazines, and stories that always had happy endings.

"They called her the Queen of the Pulps," Esther said.

Esther talked of how Daisy had nurtured and mentored dozens of many writers, many of whom had gone on to have books published. She showed Elaine the many books in the built-in bookshelves with inscriptions.

> To Daisy Bacon—who has been a powerful influence in so many careers!

> January 12, 1965. Dear Miss Bacon: this is a little late, but I've never forgotten how much I owe to your early criticism. Should have sent you copies of the other one too. This is not a good suspense novel, but it is a pretty honest story. Best wishes Winfred Van Atta.

> For my friend Daisy Bacon. New York City September 3–31. Chapter 10 isn't bad; chapter 13 with its Salvation Army incident has a bit of color in it, and I do like the march of the toys across the counter pane in the following one.

Esther told Elaine of Daisy's lover, a man named Henry Miller, who had been married to a famous writer but who had built a house for Daisy in the woods.

On March 25, 1986, Elaine left Daisy to sleep so she could attend to other work in the house. After a short while, she went back upstairs to find that Daisy had died.

Daisy was buried at the local cemetery in Port Washington with little fanfare, in a plot with a simple flat headstone. She did merit an obituary in the *New York Times*.

> Daisy Bacon, a writer and for many years an editor for the now-defunct *Love Story Magazine*, died Tuesday at her home in Port Washington, L.I. She was 87 years old.
> Miss Bacon became editor of *Love Story Magazine*, one of the first women weeklies, in January 1928 and remained in the post 22 years before retiring to devote herself exclusively to writing.... She also edited other publications for Street & Smith, the magazine's publisher, including *Smart Love Stories, Detective Stories* and *Doc Savage,* an early science-fiction magazine.

> Miss Bacon was the author of short stories and several books, including the best-selling "*Love Story Writer*," a book on how to write love stories, published in 1953.
> She is survived by a half-sister, Esther Ford Robinson of Port Washington.[7]

While the obit has several errors, at least she was given credit for some of the magazines she edited through her career. The fact that they identified *Love Story Writer* as "best-selling" would have pleased her immensely, even though the article erroneously uses 1953 as the year it was released.

Esther lived another three years. When she died, she was interred next to Clarke at Arlington National Cemetery. Interestingly, her name on her tombstone is simply "Esther Ford, his wife." In death, as in life, Esther was always content to stay in the background.

In 1991, a local Port Washington attorney stood up at the local high school commencement program. Harry Mulry cleared his throat and began to speak. He was there to introduce the Daisy Bacon Scholarship Fund.

> Even more than I have been asked the question "Have I won?" people have been inquiring: "Who is or was Daisy Bacon?" A quiet, unassuming lady who lived in Baxter Estates since the 1940s until her death two years ago, Daisy Bacon was a famous writer. She served as the editor of *Love Story Magazine,* which was the forerunner of all love and romance magazines appearing on newsstands today.
> ... Daisy Bacon was an anachronism, a successful businesswoman before most people understood that such a term existed.

Since 1991, over 250 students have benefited from the Daisy Bacon Scholarship Fund.

Epilogue

I was lost. No question about it. Google Maps had failed me. I was nowhere near what I thought was a highway. Being from Los Angeles, I needed four-lane freeways, overpass exit signs, and civilized street lamps to get my bearings. Driving dark roads—through dense woods with the threat of deer leaping onto the road out of nowhere while impatient tailgaters hugged my bumper—was not. Still, I had to keep driving. I had to get to my destination, one way or another: The mysterious spot known as "Botts."

When I first began to read Daisy's diaries, I had noticed that a certain word kept appearing.

soft rain like so many nights at house in Jersey and at Botts

Last time I was at Botts in Nov. was '39

Sometimes the word shows up several days in a row in her journals. She thinks of Botts when the wind brushes through her trees at night, or when there's a full moon. Blustery winters were "wild & cold, like so many at Botts." All of the journal entries seem to be related to her memories of Henry. Henry, I realized, was intrinsically related to this Botts in some way.

Botts was with her when she dropped off to sleep, when she picked up a book. She thinks of it when she is on Fourth Avenue in New York one day. In 1963, she marks the 23rd year since the last time she had seen it.

What the heck was Botts? A town? A hotel? A lake? A farm? A figment of her imagination?

For several weeks after obtaining Daisy's papers, I looked without success. I looked at every single piece of browned, fragile torn pieces of newspaper that she shoved into her diaries. I studied the photos, chased down the return addresses on empty envelopes and letterheads on correspondence. Nothing. I searched Botts on Google Maps in New York and New Jersey, and the only hit was a Botts Mine in Morris County, New Jersey. There was nothing to indicate there was anything else in the area.

Esther mentions many times in her journals that Daisy went to "the country" on the weekends, many times with Henry to "the farm." Was this Botts? I suspected that the farm, or the country, that her mother and sister noted in their journals, was Botts. But where was it? Nothing on the Internet seemed to help at all. I surrendered and concluded that it was one of the mysteries of her life I'd never be able to solve.

Then, one evening, I realized with some chagrin that even though I had researched Henry's name on Newspapers.com and other data sources like Ancestry.com, I had never done a straightforward Internet search on "Henry Wise Miller." I hurriedly and rather furtively type his name in, almost hoping I wouldn't find anything that would show how stupid I was for not searching for it before a title of a blog popped up.

The Smoke Rise and Kinnelon Blog:
The Land Where the Smoke Rises—In and Around Kinnelon, NJ.

The blog post, posted in 2011, is a tour of a chapel on the property of the Catholic Church in Kinnelon, New Jersey, where the Our Lady of the Magnificat church was built. "It was named after the gospel of St. Luke, "My soul doth magnify the Lord," by Henry Wise Miller, who donated the Chapel buildings and land to the Diocese of Paterson of '54," the writer explained.[1]

So, Henry had donated property to the Catholic Church. That was a beginning. And there was something about it that made me feel that this was what I was looking for.

I meandered around on a Google map for a while. The town of Kinnelon appeared to be in western New Jersey, quite a drive from New York City. I zoomed in on the map. The Our Lady of the Magnificat church is located on Miller Road, undoubtedly named for Henry for his generosity. I followed Miller Road until it stops at what appears to be a forest called Pyramid Mountain. Nothing there gave me any clues.

I then found a Boonton Road that travels almost parallel to Miller Road. I followed Boonton Road, a long winding road, until another road, High Mountain Road, that travels off of Boonton Road.

I looked at the area around High Mountain Road.

There it was.

"Botts Pond."

Now, I was on my way to Kinnelon. I wanted to see Botts: the place that Daisy had cherished.

As I drove into Kinnelon, I saw clues of what must have been the magic that Daisy dreamed and thought of for decades after her last visit: Blue jays, woodpeckers, maples, beeches, oaks, floors of forest covered with ferns. A blue heron hugged the shore of a small lake, carefully gliding out of sight by the time I recognized it. I turned off Kinnelon Road on to Fayson Lakes Road, and the road becomes even darker with the canopy of trees draping over the road.

During the 1920s, this period became a popular place for well-to-do people to escape the city. Henry was one of these people. I passed a reservoir that bookends both sides of the road, a reservoir that was not here in 1930.

I drove by the area that showed up on the map as Botts Pond. But there was nothing to indicate a pond, nor any body of water, on the street. Nothing but large, expensive homes on a quiet street. I didn't expect to find anything there that would help me; something told me that the property that he donated to the Catholic Church was the key to what I was looking for.

I turned back to Fayson Lakes Road and made a right on to Miller Road.

Daisy's legacy as a successful businesswoman has largely been forgotten. Her megaphone to the world at large, the newspaper interviews and magazine articles in which she sneaked in her philosophies on what the businesswoman of the 1930s had to put up with, can only be found on digital newspaper databases now. The hundreds of writers that were helped by Daisy's feedback and mentoring over her twenty-year career have scattered, most of them dead now. I like to think that being published in *Love Story Magazine* influenced them in some way.

There has always been a great deal of discussion over the demise of the pulps and the reasons behind it. Was it the rise of comic books? More and more television sets appearing in homes? The paperback novel? The love of the rebellion of reading a pulp underneath the covers with a flashlight? The debate continues, but more than likely it was a combination of all of these to some extent.

As for romance pulps, the reasons become a little bit more muddied and even somewhat mysterious. By the end of 1949, 20 general romance pulps and 10 western romance pulps had appeared on shelves at least at some point during that year. At the same time, the romance comic book was experiencing a manic—albeit temporary—growth in numbers. Michelle Nolan vividly describes the scene in *Love on the Racks: A History of American Romance Comics*:

> Love on the racks took a long time to bloom. Then the comic book creators, editors and publishers, the vast majority of them male, and the romance readers of America, the vast majority female, went love crazy. Stark, raving crazy…. Never before, and never again, did a single genre of the comic book—an original American commercial concept—explode in such an orgy of financial opportunism.[2]

But romance pulps held their ground, and 1950 was just as strongly represented by them as was 1949. *Love Story* even experienced a resurrection, when Popular Publications bought the title from Street & Smith and re-released it as a bimonthly magazine in 1952. But then confession magazines began to experience what would become their golden age in the 1950s, and the reader who previously was happy reading a genteel, wholesome *Love Story* novelette may have wanted something a little more titillating. Romance pulps suddenly declined at a harrowing speed. *Love Story* died a second death in 1954.

As for the paperback romance novel that became the mainstream means of delivering the romance story we know today, they didn't really begin to gain ground until the 1960s, when Ace began to publish more romance titles and Harlequin switched to focus exclusively on the romance story.

Looking at television in the blame game is a more esoteric exercise. Early on, television was blamed for juvenile delinquency (but then so were comic books and pulp magazines!), the decline of reading in general, and basically the fall of western civilization. Throw it into the mix of the demise of the romance pulp, and I'm sure that eventually it had its influence, but it's my opinion that it was minimal. Like Daisy said, readers will continue to read. The entertainment that a reader experiences reading a print book, especially a romance set in historical or even modern times, for some unexplained reason cannot be duplicated on a television screen.

In addition, it's feasible that many readers wanted to move away from pulp magazines, as they reminded them of a time that for many was a difficult period. Pulp magazines were definitely icons of the Great Depression and World War II.

Regardless of the reasons, it can't be denied that the romance pulp magazine certainly made American publishers sit up and pay attention to a specific theory: The appetite for the love story, in whatever format that is the flavor of the day, seems to be insatiable.

Some authors—and this is a very incomplete list—who wrote for the romance pulps who went on to have successful careers writing romance novels, or were writing novels simultaneously with their pulp stories are Emilie Loring, Maysie Grieg, Phyllis Gordon Demarest, Erolie Pearl Gaddis Dern (writing under the names Peggy Gaddis and Peggy Dern), Dorothy Daniels, Marcia Davenport, Hebe Elsna, Ethel Dell, Thomas Dixon, Mary

Roberts Rinehart, Denise Robins, Inez Sabastian, L.M. Montgomery, Helen Ahern, Mabel Winifred Knowles, and May Wynne.[3]

I know of at least one instance in which a real-life romance bloomed from the pages of one of Daisy's magazines. As this book was going to print, I was contacted by Lori Biederman, who was looking for a particular issue of *Romantic Range*. Her grandmother, a 23-year-old "redhead from Oklahoma," named Kay Hines, had her request for pen pals listed in the magazine's pen pal column sometime between August 1940 and September 1941. A twenty-five year old soldier stationed in South Carolina, Carl "Joe" Biederman, wrote Kay a letter in March of 1942 in response to the pen pal column. Kay eventually moved to South Carolina and in 1945, the two were married. Eventually relocating to Saint Peter, Minnesota, they were married 43 years until Kay's death in 1988.

I also learned of an interesting outcome of one particular artifact, the Packard automobile Daisy and Esther bought in 1933. A few years ago, the Packard's current owner, Alexis Francois-Poncet, contacted me and provided the chain of title. The Packard is now in France. A photograph of the car shows it looking as if it had just been driven off the showroom floor.

One of the most visible remainders of the pulp fiction era has been the art that adorned the magazine covers. While many of it has been permanently lost—there are anecdotal stories of some publishers, cleaning out their offices, leaving the art work out at the curb to be picked up with the garbage—a small portion has been saved, collected, and protected. Much of it can gain hefty prices at auctions and private sales. Dozens of books have been published celebrating the art.

As for Modest Stein, he went on to have a quiet career in portraiture. He had carved a bronze plaque for Emma Goldman's monument when she was buried in Chicago in 1940, and in 1958 he was awarded the Art League of Long Island Portraiture Prize. On February 26, 1958, two days after receiving that prize, he died in a hospital in Flushing, Queens.

One of Stein's biggest fans was Daisy Bacon. At the time of her death, she owned at least three Modest Stein pieces. I am the proud owner of one of those pieces now, given to me by Elaine Knowlden, who inherited the piece after Daisy and Esther died. I love the piece, especially because it has a marked alteration—the man's head has been replaced. More than likely, Daisy, being the perfectionist she was, didn't like Stein's first version of the piece. Being under tight production deadlines, Stein simply replaced the head rather than redo the entire piece. It was featured on the September 5, 1936, cover of *Love Story Magazine*. To me, it represents the best of romance pulp art: a lovely woman; a tall, dark, and handsome hero; and three puppies to boot.

Now driving up Miller Road, my car climbed up short steep hill before flattening out, and the dense trees that canopied the road fell away to broad lawns. I looked to the left. An imposing Catholic church with a front edifice made of glass towered through the trees. This was the property that Henry Miller had donated to the Catholic Church in the early 1950s. I then turned my attention to the right side of the road.

There, set back from the road, was Henry's chapel that he designed and saw to its completion before he died. It is a simple stone building embraced by large shrubs on each side that have almost reached the roof. It is so small and simple that drivers passing by could have easily missed it.

I got out of the car and walked slowly around the front of the chapel. As I reached the back of the building, I stopped. A small road followed down a gentle slope behind the chapel. At the bottom of the road, I saw what I had traveled 3,000 miles to see.

The original Modest Stein painting used for the September 5, 1936, now in the home of the author. You can plainly see that the man's head had been replaced (author collection).

The house at Botts, now the office and residence of the diocese of the Our Lady of the Magnificat Catholic parish (author collection).

It was the house. I had no doubt in my mind.

It is a small cottage resting in the middle of the small meadow, made of stone, with large, leaded windows and red shutters. The stone path that bordered the house is the same path that appears in many of Daisy's photographs.

The house is dwarfed by two enormous English birch trees that straddle the front pathway to the front door. They are Alice's trees, almost a hundred years old now. They are immense and cover the entire front lawn with their shade.

I returned to the parking lot. There I met Roger Huss, a local historian, who had been kind enough to contact me and arrange a visit with the monsignor of the church, Monsignor Carroll.

I was more than a little nervous. After all, I was going to write about the man whose generosity basically changed their parish forever. And here I would be exposing him as an adulterer. My book would be told around the life of his mistress. Yet, Monsignor Carroll graciously offered to take me on a tour of the chapel. They are very proud of this gift from Henry Miller.

We traded notes on what we knew about Henry Miller and the land. Roger told me the meaning behind the name "Botts": There was a family with the surname of Botts who had lived adjacent to Henry's property and probably at one time had owned the property.

Monsignor Carroll, Roger, and I toured the chapel. The interior was cool, dark and serene, with burnished mahogany pews, stone floors, and cathedral ceilings. It is purposely spartan, following the design of its inspiration. The walls and floors are a golden stone, the walls sixteen-inches thick.

Outside the entry, a bronze plaque reads:

IN LOVING MEMORY
HENRY WISE MILLER
1875–1954
BY WHOSE LOVE, LABOR AND GENEROSITY
THIS CHAPEL WAS ERECTED.
R.I.P.

The chapel had been completed on July 2, 1954, and Henry's funeral mass was the first one celebrated in the new chapel.

Henry had ended up building two more cottages on the property; one for Audrey's parents and, later, another residence. There is some confusion as to whether Henry built the main home first or secondary home set back in the clearing. But judging from the photographs in Daisy's collection, I was convinced that the main home, the home which is now the residence for the church staff, was the home that Henry and Daisy shared.

I had resigned myself to being only able to see the exterior of that house. It was now the residence for the Monsignor, a private home. I was floored when he invited me to take a tour of some of the interior.

It was exactly as I imagined it. To the left of the entryway was the living room with a large stone fireplace as the centerpiece. Gleaming apple wood paneling and leaded windows with diamond-shaped pattern. The pictures that adorned the walls, with nautical themes and of racehorses, the oriental rugs, wingback chairs, sofas—all of it could have been here in the 1930s. I could see Daisy and Henry relaxing in the wing-back chairs, next to the fireplace, listening to the radio.

As we left the house, I asked a question, the answer to which had been eluding me for some time.

"Do you know if Henry left any papers behind?" I asked him as we finished the tour.

"Unfortunately, from what I know, he had left some papers. But they had been stored in the other house. Unfortunately, there had been a rain or some flooding, and all of the paperwork was damaged beyond repair."

He paused. "It was a shame, because he knew a lot of very famous people. All of that correspondence is gone."

Including any letters from Daisy, I thought.

Viewing the property helped me to see Henry as a generous, caring man who donated this magical piece of property for the betterment of a community. But I couldn't help but think that Daisy would be seen in a different light here. She wouldn't be the head of a powerhouse publication, nor the darling of newspaper interviews. Daisy, at least on this property, would be known as "the other woman."

The next day, I traveled to New York City. I sat down in the archives in Barnard College and studied Alice Duer Miller's personal papers. I was particularly interested in a group of letters in the collection: letters written by Alice to Henry. As I read them, I began to have a cold feeling in my stomach, a feeling that almost turned to nausea.

Daisy is never mentioned in any of her letters to Henry.

Was I totally wrong in assuming that Henry and Daisy were in a relationship? I had to sit down and sort it out. All the documentation I had from Daisy's papers, and Henry's hints of his unfaithful nature in *All Our Lives*, the photographs—both the mirror images and the photos of the two of them together—and all of the journals notes by Daisy,

Esther's and Jessie's journals, of Henry's name, of his initials, of Daisy's dreams of Alice, of getting a letter from their son. All of it is compelling evidence.

In addition, the letters from Alice to Henry in the collection is a very small collection—under twenty letters—which is a very small number considering that they were married for over forty years and Alice was a prolific letter writer. Her trips abroad did not prevent her from writing to Henry sometimes on a daily basis. It made me suspect that Henry culled letters from the collection before donating it.

But there isn't any discussion of Daisy in Alice's letters to Alexander Woollcott in his personal paper collection at Harvard University, either.

Perhaps Alice felt that Daisy wasn't worth a mention in her letters. Perhaps she was in denial. Perhaps she really didn't know about Daisy, which I found to be very doubtful. Finally, I could not rule out the fact that Alice, Henry, Daisy—all of these people—lived in a period before the confessional, tell-all culture that emerged after the sexual revolution of the 1960s. Alice and most of her upper-class friends were brought up in a world where marital discord and affairs were not discussed in polite society. And, as it was discussed before, she and Henry lived separate lives, but lives that would intersect in times of crisis.

After Henry died, his second wife Audrey eventually moved away from Botts and remarried. Henry and Alice's son Denning died in 1981, in Florida, a long way away from the mountain in Vermont, and his wife Alison died in Vermont a few years later. There are no indications that they had children.

On my last day in Kinnelon, I had to make one more stop before heading home. When I had originally searched for the Botts property on the Google map so many months before, something else had shown up on the map that I couldn't believe was true. I had to see it for myself.

Daisy Court is roughly a half-mile from the Botts house (author collection).

I turned up Miller Road and drove past the chapel. Shortly after the church property, the area becomes residential again, full of well-to-do homes, most of them built in the last thirty years.

I drove slowly, taking in the large homes on either side of the road.

Just a half mile from the cottage at Botts, I stopped at the entrance of a cul-de-sac and got out to look at the street sign. I took a photo.

The name of the cul-de-sac is Daisy Court.

Chapter Notes

Chapter 1

1. Aron Mathieu, "Cobbler's Child," *Writer's Yearbook*, 1941.
2. Daisy Bacon, *Love Story Writer* (New York: Hermitage House, 1954; Bold Venture Press, 2016), 136. Citations are to the 1954 edition.

Chapter 2

1. Alvia H. Goldstein, "Pulp Magazine Cupid," *St. Louis Post Dispatch*, November 1, 1942, 2G.
2. Kathleen Crocker and Jane Currie, *Images of America: Westfield* (Charleston, SC: Arcadia Publishing, 2006), 24.
3. Kathleen Crocker and Jane Currie, *Images of America: Chautauqua Lake Region* (Charleston, SC: Arcadia Publishing, 2002), 106–107.
4. "Wedding Bells," *Westfield Republican*, January 4, 1888.
5. Goldstein, "Pulp Magazine Cupid."
6. Daisy Bacon, *Love Story Writer*, 32.
7. *Ibid.*, 32.
8. "Invalid's Hotel and Surgical Institute," *Invalid's Hotel Booklet*, reproduced by Mike Joki, undated, author collection; "Pierce Building," *Buffalo as an Architectural Museum web site*, http://buffaloah.com/a/main/651/index.html.
9. Elmer E. Bacon, letter to Jessie Bacon, November 6, 1899.
10. "Obituary," *Westfield Republican*, January 10, 1900, 8.
11. Pauline H. Bush, "History of Barcelona; Its People," Patterson Library, Westfield, New York, 1.
12. Virginia Lee, "Love Stories Must Mirror Life," *The Author & Journalist*, April 1934.
13. Jessie H. Bacone [sic], "The Child's Lament Song," 1903.
14. "Volunteer Captain Won by Faith Curists," *The Evening Telegram*, January 7, 1898.
15. "Bridgeton Pastor Suddenly Leaves," *The Philadelphia Inquirer*, June 27, 1901, 1; "A Pastor Gone Wrong," *The Daily Palladium*, June 28, 1901; "Back to Bridgeton to Live Down Scandal," *The Call*, July 4, 1901.
16. "David Bacon Killed," *Westfield Republican*, October 21, 1908, 1.
17. "A Summons to the Colors," *Westfield Republican,* June 27, 1917, 2.

Chapter 3

1. Daisy Bacon, Notes to Lionel Houser, Autobiographical Notes, 1.
2. "605 Lexington Avenue, Cross Streets 53rd and 54th St." Folder 20, picture 1, New York Historical Society Photograph Collection.
3. Ted Widmer, "The Other Gettysburg Address," *New York Times*, online edition, November 19, 2013.
4. Henry Wise Miller, *All Our Lives* (New York: Coward—McCann, Inc., 1945), 23.
5. *Ibid.*, 98.
6. *Ibid.*, 108.
7. *Ibid.*, 100.
8. *Ibid.*, 100.
9. *Ibid.*, 103–105.
10. Jessie Ford, diary entry, July 30, 1923.
11. *Ibid.*, September 3, 1923.
12. Daisy Bacon, diary entry, November 25, 1957.

Chapter 4

1. Quentin Reynolds, *The Fiction Factory* (New York: Random House, 1955), 18.
2. John Tebbel and Mary Ellen Zuckerman, *The Magazine in America: 1741–1990* (New York: Oxford, 1991), 27, 29.
3. Mary Ellen Zuckerman, *A History of Popular Women's Magazines in the United States, 1792–1995* (Westport, CT: Greenwood Press, 1998), 5, 11, 15.
4. Michael Denning, *Mechanic Accents: Dime Novels and Working-Class Culture in America* (New York: Verso, 1998), 193.
5. Reynolds, *Fiction Factory*, 38.
6. "Bertha M. Clay," *American Women's Dime Novel Project,* http://chnm.gmu.edu/dimenovels/the-american-womens-dime-novel.
7. J. Randolph Cox, *The Dime Novel Companion* (Westport, CT: Greenwood Press, 2000), 170–174.
8. Denning, *Mechanic Accents*, 10–12.
9. Sam Moskowitz, *Under the Moons of Mars: A History and Anthology of "The Scientific Romance" of the Munsey Magazines, 1912–1920* (New York: Holt, Rinehart, and Winston, 1970), 304.
10. Jeff Kisseloff, *You Must Remember This: An Oral History of Manhattan from the 1890s to World War II* (Baltimore: Johns Hopkins University Press, 1989), 489, 480.

11. *Ibid.*, 483.

12. Reynolds, *Fiction Factory*, 156.

Chapter 5

1. Reynolds, *Fiction Factory*, 195.

2. *Ibid.*, 195.

3. John Bakeless, *Magazine Making* (New York: The Viking Press, 1931), 36.

4. Theodore Peterson, *Magazines in the Twentieth Century* (Urbana: University of Illinois Press, 1964), 294.

5. Amita Fairgrieve, *Smith Alumnae Quarterly*, Volume XII, May 1921, 254.

6. *Ibid.*; "Alumnae Notes, Class News," *Smith Alumnae Quarterly*, Volume XIII, November 1921, 84.

7. "Love Story Notes," *Love Story Magazine*, April 18, 1942, 5.

8. Fairgrieve, *Smith Alumnae Quarterly*, Volume XIII.

9. Graham Law, Gregory Drozdz, and Debby McNally, eds., *Charlotte M. Brame (1836–1884): Towards a Primary Bibliography* (Canterbury: Canterbury Christ Church University, 2011), 45.

10. "Over the Editors Desk," *Love Story Magazine*, August 1921, 141.

11. Reynolds, *Fiction Factory*, 197.

12. "Over the Editor's Desk," *Love Story Magazine*, August 25, 1921, 138.

13. *Love Story Magazine*, September 10, 1921, inside cover.

14. Mildred E. Phillips, "Forum of Feminine Fraternity of Fourth Estaters," *Editor & Publisher*, July 23, 1921, 33.

Chapter 6

1. Daisy Bacon, "Dear Mrs. Browne," 2.

2. *Ibid.*, 1.

3. *Ibid.*, 4.

4. *Ibid.*, 3, 15.

5. *Ibid.*, 3–4.

6. *Ibid.*, 3–4.

7. *Ibid.*, 16–17.

8. [Daisy Bacon], "With Contents Unknown," *Saturday Evening Post*, August 16, 1924, 28.

9. Marjorie Shuler, Ruth Adams Knight, and Muriel Fuller, *Lady Editor* (New York: E.P. Dutton & Co., Inc., 1941), 131.

10. Frederik Pohl, *The Way the Future Was* (New York: Ballantine Books, 1978), 43.

11. Reynolds, *Fiction Factory*, 156.

12. *Ibid.*

13. Bakeless, *Magazine Making*, 54–56.

14. Jienne Alhaideri, *From Tablet to Tablet: the History of the Book*. https://sites.google.com/a/umich.edu/from-tablet-to-tablet/final-projects/the-invention-of-the-linotype-machine-jienne-alhaideri-13

15. Theodore Peterson, *Magazines in the Twentieth Century*, 104.

Chapter 7

1. Mary Frances Doner, "Searchable Sea Literature," *The Maritime Studies Program of Williams College & Mystic Seaport,* https://sites.williams.edu/searchablesealit/d/doner-mary-frances/.

2. "Anita Blackmon aka Anita Blackmon Smith (1892–1943)," *Encyclopedia of Arkansas History & Culture,* http://www.encyclopediaofarkansas.net/encyclopedia/entry-detail.aspx?search=1&entryID=8125

3. Helen R. Woodward, "Love Story's Editor Speaks," *Writer's Market*, February 1939.

4. Richard Wormser, *How to Become a Complete Nonentity* (iUniverse, Inc., 2006), Kindle edition, locator 29.

5. *Ibid.*, locator 600.

6. Reynolds, *Fiction Factory*, 157.

7. "Daisy Bacon," Author Index Cards, Love Story Magazine, 1927–1939, Box M-101, Indexes, Street & Smith Records, Special Collections Research Center, Syracuse University Libraries.

8. "Manuscript Purchase Cards, 1926–28, "Love Story Magazine," Editorial Files, Box 10, Street & Smith Records, Special Collections Research Center, Syracuse University Libraries.

9. A.M. Mathieu, "A Rose by the Same Name," *Writer's Digest*, April 1947.

10. Manuscript Purchase Card, March 16, 1928, "Love Story Magazine," Editorial Files, Box 10, Street & Smith Records.

Chapter 8

1. "Interview with Daisy Bacon and Clark Robinson." *The Writer and Your Life.* WNYZ radio recording, June 13, 1941.

2. Daisy Bacon, Notes to Houser, Autobiographical Notes, 4.

3. "Miss E.J. Ford," Author Index Cards, Love Story Magazine, 1927–1939. Indexes, Box M-101, Street & Smith Records.

4. Daisy Bacon, "Women Among Men," 4.

5. John Locke, ed., *Pulp Fictioneers: Adventures in the Storytelling Business* (Silver Spring, Maryland: Adventure House, 2004), 12.

6. Reynolds, *Fiction Factory,* 156.

7. Daisy Bacon, "Lessons Learned," 1.

8. *Ibid.*, 2.

9. Daisy Bacon, "Women Among Men," 5.

10. *Ibid.*

11. Daisy Bacon, *Love Story Writer*, 39.

12. Paul Avrich and Karen Avrich, *Sasha and Emma: The Anarchist Odyssey of Alexander Berkman and Emma Goldman* (Boston: Belknap Press of Harvard University, 2012), 73–74, 362–364, 372–374.

13. Jessie Ford, diary entries, March 10, 1931, March 14, 1932.

14. Daisy Bacon, *Love Story Writer*, 4–5.

15. *Ibid.*, 90.

16. *Ibid.*, 92.

17. Elmer Davis, letter to Daisy Bacon, September 19, 1928.

Chapter 9

1. Henry Wise Miller, *All Our Lives*, 10.

2. Harvey O'Higgins, "A Lady Who Writes," *The New Yorker*, February 19, 1927, 25.

3. Daisy Bacon, journal notes, undated.

4. Daisy Bacon, *Love Story Writer*, 151.

5. Maury Klein, *Rainbow's End: The Crash of 1929* (New York: Oxford University Press, 2001), 177.

6. Locke, ed., *Pulp Fictioneers: Adventures in the Storytelling Business*, 120.

7. Fanny Hurst in "Trend of the Literary Market for 1929," by Willard F. Hawkins, *The Author & Journalist*, March 1929, 5–10.

8. Willard F. Hawkins, "Trend of the Literary Market for 1929," *The Author & Journalist*, March 1929, 6.

9. "Romance Stories," *Writer's Digest*, January 1929.

10. "Literary Market Tips," *The Author & Journalist*, September 1929, 30.

11. Joa Humphrey, "Editors You Want to Know: Daisy Bacon, Editor of *Love Story Magazine*," *The Author & Journalist*, September 1929, 12.

12. Daisy Bacon, journal notes, undated.

Chapter 10

1. Daisy Bacon, journal notes, undated.

2. Alice Duer Miller, letter to Henry Wise Miller, September 17, 1927, Alice Duer Miller collection, Barnard College.

3. Daisy Bacon, Notes to Houser, Autobiographical Notes, 4.1.

4. Robert H. Uzzell, "The Love Pulps," *Scribner's Magazine*, April 1938, 38.

5. Woodward, "Love Story's Editor Speaks."

6. Jack Smalley, "Confessions of a Pulpeteer," Originally printed in *Westways*, June 1974. Reprinted on Pulp Flakes, http://pulpflakes.blogspot.com/2018/09/confessions-of-pulpeteer-jack-smalley.html

7. August Lenninger, "*Love Story Magazine*," *Writer's Digest*, May 1930.

8. Daisy Bacon, Notes to Houser, Autobiographical Notes, 4.

9. "Love Story Editor," *Parade Weekly*, September 27, 1942, 8.

10. Daisy Bacon, Notes to Houser, Autobiographical Notes, 1.

11. Gertrude Schalk; letter to Bernice Dutrieuille Shelton, no date [late 1930], Bernice Dutrieuille Shelton Papers, Historical Society of Pennsylvania.

12. Gertrude Schalk to Bernice Dutrieuille Shelton, June 5, 1931, Bernice Dutrieuille Shelton Papers.

13. Daisy Bacon, *Love Story Writer*, 48.

14. *Ibid.*, 49.

15. *Ibid.*, 58.

16. Daisy Bacon, Notes to Houser, Autobiographical Notes, 3.

17. Frederik Pohl, *The Way the Future Was* (New York, Del Rey/Ballantine, 1978), 103.

18. Manuscript Purchase Cards, January 1926–May 1938, Love Story Magazine, Box 10, Editorial Files, Street & Smith Records. To arrive at the average payments made for stories printed in *Love Story*, the author requested a random sampling of Manuscript Purchase Cards of four from each year from 1926 through 1938.

19. Audit Bureau of Circulations, *A.B.C. Blue Book Periodical Publisher's Statements For Period Ending December 31, 1929*. Information provided by the *Circulating American Magazines* digital project, Brooks Hefner and Ed Timke, co-directors.

20. Daisy Bacon, Notes to Houser, Autobiographical Notes, 9.

21. Daisy Bacon, "Careers in the All-Fiction Field," *The Writer*, April 1947; Daisy Bacon, Notes to Lionel Houser, Autobiographical Notes, 4; "Author Index Card" for Esther Ford, Street & Smith Records.

22. Jessie Ford, diary entry, June 2, 1930.

23. Daisy Bacon, diary entry, June 28, 1958.

24. Foster & Reynolds, *New York: The Metropolis of the Western World* (New York: Foster & Reynolds Co. 1901, rev. 1924), 74.

Chapter 11

1. H. Bedford Jones, "The Changing Market," *The Author & Journalist*, February 1931.

2. Daisy Bacon, "Women Among Men," 2.

3. Harold Hersey, *The New Pulpwood Editor* (Frederick A. Stokes Company, 1937, Adventure House, 2002), 15. Citations are to the Adventure House edition.

4. Minna Bardon, "Plots from the Lovelorn," *Writer's Digest*, January 1933.

5. Daisy Bacon, Notes to Houser, Autobiographical Notes, 5.

6. Laura Alston Brown [pseu.], "The Friend in Need," *Love Story Magazine*, April 16, 1932, 159.

7. Daisy Bacon, Notes to Houser, Autobiographical Notes, 10.

8. Daisy Bacon, diary entry, November 22, 1951.

9. Daisy Bacon, "Wife of Tin Pan Alley," *Short Shorts*, September 1932, 13–14.

10. Alice Duer Miller, *Forsaking All Others* (New York: Simon and Schuster, 1931), 7.

11. *Ibid.*, 52.

12. Henry Wise Miller, *All Our Lives*, 43.

13. *Ibid.*, 193.

14. Jessie Ford, diary entry, June 10, 1931.

15. "Modern Miss Doesn't Want the Old Hokum," *Boston Sunday Globe*, May 31, 1931, 62.

16. Marion Clyde McCarroll, "Men More Domestic at Heart Than Women, Says Editor of *Love Story Magazine*," *New York Evening Post*, July 9, 1931, 6.

17. Daisy Bacon, "The Sex Complex in Business," Daisy Bacon collection.

18. Daisy Bacon, Notes to Houser, Autobiographical Notes, 4.

19. Will Murray, personal email to the author, May 26, 2018.

20. Frank Robinson and Lawrence Davidson. *Pulp Culture: The Art of Fiction Magazines* (Portland: Collectors Press, Inc. 2001), 85.

21. Locke, ed., *Pulp Fictioneers: Adventures in the Storytelling Business*, 37.

22. "12 'Pulp' Magazines Stop Production," *New York Times*, December 28, 1932, 19.

23. Frank Blackwell in *Pulpwood Days, Volume One: Editors You Want to Know*, John Locke, ed. (Elkhorn, CA: Off-Trail Publications, 2007), 21.

24. Bold Venture Press, "Plot Genie by Wycliffe A. Hill," https://boldventurepress.com/the-magic-of-plot-genie/

25. "Literary Market," *The Author & Journalist*, January 1934, 16.

26. Ruth Rukin, "Goldilocks—1931," *Writer's Digest*, February 1931.

27. Daisy Bacon, Notes to Houser, Autobiographical Notes, 12.

28. Daisy Bacon, *Love Story Writer,* 4, 5–6.

29. "Munsey Company Adopts Policy to Defeat Plagiarists," *The Author & Journalist,* January 1933, 16–18.

30. "Railroad Men Cited for Rescue of Cat," *New York Times,* January 11, 1933, 5.

31. Daisy Bacon, *Love Story Writer,* 29.

32. Tim DeForest, *Storytelling in the Pulps, Comics, and Radio: How Technology Changed Popular Fiction in America.* (Jefferson, North Carolina: McFarland, 2004), 152.

Chapter 12

1. James Aswell, "My New York," *Chester Times,* January 31, 1934.

2. Daisy Bacon, "Women Among Men," 1–2.

3. Walter Winchell, "On Broadway," *Wisconsin State Journal,* October 29, 1934, 4.

4. Daisy Bacon, Notes to Houser, Autobiographical Notes, 5.

5. Marcus Duffield, "The Pulps: Day Dreams for the Masses," *Vanity Fair,* June 1933, 26–27, 51–60.

6. Alvin Barclay in *The New Republic,* quoted in *Wordslingers* by William P. Murray (Altus Press: 2013), 66.

7. Minna Bardon, "Love in the Pulps," *Writer's Digest,* March 1932.

8. "Literary Market Tips," *The Author & Journalist,* October 1928, 24.

9. Helen Welshimer, "How Do Women Like their Men?" *Lubbock Morning Avalanche,* August 10, 1934, 14.

10. Robert Kenneth Jones, *The Shudder Pulps* (FAX Collector's Edition: 1975), 39.

11. Daisy Bacon, Notes to Houser, Autobiographical Notes, 9.

12. James Aswell, "My New York," *Aberdeen Daily News,* August 7, 1934, 6.

13. Harriet Bradfield, "Revival of the Fittest," *Writer's Digest,* September 1934.

14. Daisy Bacon, *Love Story Editor* (New York: Gemini Books, 1963), preface.

15. Earle R. Buell, "Broken Vows," *Ainslee's Smart Love Stories,* July 1935, 56.

16. Hortense McRaven, "The Love-Pulp Heroine Steps Out," *The Author &Journalist,* August 1935, 4–6.

17. Jack Woodford, "If You Must…," *The Author & Journalist,* June 1931, 5–8.

18. Virginia Lee, "Love Stories Must Mirror Life, Says Daisy Bacon," *The Author & Journalist,* April 1934.

19. "Walla, William Morrow & Company," letter to Daisy Bacon, April 9, 1935.

Chapter 13

1. Esther Ford, diary entries, January 14–15, 1937.

2. Daisy Bacon, "Enjoy 1936" memo pads.

3. John Robert Gregg, S.C.D., *Gregg Dictionary of Shorthand.* (New York: Gregg Publishing Company, 1930). Gregg.angelfishy.net/gsd.pdf; p. 232.

4. Minna Bardon, "The Rhinestone Princess," *Writer's Digest,* December 1936.

5. Peterson, *Magazines in the Twentieth Century,* 79.

6. Bardon, "The Rhinestone Princess."

7. Vivian Grey, "Go West Young Woman," *Spokane Daily Chronicle,* February 1, 1936.

8. Susan Ware, *Holding Their Own: American Women in the 1930s.* (Boston: Twayne Publishers, 1982), 27.

9. Marie Girard, "Marie Girard's Story," quoted in *Making Do,* by Jeanne Westin (Kindle version: 2012, location 2496).

10. Daisy Bacon, Women Among Men, *The New York Woman,* October 21, 1936, 11.

11. Anonymous, "Letter to the Editor," *The New York Woman,* November 18, 1936.

12. Milton Adelmann, "Letter to the Editor," *The New York Woman,* November 25, 1936.

13. Daisy Bacon, letter to Gerard Chapman, June 13, 1948, International Press Bureau Fonds, 1904–1953, University of Waterloo.

Chapter 14

1. Daisy Bacon, diary entry, November 11, 1957.

2. Walter Winchell, "Walter Winchell on Broadway," *Logansport Pharos-Tribune,* February 24, 1937, 7.

3. "Clarke Robinson, Retired Author," *New York Times,* January 29, 1962, 31.

4. Clarke Robinson, "Rainbows in Cellophane," *Smart Love Stories,* June 1937, 95.

5. Daisy Bacon, diary entry, February 8, 1955.

6. Alice Duer Miller, letter to Alexander Woollcott, letters #47195558–18–18 and 20–20, Alexander Woollcott collection, Houghton Library, Harvard University.

7. Marie Belloc Lowndes, letter to daughter Elizabeth in *Diaries and Letters of Marie Belloc Lowndes, 1911–1947,* Susan Lowndes, ed. (London: Chatto & Windus, 1971), 234.

8. Marie Belloc Lowndes, letter to Alexander Woollcott, September 15, 1942, Alexander Woollcott collection.

9. Daisy, Bacon, "The Golden Age of the Iron Maiden," *Round-up Magazine,* April 1975, 1.

10. "Memoranda: Editorial Department organization, Sept. 27, 1937," Miscellaneous Editorial Files, Box 41, Street & Smith Records.

11. Daisy Bacon, "The Golden Age of the Iron Maiden," 1.

12. William Winter, letter to William Murray, June 15, 1985; letter to Charles Verral, September 19, 1995, private collection.

13. Robert Uzzell, "The Love Pulps," *Scribner's Magazine,* April 1938, 36–41.

14. *Ibid.,* 38.

15. *Ibid.,* 41.

16. *Ibid.,* 37.

17. Daisy Bacon, diary entry, March 30, 1959.

18. "Doctor's Hospital Keeps Cures Hidden," *New York Times,* February 10, 1930, 12.

Chapter 15

1. Daisy Bacon, *Love Story Writer,* 50.

2. Daisy Bacon, "The Golden Age of the Iron Maiden," *Round-up Magazine,* April 1975, 2.

3. *Ibid.*, 2.

4. Francis Stebbins, letter to Paul Powers, May 8, 1940, Paul S. Powers collection, Rare Books and Manuscripts Library, Ohio State University.

5. Alice Duer Miller, letter to Alexander Woollcott, August 19, 1939, Alexander Woollcott collection.

6. Alice Duer Miller, letter to Alexander Woollcott, undated.

7. Daisy Bacon, diary entry, November 30, 1968.

8. Daisy Bacon, "He Liked Them Helpless Looking," unpublished short story, no date.

9. Daisy Bacon, diary entry, October 21, 1956.

10. Lynn Fontanne, letter to Alexander Woollcott, July 17, 1940, Alexander Woollcott collection.

11. Alice Duer Miller, *The White Cliffs* (New York: Coward-McCann, Inc., 1940).

Chapter 16

1. Daisy Bacon, journal notes.

2. Locke, ed., *Pulp Fictioneers,* 113.

3. Marjorie Shuler, et al., *Lady Editor,* 131.

4. Adelaide Kerr, "Editor Sells Romance to Lonely Wives, But Has No Love Herself," *Binghampton Press,* March 20, 1941, 28.

5. Ed Hulse, *The Blood 'n' Thunder Guide to Pulp Fiction* (Morristown, N.J: Murania Press, 2013), 141.

6. "Editor Notes," Writer's Digest, January 1941.

7. William Bogart, Letter to Lester Dent, May 27, 1941, private collection.

8. *Ibid.*

9. Bogart, letter to Dent, September 11, 1941, private collection.

10. Bogart to Dent, May 27, 1941.

11. Joan Younger, "Women in the News," *Statesville Daily Record,* June 4, 1941, 5.

12. "Modern Women," *Trenton Evening Times,* November 1, 1941, 5.

13. A.M. Mathieu, "Cobber's Child," *Writer's Yearbook,* 1941.

14. Daisy Bacon, "Love Story," *Writer's Yearbook,* 1941.

Chapter 17

1. "Daisy Bacon is the Timeliest of Editors Thanks to Her Subconscious," *Writer's Journal,* February 1942.

2. Locke ed., *Pulp Fictioneers,* 136.

3. "Churches Would Ban Pulp," *New York Times,* February 16, 1942, 25.

4. John A. Dinan, *The Pulp Western: A Popular History of the Western Fiction Magazine in America* (Borgo Press, 1989; BearManor, 2003), 8. Citations are to the BearManor edition.

5. Daisy Bacon, "The All-Fiction Field," *The Writer,* July 1946.

6. Denning Miller, letter to Alexander Woollcott, February 8, 1942.

Chapter 18

1. "Calls on Printers to Use Less Paper," *New York Times,* September 18, 1942, 15.

2. Stephen G. Clow, "Arbiter of Smut," *The Author & Journalist,* November 1934, 9.

3. "Moss Bans 11 Magazines," *New York Times,* May 10, 1943.

4. Lee Server, *Danger Is My Business* (San Francisco: Chronicle Books, 1993), 136.

5. Daisy Bacon, "Writing Your First Story," *Writer's Market,* April 1942.

6. Wolff H. Salz, "Mission to Manhattan," in *Pulpwood Days,* John Locke, ed., 127.

7. *Ibid.*

8. Daisy Bacon, *Love Story Writer,* 129.

9. Daisy Bacon, diary entry, November 11, 1957.

Chapter 19

1. Henry Wise Miller, *All Our Lives,* 185.

2. *Ibid.,* 193.

3. *Ibid.,* 109.

4. *Ibid.,* 88, 64.

5. Samuel Hopkins Adams, "A Happy Marriage," *New York Times,* June 24, 1945, 77.

6. Esther Ford Robinson, diary entry, May 19, 1946.

7. *Ibid.,* September 26, 1946.

8. Michelle Nolan, *Love on the Racks: A History of American Romance Comics* (Jefferson, NC: McFarland, 2008), 9.

9. Daisy Bacon, letters to Gerard Chapman, June 1948–December 1948, International Press Bureau Fonds, 1904–1953.

10. Lester Dent, letter to William Bogart, May 20, 1948, private collection.

Chapter 20

1. Daisy Bacon, *Love Story Writer,* 56–57.

2. Will Murray, "Interlude," *Doc Savage #87,* Anthony Tollin, ed. (San Antonio, TX: Sanctum Books: 2016), 88–91.

3. Daisy Bacon, letter to Gerard Chapman, undated, International Press Bureau Fonds, 1904–1953.

4. Will Murray, "Interlude," *Doc Savage #47,* Anthony Tollin, ed. (San Antonio, TX: Sanctum Books, 2011), 86–88.

5. Daisy Bacon, letter to Lester Dent, September 20, 1948, in "Sunset for a Superman," by Will Murray.

6. Will Murray, "Intermission," *Doc Savage #15,* Anthony Tollin, ed. (San Antonio, TX: Sanctum Books: 2008), 71–73.

7. *Ibid.*

8. Daisy Bacon, letter to Dent, dated November 19, 1948, "Sunset for a Superman," by Will Murray.

9. Will Murray, "Interlude," *Doc Savage #87.*

10. Daisy Bacon, letter to Dent, April 4, 1949, "Sunset for a Superman," by Will Murray.

11. Will Murray, "Intermission," *Doc Savage #15.*

12. Daisy Bacon, "The Golden Age of the Iron Maiden, 7, 9.

13. "Street & Smith Giving Up Pulps," *New York Times,* April 9, 1949, 19.

14. Daisy Bacon, "The Golden Age of the Iron Maiden."

15. Aaron Mathieu, "Cobbler's Child," Writer's Yearbook, 1941.

16. Esther Ford Robinson, diary entry, May 11, 1949.

Chapter 21

1. Daisy Bacon, "Jerry Siegel memo."
2. The only surviving diaries attributed to Daisy begin in 1950. If she kept diaries prior to that time, they have not survived. It is possible that she kept diaries but destroyed them after she retired. But it is also possible that she did not keep them during her working life due to her hectic schedule.
3. Daisy Bacon, diary entry, December 26, 1950.
4. *Ibid.*, February 15, 1951.
5. *Ibid.*, March 4, 1951.
6. *Ibid.*, March 12, 1951.
7. *Ibid.*, April 5, 1951.
8. *Ibid.*, August 5, 1951.
9. *Ibid.*, November 10, 1951.
10. *Ibid.*, February 29, 1952.
11. Daisy Bacon, *Love Story Writer*, 3.
12. *Ibid.*, 86.
13. Daisy Bacon, diary entry, March 13, 1953.
14. "OLM [Our Lady of the Magnificat]: The Early Years," 5.
15. "Henry W. Miller, Stockbroker, 78," *New York Times*, September 16, 1954, 29.

Chapter 22

1. Daisy Bacon, diary entry, March 17, 1951.
2. *Ibid.*, October 20, 1956.
3. *Ibid.*, July 17, 1960.
4. Esther Ford Robinson, letter to Daisy Bacon, October 17, 1961.
5. "Women and Men, Too!" *Port Angeles Evening News*, January 24, 1965, 6.
6. Daisy Bacon, letter to John Dinan, July 2, 1975.
7. "Daisy Bacon," *New York Times,* March 27, 1986, 110.

Epilogue

1. Cornie Hubner. "Our Lady of the Magnificat: Didja Know?" *The Smoke Rise and Kinnelon Blog*, October 9, 2011. http://smokerise-nj.blogspot.com/2011/10/our-lady-of-magnificat-didja-know-by.html
2. Michelle Nolan, *Love on the Racks*, 43.
3. Aruna E. Vasudevan, ed., *Twentieth-Century Romance & Historical Writers* (London: St. James Press, 1994, third edition).

Bibliography

Magazines, Newspapers and Other Periodicals

Abeling, Ruth Agnes. "For Mary's Visit." *The Southeast Missourian,* May 9, 1921: 4.

_____. "The Thoughtless Girl." *The Pittsburgh Press,* July 28, 1921: 19.

_____. "When a Woman Tells." *South Bend News,* October 9, 1921:20.

Adams, Samuel Hopkins. "A Happy Marriage." *New York Times,* June 24, 1945: 77.

Aswell, James. "My New York." *Aberdeen Daily News,* August 7, 1934: 6.

_____. "My New York." *Chester Times,* January 31, 1934: 14.

The Author & Journalist. "Literary Market Tips." January 1934.

_____. "Literary Market Tips." October 1928: 24.

_____. "Literary Market Tips." September 1929: 30.

_____. "Munsey Company Adopts Policy to Defeat Plagiarists." January 1933: 16–18.

Bacon, Daisy. "The All-Fiction Field," *The Writer,* July 1946.

_____. "Careers in the All-Fiction Field." *The Writer,* April 1947.

_____. "The Golden Age of the Iron Maiden," *Round-up Magazine,* April 1975: 1–2, 7–9, 16.

_____. "Love Story." *Writer's Yearbook,* 1941.

[_____]. "On The Fourteenth Floor." *Saturday Evening Post,* June 21, 1924: 9.

[_____]. "With Contents Unknown," *Saturday Evening Post,* August 16, 1924: 28.

_____. "Women Among Men." *The New York Woman,* October 21, 1936: 11.

_____. "Writing Your First Story." *Writer's Market,* April 1942.

Baker, Lucinda. "Skeletons Out of My Closet." *Writer's Digest,* December 1941.

Bardon, Minna. "Love in the Pulps." *Writer's Digest,* March 1932.

_____. "Plots from the Lovelorn." *Writer's Digest,* January 1933.

_____. "The Rhinestone Princess." *Writer's Digest,* December 1936.

Boston Sunday Globe. "Modern Miss Doesn't Want the Old Hokum." May 31, 1931: 62.

Bradfield, Harriet. "Revival of the Fittest." *Writer's Digest,* September 1934.

Brooklyn Daily Eagle. "Miss Daisy Bacon, magazine editor…" August 9, 1930: 3.

The Call. "Back to Bridgeton to Live Down Scandal." July 4, 1901.

Clow, Stephen G. "Arbiter of Smut." *The Author & Journalist,* Nov. 1934: 9.

The Daily Palladium. "Pastor Gone Wrong." June 28, 1901.

Duffield, Marcus. "The Pulps: day dreams for the masses." *Vanity Fair,* June 1933: 26–27, 51–60.

The Evening Telegram. "Volunteer Captain Won by Faith Curists." January 7, 1898.

Fairgrieve, Amita. *Smith Alumnae Quarterly,* Volume XII, May 1921: 254.

_____. *Smith Alumnae Quarterly,* Volumes XIII, November 1921: 84.

Goldstein, Alvia H. "Pulp Magazine Cupid." *St. Louis Post Dispatch,* November 1, 1942: 2G.

Grey, Vivien. "Go West, Young Woman!" *Spokane Daily Chronicle, Saturday Magazine,* February 1, 1936: 3.

Hawkins, Willard E. "Trend of the Literary Market for 1929." *The Author & Journalist,* March 1929: 5–10.

Humphrey, Joa. "Editors You Want to Know: Daisy Bacon, Editor of *Love Story Magazine.*" *The Author & Journalist,* September 1929: 13.

Jones, H. Bedford. "The Changing Market." *The Author & Journalist,* February 1931: 5–7.

Kerr, Adelaide. "Editor Sells Romance to Lonely Wives, but Has No Love Herself." *The Binghamton Press,* March 20, 1941: 28.

Latham, Larry. "The Great Transition: How Dime Novels, Story Papers, and Nickel Weeklies Yielded to the Pulps." *Blood n Thunder,* 2013–14 (Special Issue): 66–80.

Lee, Virginia. "Love Stories Must Mirror Life." *The Author & Journalist,* April 1934.

Lenninger, August. "Love Story Magazine." *Writer's Digest,* May 1930.

Mathieu, A.M. "A Rose by the Same Name." *Writer's Digest,* April 1947.

Mathieu, Aron. "Cobbler's Child." *Writer's Yearbook,* 1941.

McCarroll, Marion Clyde. "Men More Domestic at Heart Than Women, Says Editor of Love Story Magazine." *New York Evening Post,* July 9, 1931: 6.

Murray, Will. "The Thrill Book Story." *Pulp Vault* No. 14, by Tattered Pages Press. 2011.

New York Times. "Alice Duer Miller Dies at Home Here." August 23, 1942: 42.

_____. "Churches Would Ban Pulp." February 16, 1942: 25.

_____. "Clarke Robinson, Retired Author." January 29, 1962: 31.

_____. "Doctor's Hospital Keeps Cures Hidden." February 10, 1930: 12.

_____. "Henry W. Miller, Stockbroker, 78." September 16, 1954: 29.

_____. "Railroad Men Cited for Rescue of Cat." January 11, 1933: 5.

_____. "12 'Pulp' Magazines Stop Production." December 28, 1932.

_____. "Young Lady Wanted." February 21, 1926: 134.

O'Higgins, Harvey. "A Lady Who Writes." *The New Yorker.* February 19, 1927: 25–27.

Parade Weekly. "Love Story Editor." September 27, 1942: 8–11.

The Philadelphia Inquirer. "Bridgeton Pastor Suddenly Leaves." June 27, 1901: 1.

Phillips, Mildred E. "Forum of Feminine Fraternity of Fourth Estaters." *Editor & Publisher,* July 23, 1921: 33.

Porter, Amy. "Love Still Makes the World Go Round, Says Fiction Editor." *Zanesville Signal,* December 27, 1942: 2.

Ross, James. M. "Pennsylvania Lass Makes Good in Big Way; Edits Three Magazines Simultaneously." *The Nassau Daily Review-Star,* February 4, 1942: 9.

Rukin, Ruth. "Goldilocks—1931." *Writer's Digest,* February 1931.

Thomas, Ward. "The Escape of a Nation." *Writer's Digest,* May 1934.

The Times-Picayune New Orleans. "Love Stories Hold Readers Despite War." December 13, 1942: 8.

Uzzell, Thomas H. "The Love Pulps." *Scribner's,* April 1938: 36–41.

Welshimer, Helen. "How Do Women Like Their Men?" *Lubbock Morning Avalanche,* August 10, 1934: 14.

The Westfield Republican. "David Bacon Killed." October 21, 1908: 1.

_____. "Narrow Escape." December 22, 1926: 1.

_____. "Obituary." January 10, 1900: 8.

_____. "A Summons to the Colors." June 27, 1917: 2.

_____. "Wedding Bells." January 4, 1888: 1.

Winchell, Walter. "Walter Winchell On Broadway." *Logansport Pharos-Tribune,* February 24, 1937: 7.

_____. "Walter Winchell On Broadway." *Wisconsin State Journal,* October 29, 1934: 4.

Woodford, Jack. "If You Must…" *The Author & Journalist,* June 1931: 5–8.

Woodward, Helen. R. "Love Story's Editor Speaks." *Writer's Market,* February 1939.

Writer's Digest. "Editor Notes." January 1941.

_____. "Romance Stories." January 1929.

Writer's Journal. "Bacon is the Timeliest of Editors, Thanks to Her 'Subconscious.'" February 1942.

Younger, Joan. "Women in the News." *Statesville Daily Record.* June 4, 1941: 5.

Books

Allen, Charles Laurel. *The Journalist's Manual of Printing.* New York: Thomas Nelson and Sons, 1929.

Allen, Frederick Lewis. *Only Yesterday and Since Yesterday.* New York: Bonanza Books, 1986.

Avrich, Paul and Karen Avrich. *Sasha and Emma: The Anarchist Odyssey of Alexander Berkman and Emma Goldman.* Cambridge: Belknap Press of Harvard University, 2012.

Bacon, Daisy. *Love Story Editor.* New York: Gemini Books, 1963.

_____. *Love Story Writer.* New York: Hermitage House. 1954. Reprint: Bold Venture Press, 2016.

Bakeless, John. *Magazine Making.* New York: The Viking Press, 1931.

Barrett, Mary Ellin. *Irving Berlin: A Daughter's Memoir.* New York: Simon & Schuster, 1994.

Burns, Ric and James Sanders. *New York: An Illustrated History.* New York: Knopf, 1999.

Cox, J. Randolph. *The Dime Novel Companion.* Westport, CT: Greenwood Press, 2000.

Crocker, Kathleen and Jane Currie. *Images of America: Chautauqua Lake Region.* Charleston, SC: Arcadia Publishing, 2002.

_____. *Images of America: Westfield.* Chicago: Arcadia Publishing, 2006.

DeForest, Tim. *Story Telling in the Pulps, Comics, and Radio: How Technology Changed Popular Fiction in America.* Jefferson, NC: McFarland, 2004.

Denning, Michael. *Mechanic Accents: Dime Novels and Working-Class Culture in America.* New York: Verso, 1998.

Dinan, John A. *The Pulp Western: A Popular History of the Western Fiction Magazine in America* (Borgo Press, 1989; BearManor Media: 2003).

Ellis, Doug, Ed Hulse, and Robert Weinberg, eds. *The Art of the Pulps: An Illustrated History.* San Diego: IDW Publishing. 2017.

Ellis, Doug, John Locke, and John Gunnison. *The Adventure House Guide to the Pulps.* Silver Spring, Maryland: Adventure House, 2000.

Federal Writers' Project of the Works Progress Administration. *The WPA Guide to New York City: The Federal Writers' Project Guide to 1930s New York.* New York: Random House, 1939. Reprinted by The New Press, 1992.

Foster & Reynolds. *New York: The Metropolis of the Western World.* New York: Foster & Reynolds Co., 1901. 1924 edition.

Foy, Sally Fairchild and Linda Z. Winterberg. *Mac-*

culloch Hall: A Family Album. Morristown: Junior League of Morristown, 1980.

Gaines, James R. *Wit's End: Days and Nights of the Algonquin Round Table*. New York: Harcourt Brace & Jovanovich, 1977.

Gallagher, Brian. *Anything Goes: The Jazz Age Adventures of Neysa McMein and Her Extravagant Circle of Friends*. New York: Times Books, 1987.

Gleason, William A. "Postbellum, Pre-Harlequin: American Romance Publishing in the Late Nineteenth and Early Twentieth Century." In Gleason, William A. and Eric Murphy Selinger, eds. *Romance Fiction and American Culture: Love as the Practice of Freedom?* Surrey, England and Burlington, Vermont: Ashgate Publishing Limited, 2016: 58–70.

Goodstone, Tony, ed. *The Pulps: Fifty Years of American Pop Culture*. New York: Chelsea House. 1970.

Grant, Jane. *Ross, the New Yorker and Me*. New York: Reynal and Company, 1968.

Gruber, Frank. *The Pulp Jungle*. Los Angeles: Sherbourne Press, Inc. 1967.

Hennessey, Joseph, ed. *The Portable Woollcott*. New York: Viking Press, 1946.

Hersey, Harold. *The New Pulpwood Editor*. Frederick A. Stokes Company, 1937; reprinted with Foreword by Adventure House, 2002.

Hill, Wycliffe A. *The Plot Genie: Romance*. Hollywood: The Gagnon Company, 1931. Reprinted by Bold Venture Press, 2015.

Hulse, Ed. *The Blood 'n' Thunder Guide to Pulp Fiction*. Morristown, New Jersey: Murania Press, 2013.

Invalid's Hotel. Reproduced by Mike Joki. Original printing date unknown.

James, Edward T. *Notable American Women, 1607–1950: A Biographical Dictionary; Volume II, G–O*. Cambridge, MA: The Belknap Press of Harvard University Press, 1971.

Jones, Robert Kenneth. *The Shudder Pulps: A History of the Weird Menace Magazines of the 1930s*. West Linn, Oregon: FAX Collector's Editions, 1975.

Kaufman, Beatrice and Joseph Hennessey, eds. *The Letters of Alexander Woollcott*. New York: Viking Press, 1944.

Kisseloff, Jeff. *You Must Remember This: An Oral History of Manhattan from the 1890s to World War II*. Baltimore: Johns Hopkins University Press, 1989.

Klein, Maury. *Rainbow's End: The Crash of 1929*. New York: Oxford University Press, 2001.

Langstaff, John Brett. *New Jersey Generations: Macculloch Hall, Morristown*. New York: Vantage Press, 1964.

Law, Graham, Gregory Drozdz, and Debby McNally, eds.; *Charlotte M. Brame (1836–1884): Towards a Primary Bibliography*. Canterbury: Canterbury Christ Church University, 2011.

Locke, John, Ed. *Pulp Fictioneers: Adventures in the Storytelling Business*. Silver Spring, Maryland: Adventure House, 2004.

_____. *Pulpwood Days. Volume One: Editors You Want to Know*. Castroville, CA: Off-Trail Publications, 2007.

_____. *Pulpwood Days. Volume Two: Lives of the Pulp Writers*. Elkhorn, CA: Off-Trail Publications, 2013.

Lowndes, Susan, ed. *Diaries and Letters of Marie Belloc Lowndes, 1911–1947*. London: Chatto & Windus, 1971.

Marx, Harpo and Rowland Barber. *Harpo Speaks!* New York: Limelight Editions. 1981. 1988 Edition.

Meyers, Lucy A. *Kinnelon—A History*. Kinnelon Bicentennial Committee, 1976.

Miller, Alice Duer. *Forsaking All Others*. New York: Simon & Schuster, 1931.

_____. *The White Cliffs*. New York: Coward-McCann, Inc., 1940.

Miller, Henry Wise. *All Our Lives*. New York: Coward-McCann, Inc., 1945.

Moskowitz, Sam. *Under the Moons of Mars: A History and Anthology of "The Scientific Romance" of the Munsey Magazines, 1912–1920*. New York: Holt, Rinehart, and Winston, 1970.

Murray, Will. "Interlude." *Doc Savage #47*. Anthony Tollin, ed. San Antonio, TX: Sanctum Books, 2011: 86–88.

_____. "Interlude." *Doc Savage #87*. Anthony Tollin, ed. San Antonio, TX: Sanctum Books, 2016: 88–91.

_____. "Intermission." *Doc Savage #15*. Anthony Tollin, ed. San Antonio, TX: Sanctum Books, 2008: 71–73.

_____. *Wordslingers: An Epitaph for the Western*. Altus Press, 2013.

Nolan, Michelle. *Love on the Racks: A History of American Romance Comics*. Jefferson, NC: McFarland, 2008.

Peterson, Theodore. *Magazines in the Twentieth Century*. Urbana: University of Illinois Press, 1964.

Pohl, Frederik. *The Way The Future Was*. New York: Ballantine Books, 1978.

Reynolds, Quentin. *The Fiction Factory*. New York: Random House, 1955.

Robinson, Frank and Lawrence Davidson. *Pulp Culture: The Art of Fiction Magazines*. Portland: Collectors Press, Inc., 2001.

Romalov, Nancy Tillman. "Unearthing the Historical Reader, or, Reading Girls' Reading." In *Pioneers, Passionate Ladies, and Private Eyes: Dime Novels, Series Books, and Paperbacks*. Sullivan, Larry E. and Lydia C. Schurman, eds. New York: Haworth Press, 1996: 87–101.

Salz, H. Wolff. "Mission to Manhattan." In *Pulpwood Days. Volume One: Editors You Want to Know*. Locke, John, ed., Castroville, CA: Off-Trail Publications, 2007: 127.

Server, Lee. *Danger Is My Business*. San Francisco: Chronicle Books, 1993.

Shuler, Marjorie, Ruth Adams Knight, and Muriel Fuller. *Lady Editor*. New York: E.P. Dutton & Co., Inc., 1941.

Tebbel, John and Mary Ellen Zuckerman. *The Magazine in America: 1741–1990.* New York: Oxford, 1991.

Tollin, Anthony. "From Pulp to Radio … and Back Again!" *Doc Savage #63.* Anthony Tollin, ed. San Antonio: Sanctum Books, 2012: 121.

Vasudevan Aruna. *Twentieth Century Romance and Historical Writers.* London: St. James Press, 1994. Third edition.

Ware, Susan. *Holding Their Own: American Women in the 1930s.* Boston: Twayne Publishers, 1982.

Westin, Jeane. *Making Do: How Women Survived the '30s.* Amazon Digital Services, 2012.

Wolseley, Roland E. *Understanding Magazines.* Ames, Iowa: Iowa State University Press. Second edition, 1969.

Wormser, Richard. *How to Become a Complete Nonentity.* iUniverse, Inc., 2006. Kindle edition.

Yagoda, Ben. *About Town: The New Yorker and the World It Made.* New York: Scribner's, 2000.

Young, William H. and Nancy K. *American Popular Culture Through History Series: 1930s.* Westport, Connecticut: Greenwood Press, 2002.

Zuckerman, Mary Ellen. *A History of Popular Women's Magazines in the United States, 1792–1995.* Westport, Connecticut: Greenwood Press, 1998.

Archives

Alexander Woollcott correspondence, 1856–1943. Alexander Woollcott collection. Houghton Library, Harvard University.

Alice Duer Miller Personal Paper Collection. Barnard College, New York.

Audit Bureau of Circulations. *A.B.C. Blue Book Periodical Publisher's Statements For Period Ending December 31, 1929.* Information provided by the *Circulating American Magazines* digital project. Brooks Hefner and Ed Timke, co-directors.

Bernice Dutrieuille Shelton Papers, Historical Society of Pennsylvania.

Bush, Pauline H. "History of Barcelona; Its People." Patterson Library. Westfield, New York.

Editorial files, Miscellaneous Editorial files, and Indexes. Street & Smith Records, Special Collections Research Center, Syracuse University Libraries.

International Press Bureau Fonds, 1904–1953; University of Waterloo, Waterloo, Ontario, Canada; June 1948–December 1948. https://uwaterloo.ca/library/special-collections-archives/sites/ca.library.special-collections-archives/files/uploads/files/ga1.pdf

New York Historical Society. Photograph collection.

"OLM: The Early Years." Provided by Our Lady of the Magnificat office.

Paul S. Powers collection. Rare Books and Manuscripts Library, Ohio State University.

Daisy Bacon Collection

Bacon, Daisy. Autobiographical notes, pp. 1–14, c. 1935.

_____. "Dear Mrs. Browne." No date.

_____. Diaries. 1951–1977.

_____. "He Liked Them Helpless Looking," unpublished short story, no date.

_____. "Learning Tricks of the Trade." No date.

_____. "1936" memo, personal papers, undated.

_____. "The Sex Complex in Business."

_____. "Women Among Men."

Bacon, Elmer E. Letter to Jessie Bacon, Nov. 6, 1899.

Bacon, Jessie. Diaries. 1898–1899, 1922–1934.

Bacone, [sic] Jessie H. "The Child's Lament Song." 1903.

Davis, Elmer. Letter to Daisy Bacon. September 19, 1928.

"Interview with Daisy Bacon and Clark Robinson." *The Writer and Your Life.* WNYZ radio recording, June 13, 1941.

[Miller, Henry]. Cable to Daisy Bacon. January 13, 1930.

Robinson, Esther Ford. Diaries. 1937–1980.

"Walla." William Morrow & Co. Letter to Daisy Bacon. April 9, 1935.

Web Sites

Alhaideri, Jienne. *From Tablet to Tablet: the History of the Book.* https://sites.google.com/a/umich.edu/from-tablet-to-tablet/final-projects/the-invention-of-the-linotype-machine-jienne-alhaideri-13

"Anita Blackmon aka Anita Blackmon Smith (1892–1943)." *Encyclopedia of Arkansas History & Culture.* http://www.encyclopediaofarkansas.net/encyclopedia/entry-detail.aspx?search=1&entryID=8125

"Bertha M. Clay." *American Women's Dime Novel Project.* http://chnm.gmu.edu/dimenovels/the-american-womens-dime-novel

Doner, Mary Frances. "Searchable Sea Literature." *The Maritime Studies Program of Williams College & Mystic Seaport.* https://sites.williams.edu/searchablesealit/d/doner-mary-frances/

Gregg, John Robert, S.C.D. *Gregg Dictionary of Shorthand.* New York: Gregg Publishing Company, 1930. Gregg.angelfishy.net/gsd.pdf.: 232. Retrieved 10.1.2018

History of Kinnelon. http://nynjctbotany.org/njhltofc/kinnelonboro.html

Hubner, Cornie and Christina B. Whitmore. "Our Lady of the Magnificat: Didja Know?" *The Smoke Rise and Kinnelon Blog,* October 9, 2011. http://smokerise-nj.blogspot.com/2011/10/our-lady-of-magnificat-didja-know-by.html

Hutchinson, Peter. *A Publisher's History of American Magazines—Magazine Growth in the Nineteenth Century.* http://www.themagazinist.com/uploads/Part_2_Paper_Printing.pdf

"Pierce Building." *Buffalo as an Architectural Mu-*

seum. http://buffaloah.com/a/main/651/index. html; retrieved October 21, 2018.

"Pulp Fiction Magazines Database." *Galactic Central.* http://philsp.com/

Smalley, Jack. "Amazing Confessions of a Pulpeteer." *Westways.* June 1974. Reprinted on *Pulp Flakes,* September 8, 2018. http://pulpflakes.blogspot.com/2018/09/confessions-of-pulpeteer-jack-smalley.html

U.S. Bureau of Labor Statistics. *100 Years of Consumer Spending: 1934–36.* www.bls.gov/opub/uses/1934–36

Widmer, Ted. "The Other Gettysburg Address." *New York Times.* November 19, 2013. Online edition. https://opinionator.blogs.nytimes.com/2013/11/19/the-other-gettysburg-address/

Index

Numbers in **bold italics** indicate pages with illustrations